# THE DAILY STUDY BIBLE

*THE REVELATION OF JOHN*

VOL. 2: CH. 6–22

REVISED EDITION

# THE REVELATION OF
# JOHN

VOLUME TWO—CHAPTERS 6 TO 22

REVISED EDITION

## WILLIAM BARCLAY

THE SAINT ANDREW PRESS
EDINBURGH

TO
ALL THOSE READERS
WHO BEGAN WITH ME
AT THE BEGINNING OF THIS SERIES
AND WHO HAVE PERSEVERED WITH ME
TO THIS THE END

Published by
THE SAINT ANDREW PRESS
121 George Street, Edinburgh

© William Barclay 1976
First Edition 1959
Revised Edition 1976

*For copyright reasons not for sale in the USA*

ISBN 0 7152 0286 3 (Limp)
ISBN 0 7152 0314 2 (Cased)

Photoset by McCorquodale (Scotland) Ltd., Glasgow
Printed and Bound by T. & A. Constable Ltd., Edinburgh

# GENERAL INTRODUCTION

*The Daily Study Bible* series has always had one aim—to convey the results of scholarship to the ordinary reader. A. S. Peake delighted in the saying that he was a "theological middleman", and I would be happy if the same could be said of me in regard to these volumes. And yet the primary aim of the series has never been academic. It could be summed up in the famous words of Richard of Chichester's prayer—to enable men and women "to know Jesus Christ more clearly, to love him more dearly, and to follow him more nearly".

It is all of twenty years since the first volume of *The Daily Study Bible* was published. The series was the brain-child of the late Rev. Andrew McCosh, M.A., S.T.M., the then Secretary and Manager of the Committee on Publications of the Church of Scotland, and of the late Rev. R. G. Macdonald, O.B.E., M.A., D.D., its Convener.

It is a great joy to me to know that all through the years *The Daily Study Bible* has been used at home and abroad, by minister, by missionary, by student and by layman, and that it has been translated into many different languages. Now, after so many printings, it has become necessary to renew the printer's type and the opportunity has been taken to restyle the books, to correct some errors in the text and to remove some references which have become outdated. At the same time, the Biblical quotations within the text have been changed to use the Revised Standard Version, but my own original translation of the New Testament passages has been retained at the beginning of each daily section.

There is one debt which I would be sadly lacking in courtesy if I did not acknowledge. The work of revision and correction has been done entirely by the Rev. James Martin, M.A., B.D., minister of High Carntyne Church, Glasgow. Had it not been for him this task would never have been undertaken, and it is

impossible for me to thank him enough for the selfless toil he
has put into the revision of these books.

It is my prayer that God may continue to use *The Daily
Study Bible* to enable men better to understand His word.

Glasgow                                  WILLIAM  BARCLAY

# CONTENTS

# THE OPENING OF THE SEALS

As one by one the seals of the roll are opened, history unfolds itself before John's eyes.

As we study this section, we must remember one general fact which is basic to its understanding. In this series of visions John is seeing in advance the end of terror and judgment which could bring in the golden age of God.

Before we study the section in detail, we note one general point. In the first section of the visions, 6: 1–8, the Authorized Version consistently follows a form of the Greek text which makes each of the four living creatures say: "Come and see!" (verses 1, 3, 5, 7). In all the best Greek manuscripts it is simply, "Come!" as translated in the Revised Standard Version. This is not an invitation to John to come and see; it is a summons to the four horses and their riders one by one to come forward on the stage of history.

## THE FOUR HORSES AND THEIR RIDERS

*Revelation* 6: 1–8

And I saw when the Lamb opened the first of the seven seals, and I heard one of the four living creatures saying with a loud voice like the sound of thunder, "Come!" And I saw, and, behold, a white horse, and he who was seated on it had a bow, and a conqueror's crown was given to him, and he went forth conquering and to conquer.

And, when he had opened the second seal, I heard the second living creature say, "Come!" And there came forth another horse blood-red in colour, and to him that sat upon it there was given to take peace from the earth, and to bring it about that men slay one another, and a great sword was given to him.

And, when he had opened the third seal, I heard the third living creature say, "Come!" And, behold, there came a black horse, and he who sat upon it had the beam of a balance in his hand. And I heard as it were a voice in the middle of the four living creatures saying: "A measure of wheat for a *denarius*, and three measures of barley for a *denarius*. But you must not injure the oil and the wine."

And, when he had opened the fourth seal, I heard the voice of the fourth living creature saying, "Come!" And I saw, and, behold, there came a pale horse, and the name of him who sat upon it was Death, and Hades followed with him; and they were given power over a fourth part of the earth, to kill with the sword, and with famine, and with pestilence, and by the wild beasts of the earth.

BEFORE we embark on a detailed interpretation of this vision, we note two important points.

(i) We note that the *origin* of this vision is in *Zechariah* 6: 1–8. Zechariah sees four horses which are let loose upon the earth to deal out vengeance on Babylon and Egypt and the nations which have oppressed God's people. "These are going forth to the four winds of heaven, after presenting themselves before the Lord of all the earth" (*Zechariah* 6: 5). The horses stand for the four mighty winds which God is about to let loose on the earth with a blast of destruction. John does not keep the details the same; but for him, too, the horses and their riders are the instruments of the avenging judgment of God.

(ii) We must explain the method of interpretation which we think must be used. The four horses and their riders stand for four great destructive forces which are in the times before the end to be despatched against the evil world by the holy wrath of God. But, John sees these forces in terms of actual events in the world which he knew where life seemed a chaos, the world seemed to be disintegrating, and the earth seemed to be full of terrors. The horses and their riders are forces of destruction and agents of wrath; they are not to be identified with any historical figures but in the events of his own time John saw symbols and types of the destruction to come.

Our method of interpretation will, therefore, be to define the destructive force for which each of the horses stands, and then, where possible, to find circumstances in the history of John's own time which illustrate the destruction to come. We will further see that in more than one case John is dealing in pictures and ideas which were part of the stock in trade of the writers of these visions of the days of the end.

## THE WHITE HORSE OF CONQUEST

*Revelation* 6 : 1, 2

> And I saw, when the Lamb opened the first of the seals, and I heard one of the four living creatures saying with a loud voice like the sound of thunder: "Come!" And I saw, and, behold a white horse, and he who was seated on it had a bow, and a conqueror's crown was given to him, and he went forth conquering and to conquer.

As each of the seven seals is broken and opened, a new terror falls upon the earth. The first terror is depicted under the form of a white horse and its rider. What do they represent? Two explanations have been suggested, one of which is certainly wrong.

(i) It has been suggested that the rider on the white horse is the victorious Christ himself. This conclusion is drawn because this picture is connected by some commentators with that in *Revelation* 19: 11, 12 which tells of a white horse and on it a rider, called Faithful and True and crowned with many crowns, who is the victorious Christ. It is to be noted that the crown in this passage is different from that in *Revelation* 19. Here the crown is *stephanos*, which is the *victor's* crown; in *Revelation* 19 it is *diadēma*, which is the royal crown. The passage we are here studying is telling of woe upon woe and disaster upon disaster; any picture of the victorious Christ is quite out of place in it. This picture tells of the coming not of the victor Christ but of the terrors of the wrath of God.

(ii) Quite certainly, the white horse and its rider stand for conquest in war. When a Roman general celebrated a triumph, that is, when he paraded through the streets of Rome with his armies and his captives and his spoils after some great victory, his chariot was drawn by white horses, the symbol of victory.

But, as we said in the introduction to this passage, John is clothing his predictions of the future in pictures of the present which his readers would recognize. The rider of the horse had in his hand a *bow*. In the Old Testament the bow is always the sign of military power. In the final defeat of Babylon her mighty men are taken and their bows—that is, their military power—destroyed (*Jeremiah* 51: 56). God will break the bow of Israel in the valley of Jezreel (*Hosea* 1: 5). God breaks the bow and shatters the spear in sunder and burns the chariots with fire; that is, against him no human military power can stand (*Psalm* 46: 9). The bow, then, would always stand for military power. But there is one particular picture which the Romans and all who dwelt in Asia would at once recognize. The one enemy whom the Romans feared was the Parthian power. The Parthians dwelt on the far eastern frontiers of the Empire and were the scourge of Rome. In A.D. 62 an unprecedented event had occurred; a Roman army had actually surrendered to Vologeses, the king of the Parthians. The Parthians rode white horses and were the most famous bowmen in the world. A "Parthian shot" still means a final, devastating blow, to which there is no possible answer.

So, then, the white horse and its rider with the bow stand for militarism and conquest.

Here is something which it has taken men long to learn. Military conquest has been presented as a thing of glamour; but it is always tragedy. When Euripides wished to depict warfare upon the stage, he did not bring on an army with banners. He brought on a bent and bewildered old woman leading by the hand a weeping child who had lost his parents. During the Spanish civil war a journalist told how he suddenly realized what war was. He was in a Spanish city in which the opposing parties were waging guerrilla warfare. He saw walking along the pavement a little boy, obviously lost, and bewildered and terrified, dragging along a toy which had lost its wheels. Suddenly there was the crack of a rifle

shot; and the little boy pitched on the ground, dead. That is
war. First among the tragic terrors of the terrible times John
sets the white horse and the man with the bow, the vision of
the tragedy of militaristic conquest.

## THE BLOOD-RED HORSE OF STRIFE

*Revelation* 6: 3, 4

When he had opened the second seal, I heard the second living
creature say: "Come!" And there came forth another horse,
blood-red in colour, and to him that sat upon it there was given to
take peace from the earth, and to bring it about that men should
slay each other, and a great sword was given to him.

THE function of the second horse and its rider is to take
peace from the earth. They stand for that destructive strife
which sets man against man and nation against nation in a
chaos of tragic destruction. There are two backgrounds to this.

(i) John was writing in a time when internecine strife was
tearing the world apart. In the thirty years before the reign of
Herod the Great, 67 to 37 B.C., in Palestine alone no
fewer than 100,000 men had perished in abortive revolutions.
In A.D. 61 in Britain there had arisen the rebellion connected
with the name of Queen Boadicea. The Romans crushed it,
Boadicea committed suicide and 150,000 men perished.

(ii) In the Jewish pictures of the end time, an essential
element is the complete disintegration of all human relationships. Brother will fight against brother, neighbour against
neighbour, city will rise against city, and kingdom against
kingdom (*Isaiah* 19: 2). Every man's hand shall be against
the hand of his neighbour (*Zechariah* 14: 13). From dawn to
sunset they will slay each other (*Enoch* 100: 12). Friend shall
war against friend; friends will attack one another suddenly
(4 *Ezra* 5: 9; 6: 24). Some of them shall fall in battle, and
some of them shall perish in anguish, and some of them
shall be destroyed by their own (2 *Baruch* 70: 2–8). Many shall

be stirred up in anger to injure many, and they shall rouse up all men in order to shed blood, and in the end they will all perish together (2 *Baruch* 48: 37).

The vision of the end was a vision of a time when all human relationships would be destroyed and the world a seething cauldron of embittered hate.

It is still true that the nation in which there is division between man and man and class and class and hatred based on competitive ambition and selfish desire is doomed; and the world in which nation is set against nation is hastening to its end.

## THE BLACK HORSE OF FAMINE

*Revelation* 6: 5, 6

> When he had opened the third seal, I heard the third living creature say: "Come!" And, behold, there came a black horse, and he who sat upon it had the beam of a balance in his hand. And I heard, as it were, a voice in the midst of the four living creatures saying: "A measure of wheat for a *denarius*, and three measures of barley for a *denarius*. But you must not injure the oil and the wine."

IT will help us to understand the idea behind this passage if we remember that John is giving an account not of the end of things, but of the signs and events which precede the end. So here the black horse and its rider represent famine, a famine which is very severe and causes great hardship, but which is not desperate enough to kill. There is wheat—at a prohibitive price; and the wine and the oil are not affected.

The three main crops of Palestine were the corn, the wine and the oil; and it is these three which are always mentioned when the crops of the land are being described (*Deuteronomy* 7: 13; 11: 14; 28: 51; *Hosea* 2: 8, 22). The rider of the horse had the cross-beam of a balance in his hand. In the Old Testament the phrase *to eat bread by weight* indicates the greatest scarcity. In *Leviticus* it is the threat of God that, if the people are disobedient "they shall deliver your bread again by weight" (*Leviticus* 26 : 26). It is the threat of God to Ezekiel: "I will break the staff of bread in Jerusalem; they shall eat bread by weight and with fearfulness" (*Ezekiel* 4 : 16).

It was not entirely abnormal that there should be wine and oil when there was no corn. The olive and the vine were much more deeply-rooted than the corn; and they could stand a drought which would wipe out the corn crop. When Jacob had to send down to Egypt for corn in the days of the famine in the time of Joseph, he was still able to send with his sons a gift of "the choice fruits of the land" (*Genesis* 43: 11). But it is true that a situation in which wine and oil were plentiful and corn prohibitively dear would be the equivalent of one in which luxuries were plentiful and necessities scarce.

We can see the extent of the scarcity from the statement of the voice from amidst the four living creatures. A measure of wheat or three measures of barley was to cost a *denarius*. The measure was a *choinix*, equivalent to two pints and consistently defined in the ancient world as a man's ration for a day. A *denarius* was the equivalent of four pence and was a working man's wage for a day. Normally one *denarius* bought anything from eight to sixteen measures of corn and three to four times as much barley. What John is foretelling is a situation in which a man's whole working wage would be needed to buy enough corn for himself for a day, leaving absolutely nothing to buy any of the other necessities of life and absolutely nothing for his wife and family. If instead of corn he bought the much inferior barley, he might manage to give some to his wife and family but again he would have nothing to buy anything else.

We have seen that, although John was telling of the signs which were to precede the end, he was nevertheless painting them in terms of actual historical situations which men would recognize. There had been desperate famines in the time of Nero which left the luxury of the rich untouched. There was an occasion when a ship arrived in Italy from Alexandria. The starving populace thought it was a cornship, for all the cornships came from Alexandria; and they rioted when they discovered that the cargo was not corn but a special kind of sand from the Nile Delta to spread upon the ground of the arena for a gladiatorial show. This passage finds an amazing echo in certain events during the reign of Domitian, at the very time when John was writing. There was a very serious shortage of grain and also a superabundance of wine. Domitian took the drastic step of enacting that no fresh vineyards should be planted and that half the vineyards in the provinces should be cut down. At this edict the people of the province of Asia, in which John was writing, came very near to rebelling for their vineyards were one of their principal sources of revenue. In view of the violent reaction of the people of Asia, Domitian rescinded his edict and actually enacted that those who allowed their vineyards to go out of cultivation should be prosecuted. Here is the very picture of a situation in which corn was scarce and it was yet forbidden to interfere with the supply of wine and oil.

So, then, this is a picture of famine set alongside luxury. There is always something radically wrong with a situation in which some have too much and others too little. This is always a sign that the society in which it occurs is hastening to its ruin.

There is one other interesting point which, it has been suggested, is in this passage. It is from the midst of the four living creatures that there comes the voice telling of the famine prices of corn. We have already seen that the four living creatures may well symbolize all that is best in nature; and this may well be taken to be nature's protest against famine amidst men. The tragedy has nearly always been that nature produces enough, and more than enough, but that there are many people to whom that abundance never comes. It is as if John was symbolically indicating that nature herself protests when the gifts she offers are used selfishly and irresponsibly for the luxury of the few at the expense of the many.

## THE PALE HORSE OF PESTILENCE AND DEATH

*Revelation* 6: 7, 8

When he had opened the fourth seal, I heard the voice of the fourth living creature saying: "Come!" And I saw, and, behold, there came a pale horse, and the name of him who sat upon it was Death, and Hades followed with him; and they were given power over a fourth part of the earth, to kill with the sword, and with famine, and with pestilence and by the wild beasts of the earth.

As we approach this passage we must once again remember that it is telling not of the final end but of the signs which precede it. That is why it is a fourth part of the earth which is involved in death and disaster. This is a terrible time but it is not the time of total destruction.

The picture is a grim one. The horse is *pale* in colour. The word is *chlōros* which means pale in the sense of livid and is used of a face blenched with terror. The passage is complicated by the fact that the Greek word *thanatos* is used in a double sense. In verse 8 it is used to mean both *death* and *pestilence*.

John was writing in a time when famine and pestilence did devastate the world; but in this case he is thinking in terms provided by the Old Testament which more than once speaks of "the four sore judgments." Ezekiel hears God tell of the time when he will send his "four sore acts of judgment upon Jerusalem"—sword, famine, evil beasts, and pestilence (*Ezekiel* 14: 21). In *Leviticus* there is a passage which tells of the penalties which God will send upon his people because of their disobedience. Wild beasts will rob them of their children and destroy their cattle and make them few in number. The sword will avenge their breaches of the covenant. When they are gathered in their cities the pestilence will be among them. He will break the staff of bread and they will eat and not be satisfied (*Leviticus* 26: 21–26).

Here John is using a traditional picture of what is to happen when God despatches his wrath upon his disobedient people. At the back of it all is the permanent truth that no man or nation can escape the consequences of their sin.

## THE SOULS OF THE MARTYRS

*Revelation* 6: 9–11

When he opened the fifth seal, I saw beneath the altar the souls of those who had been slain for the sake of the word of God and because of the witness which they bore. And they cried with a loud voice: "How long, Lord, Holy and True, will you refrain from judging and avenging our blood on those who dwell upon the earth?" And to each of them was given a white robe, and they were told to rest for still a little while, until there should be completed the number of their fellow-servants and of their brothers who must be killed.

AT the breaking of the fifth seal comes the vision of the souls of those who had died for their faith.

Jesus left his followers in no doubt as to the suffering and the martyrdom they would be called upon to endure. "Then they will deliver you up to tribulation, and put you to death; and you will be hated of all nations for my name's sake" (*Matthew* 24: 9; *Mark* 13: 9–13; *Luke* 21: 12, 18). The day would come when those who killed Christians would think they were doing a service for God (*John* 16: 2).

The idea of an altar in heaven is one that occurs more than once in the *Revelation* (8: 5; 14: 18). It is not by any means a new idea. When the furnishings of the tabernacle were to be made, they were all to be constructed according to the pattern which God possessed and would show (*Exodus* 25: 9, 40; *Numbers* 8: 4; *Hebrews* 8: 5; 9: 23). It is the consistent idea of those who wrote about the Tabernacle and the Temple that the pattern of all the holy things already existed in heaven.

The souls of those who had been slain were there beneath the altar. That picture is taken directly from the sacrificial ritual of the Temple. For a Jew the most sacred part of any sacrifice was the blood; the blood was regarded as being the life and the life belonged to God (*Leviticus* 17: 11–14). Because of that, there were special regulations for the offering of the blood.

"The rest of the blood of the bull the priest shall pour out at the base of the altar of burnt offering" (*Leviticus* 4: 7). That is to say, the blood is offered at the foot of the altar.

This gives us the meaning of our passage here. The souls of the martyrs are *beneath the altar*. That is to say, their life-blood has been poured out as an offering to God. The idea of the martyr's life as a sacrifice to God is in the mind of Paul. He says that he will rejoice, if he is *offered up* on the sacrifice and the service of the faith of the Philippians (*Philippians* 2: 17). "I am already," he says, "on the point of being sacrificed" (2 *Timothy* 4: 6). In the time of the Maccabees the Jews suffered terribly for their faith. There was a mother whose seven sons were threatened with death because of their loyalty to their Jewish beliefs. She encouraged them not to yield and reminded them how Abraham had not refused to offer Isaac. She told them that, when they reached their glory, they must tell Abraham that he had built one altar of sacrifice but their mother had built seven. In later Judaism it was said that Michael, the archangel, sacrificed on the heavenly altar the souls of the righteous and of those who had been faithful students of the law. When Ignatius of Antioch was on his way to Rome to be burned, his prayer was that he should be found a sacrifice belonging to God.

There is a great and uplifting truth here. When a good man dies for the sake of goodness, it may look like tragedy, like the waste of a fine life; like the work of evil men; and, indeed, it may be all these things. But every life laid down for right and truth and God is ultimately more than any of these things—it is an offering made to God.

## THE CRY OF THE MARTYRS

*Revelation* 6: 9–11 (*continued*)

THERE are three things in this section which we must note.

(i) We have the eternal cry of the suffering righteous—"How long?" This was the cry of the Psalmist. How long were the heathen to be allowed to afflict God's righteous people?

How long were they to be allowed to taunt his people by asking where God was and what he was doing? (*Psalm* 79: 5–10). The thing to remember is that when the saints of God uttered this cry, they were bewildered by God's seeming inactivity but they never doubted his ultimate action, and the ultimate vindication of the righteous.

(ii) We have a picture which is easy to criticize. The saints actually wished to *see* the punishment of their persecutors. It is hard for us to understand the idea that part of the joy of heaven was to see the punishment of the sinners in Hell. In the *Assumption of Moses* the Jewish writer (10: 10) hears God promise:

> And thou shalt look from on high and shalt see thy enemies in
>     Gehenna.
> And thou shalt recognize them and rejoice,
> And thou shalt give thanks and confess thy Creator.

In later times Tertullian (*Concerning Spectacles* 30) was to taunt the heathen with their love of spectacles and to say that the spectacle to which the Christian most looked forward was to see his one-time persecutors writhing in Hell.

> You are fond of spectacles; expect the greatest of all spectacles, the last and eternal judgment of the universe. How shall I admire, how laugh, how rejoice, how exult, when I behold so many proud monarchs, and fancied gods, groaning in the lowest abyss of darkness; so many magistrates who persecuted the name of the Lord, liquefying in fiercer flames than they ever kindled against the Christians; so many sage philosophers blushing in red hot flames with their deluded scholars; so many celebrated poets trembling before the tribunal, not of Minos, but of Christ; so many tragedians more tuneful in the expression of their own sufferings; so many dancers writhing in the flames.

It is easy to stand aghast at the spirit of vengeance which could write like that. But we must remember what these men went through, the agony of the flames, of the arena and the wild beasts, of the sadistic torture which they suffered. We have the right to criticize only when we have gone through the same agony.

(iii) The martyrs must rest in peace for a little longer until their number is made up. The Jews had the conviction that the drama of history had to be played out in full before the end could come. God would not stir until the measure appointed had been fulfilled (2 *Esdras* 4: 36). The number of the righteous first has to be offered (*Enoch* 47: 4). The Messiah would not come until all the souls which were to be born had been born. The same idea finds its echo in the burial prayer in the Anglican Prayer Book that "it may please thee shortly to accomplish the number of thine elect and to hasten thy kingdom." It is a curious notion but at the back of it is the idea that all history is in the hand of God, and that in it and through it all he is working his purpose out to its certain end.

## THE SHATTERED UNIVERSE

*Revelation* 6: 12–14

> I saw when he opened the sixth seal, and there was a great earthquake, and the sun became black like sackcloth made of hair, and the whole moon became like blood; and the stars of the heaven fell upon the earth, as a fig-tree casts its figs, when it is shaken by a high wind; and the heavens were split like a roll that is rolled up, and the hills and islands were moved from their places.

JOHN is using pictures very familiar to his Jewish readers. The Jews always regarded the end as a time when the earth would be shattered and there would be cosmic upheaval and destruction. In the picture there are, as it were, five elements which can all be abundantly illustrated from the Old Testament and from the books written between the Testaments.

(i) There is the *earthquake*. At the coming of the Lord the earth will tremble (*Amos* 8: 8). There will be a great shaking in the land of Israel (*Ezekiel* 38: 19). The earth will quake and the heavens will tremble (*Joel* 2: 10). God will shake the heavens and the earth and the sea and the dry land (*Haggai* 2: 6). The earth will tremble and be shaken to its bounds; the hills will be shaken and fall (*Assumption of Moses* 10: 4). The earth shall open and fire burst forth (2 *Esdras* 5: 8). Whoever gets out of the war will die in the earthquake; and whoever gets out of the earthquake will die in the fire, and whoever gets out of the fire will perish in the famine (2 *Baruch* 70: 8). The Jewish prophets and seers saw a time when earth would be shattered and a tide of destruction would flow ever the old world before the new world was born.

(ii) There is *the darkening of the sun and moon*. The sun will set at midday, and earth will grow dark in the clear day light (*Amos* 8: 9). The stars will not shine; the sun will be darkened in his going forth and the moon will not cause her light to shine (*Isaiah* 13: 10). God will clothe the heavens with blackness and will make sackcloth their covering (*Isaiah* 50: 3). God will make the stars dark and cover the sun with a cloud (*Ezekiel* 32: 7). The sun will be turned into darkness and the moon into blood (*Joel* 2: 31). The horns of the sun will be broken and he will be turned into darkness, the moon will not give her light, and will be turned into blood; and the circle of the stars will be disturbed (*Assumption of Moses* 10: 4, 5). The sun will be darkened and the moon will not give her light (*Matthew* 24: 29; *Mark* 13: 24; *Luke* 23: 45).

(iii) There is *the falling of the stars*. To the Jew this idea was specially terrible, for the order of the heavens was the very guarantee of the unchanging fidelity of God. Take away the reliability of the heavens and there was nothing left but chaos. The angel tells Enoch to behold the heavens, to see how the heavenly bodies never change their orbits or transgress against their appointed order (*Enoch* 2: 1). Enoch saw the chambers of the sun and moon, how they go out and come in, how they never leave their orbit, and add nothing to it and take nothing from it (*Enoch* 41: 5). To the Jew the last word in chaos was a world of falling stars. But in the end time the host of heaven would be dissolved and fall down as the leaf falls from the vine and the fig from the fig-tree (*Isaiah* 34: 4). The stars will fall from heaven and the powers of heaven shall be shaken (*Matthew* 24: 29). The firmament shall fall on the sea and a cataract of fire will reduce the heavens and the stars to a molten mass (*Sibylline Oracles* 3: 83). The stars will transgress their order and alter their orbits (*Enoch* 80: 5, 6). The outgoings of the stars will change (2 *Esdras* 5: 4). The end will be a time when the most reliable things in the universe will become a disorderly and terrifying chaos.

(iv) There is *the folding up of the heavens*. The picture in this passage is of a roll stretched out and held open, and then suddenly split down the middle so that each half recoils and rolls up. God will shake the heavens (*Isaiah* 13: 13). The heavens will be rolled together as a scroll (*Isaiah* 34: 4). They will be changed like a garment and folded up (*Psalm* 102: 25, 26). At the end the eternal heavens themselves will be rent in two.

(v) There is *the moving of the hills and of the islands of the sea*. The mountains will tremble and the hills will be moved (*Jeremiah* 4: 24). The mountains will quake and the hills will melt (*Nahum* 1: 5). John saw a time when the most unshakeable things would be shaken and when even rocky isles like Patmos would be lifted from their foundation.

Strange as John's pictures may seem to us, there is not a single detail which is not in the pictures of the end time in the Old Testament and in the books written between the Testaments. We must not think that these pictures are to be taken literally. Their point is that John is taking every terrifying thing that can be imagined and piling them all together to give a picture of the terrors of the end time. Today, with our increased scientific knowledge, we might well paint the picture in different terms; but it is not the picture that matters. What matters is the terrors which John and the Jewish seers foresaw when God would invade the earth when time was coming to an end.

## THE TIME OF TERROR

*Revelation* 6: 15–17

And the kings of the earth and the great ones and the captains

and the rich and the strong, and every slave and every free person
hid themselves in the caves and the rocks of the hills, and said to
the mountains and to the rocks: "Fall on us, and hide us from the
face of him who is seated on the throne, and from the wrath
of the Lamb, because the great day of their wrath has come, and
who can stand?"

As John saw it in his vision, the end time was to be one of
universal terror. Here again he is working with pictures
familiar to all who knew the Old Testament and the later
Jewish writings. When the Day of the Lord came, men would
be afraid; pangs and sorrows would take hold of them; they
would be in pain as a woman who travails; and they would
be amazed at one another (*Isaiah* 13: 6, 8). At that time even
the mighty man would cry bitterly (*Zephaniah* 1: 14). The
inhabitants of the land would tremble (*Joel* 2: 1). They would
be frighted with fear; there would be no place to which to
flee and no place in which to hide; the children of earth would
tremble and quake (*Enoch* 102: 1, 3). God would come to
be a witness against his sinning people (*Micah* 1: 1–4). He
would be like a refiner's fire, and who might abide the day
of his coming? (*Malachi* 3: 1–3). The Day of the Lord would
be great and terrible, and who could endure it? (*Joel* 2: 11).
Men would say to the mountains, "Cover us," and to the hills,
"Fall on us" (*Hosea* 10: 8), words which Jesus quoted on the
way to the Cross (*Luke* 23: 30).

This passage has two significant things to say about this fear.

(i) It is universal. Verse 15 speaks of the kings, the captains,
the great ones, the rich, the strong, the slave and the free. It has
been pointed out that these seven words include "the whole
fabric of human society." No one is exempt from the
judgment of God. The great ones may well be the Roman
governors who persecute the Church; the captains are the
military authorities. However great a governor a man is and
however much power he wields, he is still subject to the
judgment of God. However rich a man may be, however
strong, however free he may count himself, however much of

a slave, however insignificant, he does not escape the judgment of God.

(ii) When the day of the Lord comes, John sees people seeking somewhere to hide. Here is the great truth that the first instinct of sin is to hide. In the Garden of Eden Adam and Eve sought to hide themselves (*Genesis* 3: 8). H. B. Swete says: "What sinners dread most is not death, but the revealed presence of God." The terrible thing about sin is that it makes a man a fugitive from God; and the supreme thing about the work of Jesus Christ is that it puts a man into a relationship with God in which he no longer need seek to hide, knowing that he can cast himself on the love and the mercy of God.

(iii) We note one last thing. That from which men flee is *the wrath of the Lamb*. Here is paradox; we do not readily associate wrath with the Lamb but rather gentleness and kindness. But the wrath of God is the wrath of love, which is not out to destroy but even in anger is out to save the one it loves.

## RESCUE AND REWARD

*Revelation* 7: 1–3

> After this I saw four angels standing at the four corners of the earth, restraining the four winds of the earth so that the wind might not blow upon the earth, or upon the sea, or against any tree. And I saw another angel going up from where the sun rises, with a seal which belonged to the living God, and he shouted with a great voice to the four angels to whom was given power to harm the earth and the sea: "Do not harm the earth and the sea or the trees until we seal the servants of our God upon their foreheads."

BEFORE we deal with this chapter in detail, it is better to set out the general picture behind it.

John is seeing the vision of the last terrible days and in particular the great tribulation which is to come, such as was not since the beginning of the world to this time (*Matthew* 24: 21; *Mark* 13: 19). In this coming tribulation there was to be a final assault by every evil power and a final devastation of the earth. It is to play their part in this devastation that the winds are waiting and from which for a little while they are being held in check.

Before this time of terror and devastation comes, the faithful are to be sealed with the seal of God in order that they may survive it. It is not that they are to be exempt from it but that they are to be brought safely through it.

This is a terrible picture; even if the faithful are to be brought through this terrible time, they none the less must pass through it, and this is a prospect to make even the bravest shudder.

In verse 9 the range of the seer's vision extends still further and he sees the faithful after the tribulation has passed. They are in perfect peace and satisfaction in the very presence of God. The last time will bring them unspeakable horrors, but when they have passed through it they will enter into equally unspeakable joy.

There are really three elements in this picture. (i) There is a *warning*. The last unparalleled and inconceivable time of tribulation is coming soon. (ii) There is an *assurance*. In that time of destruction the faithful will suffer terribly, but they will come out on the other side because they are sealed with the seal of God. (iii) There is a *promise*. When they have passed through that time, they will come to the blessedness in which all pain and sorrow are gone and there is nothing but peace and joy.

## THE WINDS OF GOD

*Revelation* 7: 1–3 (*continued*)

THIS vision is expressed in conceptions of the world which were the conceptions of the days in which John wrote.

The earth is a square, flat earth; and at its four corners are four angels waiting to unleash the winds of destruction. Isaiah speaks of gathering the outcasts of Judah from the four corners of the earth (*Isaiah* 11: 12). The end is come upon the four corners of the earth in Ezekiel (*Ezekiel* 7: 2).

It was the belief of the ancient peoples that the winds which came from due north, south, east and west were all favourable winds; but that those which blew diagonally across the earth were harmful. That is why the angels are at the corners of the earth. They are about to unleash the winds which blow diagonally. It was the common belief that all the forces of nature were under the charge of angels. So we read of the angel of the fire (*Revelation* 14: 18) and the angel of the waters (*Revelation* 16: 5). These angels were called "The Angels of Service." They belonged to the very lowest order of angels, because they had to be continually on duty and, therefore, could not keep the Sabbath as a day of rest. Pious Israelites who faithfully observed the Law of the Sabbath were said to rank higher than these angels of service.

The angels are bidden to restrain the winds until the work of sealing the faithful should be completed. This idea has more than one echo in Jewish literature. In *Enoch* the angels of the waters are bidden by God to hold the waters in check until Noah had built the ark (*Enoch* 66: 1, 2). In 2 *Baruch* the angels with the flaming torches are bidden to restrain their fire, when Jerusalem was sacked by the Babylonians, until the sacred vessels of the Temple could be hidden away and saved from the looting of the invaders (2 *Baruch* 6: 4). More than once we see the angels restraining the forces of destruction until the safety of the faithful has been made secure.

One of the interesting and picturesque ideas of the Old Testament is that of the winds as the servants and the agents of God. This was specially so of the Sirocco, the dread wind from the south-east, with the blast like hot air from a furnace which withered and destroyed all vegetation. Zechariah has the picture of the chariots of the winds, which go forth from standing before the Lord of all the earth (*Zechariah* 6: 1–5). Nahum speaks of the Lord who has his way in the whirlwind (the Sirocco) and the storm (*Nahum* 1: 3).

The Lord goes with the whirlwinds of the south (*Zechariah* 9: 14). The winds are God's chariots (*Jeremiah* 4: 13). God comes with his chariots like a whirlwind (*Isaiah* 66: 15). The wind is the breath of God (*Job* 37: 9, 10). The wind rends the mountains (1 *Kings* 19: 11) and withers the grass (*Isaiah* 40: 7, 24) and dries up the stream, the river and the sea (*Nahum* 1: 4; *Psalm* 18: 15).

So terrible was the effect of the Sirocco that it gained a place in the pictures of the last days. One of the terrors which was to precede the end was a terrible storm. God would destroy his enemies as stubble before the wind (*Psalm* 83: 13). God's day would be the day of the whirlwind (*Amos* 1: 14). The whirlwind of the Lord goes forth in its fury and falls on the head of the wicked (*Jeremiah* 23: 19; 30: 23). The wind of the Lord, the Sirocco, will come from the wilderness and destroy the fertility of the land (*Hosea* 13: 15). God will send his four winds upon Elam and scatter the people (*Jeremiah* 49: 36).

This is difficult for many of us to understand; the dweller in the temperate countries does not know the terror of the wind. But there is something here more far-reaching than that and more characteristic of Jewish thought, the Jews knew nothing of secondary causes. We say that atmospheric conditions, variations in temperature, land and mountain configurations, cause certain things to happen. The Jew ascribed it all to the direct action of God. He simply said, God sent the rain; God made the wind to blow; God thundered; God sent his lightning.

Surely both points of view are correct, for we may still believe that God acts through the laws by which his universe is governed.

### THE LIVING GOD

*Revelation* 7: 1–3 (*continued*)

BEFORE the great tribulation smites the earth the faithful ones are to be marked with the seal of God. There are two points to note.

(i) The angel with the seal comes from the rising of the sun, from the East. All John's pictures mean something and there may be two meanings behind this. (*a*) It is in the East that the sun, the supreme earthly giver of light and life, rises; and the angel may stand for the life and the light that God gives his people even when death and destruction are abroad. (*b*) It is just possible that John is remembering something from the story of the birth of Jesus. The wise men come to Palestine searching for the king who is to be born, for "We have seen his star in the East" (*Matthew* 2: 2). It is natural that the delivering angel should rise in the same part of the sky as the star which told of the birth of the Saviour.

(ii) The angel has the seal which belongs to the *living God*. *The living God* is a phrase in which the writers of Scripture delight and when they use it, there are certain things in their minds.

(*a*) They are thinking of the living God in contra-distinction to the dead gods of the heathen. Isaiah has a tremendous passage of sublime mockery of the heathen and their dead gods whom their own hands have made (*Isaiah* 44: 9–17). The smith takes a mass of metal and works at it with the hammer and the tongs and the coals, sweating and parched at his task of manufacturing a god. The carpenter goes out and cuts down a tree. He works at it with line and compass and plane. Part of it he uses to make a fire to warm himself; part of it he uses to make a fire to bake his bread and roast his meat; and part of it he uses to make a god. The heathen gods are dead and created by men; our God is alive and the creator of all things.

(*b*) The idea of the living God is used as an encouragement. In the midst of their struggles Joshua reminds the people that with them there is the living God and that he will show his strength in their conflicts with their enemies (*Joshua* 3: 10). When a man is up against it, the living God is with him.

(*c*) Only in the living God is there satisfaction. It is the living God for whom the soul of the psalmist longs and thirsts (*Psalm* 42: 2). Man can never find satisfaction in things but only in fellowship with a living person; and he finds his highest satisfaction in the fellowship of the living God.

(*d*) The biblical writers stress the privilege of knowing and belonging to the living God. Hosea reminds the people of Israel that once they were not a people, but in mercy they have become children of the living God (*Hosea* 1: 10). Our privilege is that there is open to us the friendship, the fellowship, the help, the power and the presence of the living God.

(*e*) In the idea of the living God there is at one and the same time a promise and a threat. *Second Kings* vividly tells the story of how the great king Sennacherib sent his envoy Rabshakeh to tell Hezekiah that he proposed to wipe out the nation of Israel. Humanly speaking, the little kingdom of Judah had no hope of survival, if the might of Assyria was launched against it. But with Israel there was the living God and he was a threat to the godlessness of Assyria and a promise to the faithful of Israel (2 *Kings* 18: 17–37).

## THE SEAL OF GOD

*Revelation* 7: 4–8

And I heard the number of those who were sealed, one hundred and forty-four thousand were sealed from every tribe of the sons of Israel. Of the tribe of Judah twelve thousand were sealed; of the tribe of Reuben, twelve thousand; of the tribe of Gad, twelve thousand; of the tribe of Asher, twelve thousand; of the tribe of Naphtali, twelve thousand; of the tribe of Manasseh, twelve thousand; of the tribe of Simeon, twelve thousand; of the tribe of Levi, twelve thousand; of the tribe of Issachar, twelve thousand; of the tribe of Zebulun, twelve thousand; of the tribe of Joseph, twelve thousand; of the tribe of Benjamin, twelve thousand.

THOSE who are to be brought safely through the great tribulation are sealed upon their foreheads. The origin of this picture is very likely in *Ezekiel* 9. In Ezekiel's picture, before the final slaughter begins, the man with the inkhorn marks the forehead of those who are faithful and the avengers are told that none so marked must be touched (*Ezekiel* 9: 1–7).

The idea of the king's seal would be very meaningful in the East. Eastern kings wore a signet ring whose seal was used to authenticate documents as really coming from the king's hand and to mark that which was the king's personal property. When Pharaoh appointed Joseph his prime minister and representative, he gave him his signet ring in token of the authority which had been delegated to him (*Genesis* 41: 42). So Ahasuerus gave his signet ring, first to Haman and then, when Haman's wicked schemes were unmasked, to Mordecai (*Esther* 3: 10; 8: 2). The stone which shut Daniel into the lion's den was sealed (*Daniel* 6: 17), as was the stone with which the Jews sought to make the tomb of Jesus secure (*Matthew* 27: 66).

Very commonly a seal indicated source or possession. A merchant would seal a package of goods to certify that it belonged to him; and the owner of a vineyard would seal jars of wine to show that they came from his vineyard and with his guarantee.

So here the seal was a sign that these people belonged to God and were under his power and authority.

In the early church this picture of sealing was specially connected with two things. (*a*) It was connected with baptism which was regularly described as sealing. It is as if, when a person was baptized, a mark was put upon him to show that he had become the property and the possession of God. (*b*) Paul regularly talks about the Christian being sealed with the gift of the Holy Spirit. The possession of the Holy Spirit is the sign that a man belongs to God. The real Christian is marked out by the seal of the Spirit which enables him to have the wisdom and the strength to cope with life in a way beyond the attainment of others.

## THE NUMBER OF THE FAITHFUL

*Revelation* 7: 4–8 (*continued*)

THERE are certain quite general things to be noted here which will greatly help towards the interpretation of this passage.

(i) Two things are to be said about the number 144,000. (*a*) It is quite certain that it does not stand for the number of the faithful in every day and generation. The 144,000 stands for those who in the time of John are sealed and preserved from the great tribulation which at that moment was coming upon them. In due time, as we see in verse 9, they are to be merged with the great crowd beyond all counting and drawn from every nation. (*b*) The number 144,000 stands, not for limitation but for completeness and perfection. It is made up of 12 multiplied by 12—the perfect square—and then rendered even more inclusive and complete by being multiplied by 1,000 This does not tell us that the number of the saved will be very small; it tells us that the number of the saved will be very great.

(ii) The enumeration in terms of the twelve tribes of Israel does not mean that this is to be read in purely Jewish terms. One of the basic thoughts of the New Testament is that the Church is the real Israel, and that the national Israel has lost all its privileges and promises to the Church. Paul writes: "He is not a real Jew who is one outwardly, nor is true circumcision something external and physical. He is a Jew who is one inwardly, and real circumcision is a matter of the heart, spiritual and not literal. His praise is not from men but from God" (*Romans* 2: 28, 29). "Not all who are descended from Israel belong to Israel," says Paul (*Romans* 9: 6, 7). If a man is Christ's, then is he Abraham's seed and an heir according to the promise (*Galatians* 3: 29). It is the Church which is the Israel of God (*Galatians* 6: 16). It is Christians who are the real circumcision, those who worship God in the spirit, who rejoice in Christ Jesus and who have no confidence in the flesh (*Philippians* 3: 3). Even if this passage is stated in terms of the twelve tribes of Israel, the reference is still to the Church of God, the new Israel, the Israel of God.

(iii) It would be a mistake to place any stress on the order in which the twelve tribes are given, because the lists of the tribes are always varying in their order. But two things stand out. (*a*) Judah comes first, thus supplanting Reuben, who was the eldest son of Jacob. That is simply explained by the fact it was from the tribe of Judah that the Messiah came. (*b*) Much more interesting is the omission of Dan. But there is also an explanation of that. In the Old Testament Dan does not hold a high place and is often connected with idolatry. In Jacob's dying speech to his sons, it is said: "Dan shall be a serpent in the way, a viper by the path, that bites the horse's heels, so that his rider falls backward" (*Genesis* 49: 17). In Judges the children of Dan are said to have set up a graven image (*Judges* 18: 30). The golden calves, which became a sin, were set up in Bethel and in Dan (1 *Kings* 12: 29). There is more. There is a curious saying in *Jeremiah* 8: 16: "The snorting of their horses is heard from Dan; at the sound of the neighing of their stallions the whole land quakes. They come and devour the land and all that fills it." That saying came to be taken as referring to Antichrist, the coming incarnation of evil; and it came to be believed among the Jewish Rabbis that Antichrist was to spring from Dan. Hippolytus (*Concerning Antichrist* 14) says: "As the Christ was born from the tribe of Judah, so will the Antichrist be born from the tribe of Dan." That is why Dan is missed out from this list and the list completed by the including of Manasseh, who is normally included in Joseph.

## THE GLORY OF THE MARTYRS

*Revelation* 7: 9, 10

After this I saw, and, behold, a great crowd, so great that none could count its number, drawn from every race and from all tribes and peoples and tongues, standing before the throne and before the

Lamb, clothed in white robes and palms in their hands. And they shouted with a great voice: "Salvation belongs to our God, who is seated upon the throne and to the Lamb."

HERE we have the beginning of the vision of the future blessedness of the martyrs.

(i) There is encouragement. There is coming upon the faithful a time of terror such as the world has never seen; and John is telling them that, if they endure to the end, the glory will be worth all the suffering. He is setting out how infinitely worthwhile it is in the long run to accept everything involved in the martyrdom which fidelity must undergo.

(ii) The number of the martyrs is beyond all counting. This may well be a memory of the promise that God made to Abraham that his descendants would one day be as the number of the stars in the heavens (*Genesis* 15: 5), and as the sand of the seashore (*Genesis* 32: 12); at the last the number of the true Israel will be beyond all reckoning.

(iii) John uses a phrase of which he is very fond. He says that God's faithful ones will come from every race and tribe and people and tongue (cp. *Revelation* 5: 9; 11: 9; 13: 7; 14: 6; 17: 15). H. B. Swete speaks of "the polyglot cosmopolitan crowd who jostled one another in the agora or on the quays of the Asian sea-port towns." In any Asian harbour or market-place there would be gathered people from many lands, speaking many different tongues. Any evangelist would feel his heart afire to bring the message of Christ to this assorted crowd of people. Here is the promise that the day will come when all this motley crowd of many nations and many tongues will become the one flock of the Lord Christ.

(iv) It is in victory that the faithful finally arrive in the presence of God and of the Lamb. They appear, not weary, battered and worn, but victorious. The white robe is the sign of victory; a Roman general celebrated his triumph clothed in white. The palm is also the sign of victory. When, under the might of the Maccabees, Jerusalem was freed from the pollutions of Antiochus Epiphanes, the people entered in with branches and fair boughs and palms and psalms (2 *Maccabees* 10: 7).

(v) The shout of the triumphant faithful ascribes salvation to God. It is God who has brought them through their trials and tribulations and distresses; and it is his glory which now they share. God is the great saviour, the great deliverer of his people. And the deliverance which he gives is not the deliverance of escape but the deliverance of conquest. It is not a deliverance which saves a man from trouble but one which brings him triumphantly through trouble. It does not make life easy, but it makes life great. It is not part of the Christian hope to look for a life in which a man is saved from all trouble and distress; the Christian hope is that a man in Christ can endure any kind of trouble and distress, and remain erect all through them, and come out to glory on the other side.

## THE PRAISE OF THE ANGELS

*Revelation* 7: 11, 12

> And all the angels stood in a circle round the throne and the elders and the four living creatures, and they fell upon their faces before the throne, and worshipped God, saying:
>> "So let it be. Blessing and glory and wisdom and thanksgiving and honour and power and strength belong to our God for ever and for ever. Amen."

THE picture is of a series of great concentric circles of the inhabitants of heaven. On the outer ring stand all the angels. Nearer the throne are the twenty-four elders; still nearer are the four living creatures; and before the throne are the white-robed martyrs. The martyrs have just sung their shout of praise to God and the angels take that song of praise and make it their own. "So let it be," say the angels; they say "Amen" to the martyrs' praises. Then they sing their own song of praise and every word in it is meaningful.

They ascribe *blessing* to God; and God's creation must always be blessing him for his goodness in creation and in redemption and in providence to all that he has created. As a great saint put it: "Thou hast made us and we are thine; thou hast redeemed us and we are doubly thine."

They ascribe *glory* to God. God is the King of kings and the Lord of lords; therefore, to him must be given glory. God is love but that love must never be cheaply sentimentalized; men must never forget the majesty of God.

They ascribe *wisdom* to God. God is the source of all truth, the giver of all knowledge. If men seek wisdom, they can find it by only two paths, by the seeking of their minds and by waiting upon God—and the one is as important as the other.

They offer *thanksgiving* to God. God is the giver of salvation and the constant provider of grace; he is the Creator of the world and the constant sustainer of all that is in it. It was the cry of the psalmist: "Bless the Lord, O my soul, and forget not all his benefits" (*Psalm* 103: 2). Shakespeare said that it was sharper than a serpent's tooth to have a thankless child. We must see to it that we are never guilty of the ugliest and the most graceless of sins, that of ingratitude.

They ascribed *honour* to God. God is to be worshipped. It may be that sometimes we come to think of him as some one to be used; but we ought not to forget the claims of worship, so that we not only ask things from him but offer ourselves and all we have to him.

They ascribe *power* to God. God's power never grows less and the wonder is that it is used in love for men. God works his purposes out throughout the ages and in the end his kingdom will come.

They ascribe *strength* to God. The problem of life is to find strength for its tasks, its responsibilities, its demands. The Christian can say: "I will go in the strength of the Lord."

There is no greater exercise in the life of devotion than to meditate on the praise of the angels and, to appropriate to ourselves everything in it.

## WASHING FROM SIN

*Revelation* 7: 13, 14

> And one of the elders said to me: "Do you know who these are
> who are clothed in white robes and where they came from?" I said
> to him: "Sir, you know." He said to me: "These are they who
> are coming out of the great tribulation, and who have washed their
> robes, and have made them white through the power of the
> blood of the Lamb."

ONE thing is to be noted before we go on to deal with this
passage in detail. The Authorized Version generalizes the
meaning by translating: "These are they who came out of great
tribulation." But the Revised Standard Version correctly
translates: "These are they who came out of *the* great
tribulation." The seer is convinced that he and his people are
standing at the end time of history and that that end time is
to be terrible beyond all imagining. The whole point of his
vision is that beyond that terrible time glory will follow. It is
not tribulation in general of which he is speaking but of
that tribulation which Jesus foretold when he said, "In those
days there will be such tribulation as has not been from
the beginning of the creation which God created until
now, and never will be" (*Mark* 13: 19; *Matthew* 24: 21).
Nowadays we read this passage as speaking about tribulation
in general and in that sense find it very precious; and we
are right to read it so because the promises of God are for
ever. At the same time it is right to remember that
originally it referred to the immediate circumstances of the
people to whom John was writing.

This passage has two pictures which are very common in
the Bible. We first look at these pictures separately and then
we put them together in order to find the total meaning of the
passage.

The great crowd of the blessed ones are in *white robes*.
The Bible has much to say both about white robes and
about soiled robes. In the ancient world this was a very
natural picture, for it was forbidden to approach a god with

robes which were unclean. The picture was still further intensified by the fact that often when a Christian was baptized he was dressed in new white robes. These robes were taken to symbolize his new life and to soil them was the symbolic way of expressing failure to be true to the baptismal vows.

Isaiah says: "We have become like one who is unclean, and all our righteous deeds are like a polluted garment" (*Isaiah* 64: 6). Zechariah sees the high priest Joshua clothed in filthy garments and hears God say: "Remove the filthy garments from him . . . Behold, I have taken your iniquity away from you, and I will clothe you with rich apparel" (*Zechariah* 3: 1–5). In preparation for the receiving of the commandments from God, Moses orders the people wash their garments (*Exodus* 19: 10, 14). The Psalmist prays to God to wash him thoroughly from his iniquity, to purge him with hyssop, to wash him until he is whiter than snow (*Psalm* 51: 1–7). The prophet hears the promise that the sins which are as scarlet will be as white as snow and those that were red like crimson will be as wool (*Isaiah* 1: 18). Paul reminds his people in Corinth that they have been washed and sanctified (1 *Corinthians* 6: 11).

Here is a picture which is present all through scripture, of the man who has stained his garments with sin and who has been cleansed by the grace of God. It is of the greatest importance to remember that this love of God does not only forgive a man his stained garments, it makes them clean.

## THE BLOOD OF JESUS CHRIST

*Revelation* 7: 13, 14 (*continued*)

THIS passage speaks of *the blood of the Lamb*. The New Testament has much to say about the blood of Jesus Christ. We must be careful to give this phrase its full meaning. To us *blood* indicates *death,* and certainly the blood of

Jesus Christ speaks of his death. But to the Hebrews *the blood* stood for *the life*. That was why the orthodox Jew never would—and still will not—eat anything which had blood in it (*Genesis* 9: 4). The blood is the life and the life belongs to God; and the blood must always be sacrificed to him. The identification of blood and life is not unnatural. When a man's blood ebbs away, so does his life. When the New Testament speaks about the blood of Jesus Christ, it means not only his death but his *life and death*. The *blood of Christ* stands for all Christ did for us and means for us in his life and in his death. With that in our minds let us see what the New Testament says about that blood.

It is the blood of Jesus Christ which is cleansing us from all sin (1 *John* 1: 7). It is the blood of Jesus Christ which makes expiation for us (*Romans* 3: 25), and it is through his blood that we are justified (*Romans* 5: 9). It is through his blood that we have redemption (*Ephesians* 1: 7), and we are redeemed with the precious blood of Christ as of a lamb without blemish and without spot (1 *Peter* 1: 19). It is through his blood that we have peace with God (*Colossians* 1: 20). His blood purges our conscience from dead works to serve the living God (*Hebrews* 9: 14).

There are four ideas here, the first being the main idea from which the others spring.

(i) The main idea is based on *sacrifice*. Sacrifice is essentially something designed to restore a lost relationship with God. God gives man his law; man breaks that law; that breach of the law interrupts the relationship between God and man; and sacrifice is designed to atone for the breach and to restore the lost relationship. The great work of Jesus Christ in his life and in his death is to restore the lost relationship between God and man.

(ii) This work of Christ has something to do with *the past*. It wins for man forgiveness for past sins and liberates him from his slavery to sin.

(iii) This work of Christ has something to do with *the present*. It gives a man here and now, upon earth, in spite of failure and of sin, a new and intimate relationship with God, in which fear is gone and in which love is the bond.

(iv) This work of Christ has something to do with *the future*. It frees a man from the power of evil and enables him to live a new life in the time to come.

## THE SAINTS WHO HAVE WASHED THEIR ROBES IN THE BLOOD OF THE LAMB

*Revelation* 7: 13, 14 (*continued*)

LET us now unite the two ideas of which we have been thinking. The blessed ones have washed their robes and made them white in the blood of the Lamb. Let us try to express as simply as possible what that means.

The white robes always stand for two things. They stand for *purity*, for the life cleansed from the taint of past sin, the infection of present sin and the attack of future sin. They stand for *victory*, for the life which has found the secret of victorious living. Put at its very simplest, this means that the blessed ones have found the secret of purity and the secret of victory in all that Jesus Christ did for them in his life and in his death.

Now let us try to see the meaning of *in the blood of the Lamb*. There are two possibilities.

(i) It may mean *in the power of the blood of the Lamb* or *at the cost of the blood of the Lamb*. This would then be a vivid way of saying that this purity and victory were won in the power and at the cost of all that Jesus did for men in his life and in his death.

(ii) But it may be even more probable that the picture is to be taken literally; and that John conceives of the blessed ones as having washed their robes in the blood which flows from the wounds of Jesus Christ. To us that is a strange and perhaps even repulsive picture; and it is paradoxical to think of robes becoming white when washed in the scarlet of blood. But it would not seem strange to the people of John's day; to many of them it would be literally familiar. The greatest religious force of the time was the Mystery Religions. These were dramatic religions which by deeply moving ceremonies offered to men a rebirth and a promise of eternal life. Perhaps the most famous was Mithraism, at whose centre was the god Mithra. Mithraism had its devotees all over the world; it was the favourite religion of the Roman army and even in Britain there are relics of the chapels of Mithra where the Roman soldiers met for worship. The most sacred ceremony of Mithraism was the *taurobolium*, the bath of bull's blood. It is described by the Christian poet Prudentius. "A trench was dug, over which was erected a platform of planks, which were perforated with holes. Upon this platform a sacrificial bull was slaughtered. Below the platform knelt the worshipper who was to be initiated. The blood of the slaughtered bull dripped through on to the worshipper below. He exposed his head and all his garments to be saturated with blood; and then he turned round and held up his neck that the blood might trickle upon his lips, ears, eyes and nostrils; he moistened his tongue with the blood which he then drank as a sacramental act. He came out from this certain that he was *renatus in aeternum,* reborn for all eternity."

This may sound grim and terrible to us; but in the last analysis it is not the picture which matters but the truth behind the picture. And the great and unchanging truth is that through the life and death of Jesus Christ, there has come to the Christian that purity and victory which he could never achieve for himself.

## CHRIST'S SACRIFICE AND MAN'S APPROPRIATION

*Revelation* 7: 13, 14 (*continued*)

ONE thing in this passage remains to be noted, and it is of the first importance. It is said of the blessed ones that "they washed their robes and made them white in the blood of the Lamb."

Here is symbolically laid down man's part in his own salvation; the blessed ones washed their own robes. That is to say, the act of man's redemption is Christ's, but the effect is not passive and man has to appropriate it. There might be available to a man all the apparatus to cleanse his garments, but it remains ineffective until he uses it for himself.

How does a man avail himself of the sacrifice of Christ?

He does so through *penitence*. He must begin with sorrow for his sin and the desire for amendment. He does so through *faith*. He must believe with all his heart that Christ lived and died for us men and for our salvation, and that his sacrifice is mighty to save. He does so through using the *means of grace*. The *Scriptures* will awaken his penitence and his faith and kindle his heart; *prayer* will keep him ever close to Christ and daily increase his intimacy with him; the *Sacraments* will be channels through which by faith renewing grace will flow to him. He does so through daily loyalty and vigilance and living with Christ.

## THE SERVICE IN THE GLORY

*Revelation* 7: 15

> That is why they are before the throne of God, and serve him day and night in his temple; and he who sits upon the throne will spread the covering of his glory over them.

THOSE who have been faithful will have the entry into the very presence of God. Jesus said: "Blessed are the pure in heart, for they shall see God" (*Matthew* 5: 8).

There is a very significant fact hidden here. Serving God day and night was part of the task of the Levites and the priests (1 *Chronicles* 9: 33). Now those who are before the throne of God in this vision are, as we have already seen in verse 9, drawn from every race and tribe and people and tongue. Here is a revolution. In the earthly Temple in Jerusalem no Gentile could go beyond the Court of the

Gentiles on pain of death. An Israelite could pass through the Court of the Women and enter into the Court of the Israelites, but no further. Beyond that was the Court of the Priests, which was for priests alone. But in the heavenly temple the way to the presence of God is open to people of every race. Here is a picture of heaven with the barriers down. Distinctions of race and of status exist no more; the way into the presence of God is open to every faithful soul.

There is one other half-hidden fact here. In verse 15 the Authorized Version has it that he who sits upon the throne shall *dwell* among them. That is a perfectly correct translation, but there is more in it than meets the eye. The Greek for *to dwell* is *skēnoun,* from *skēnē* which means a *tent*. It is the same word as is used when John says that the Word became flesh and *dwelt* among us (*John* 1: 14). The Jews always connected this with a certain Hebrew word which was somewhat similar in sound although quite unrelated in meaning. This was the word *shechinah*, the visible presence of the glory of God. Usually that presence took the form of a luminous cloud. So when the Ten Commandments were given, "the glory of the Lord settled on Mount Sinai, and the cloud covered it six days. . . . And the appearance of the glory of the Lord was like a devouring fire on the top of the mountain" (*Exodus* 24: 16–18). It was the same with the Tabernacle. The cloud covered the tent of the congregation and the glory of the Lord filled the tabernacle. Moses could not enter into the Tabernacle because of the glory of the Lord. This was the cloud which guided the Israelites by day and the fire that guided them by night (*Exodus* 40: 34–38). At the dedication of Solomon's temple the glory of the Lord filled it so that the priests could not enter (2 *Chronicles* 7: 1–3).

*Skēnoun* always turned the thoughts of a Jew to *shechinah*: and to say that God *dwelt* in any place was to say that his glory was there.

This was always so for a Jew, but as time went on it became more and more so. The Jews came to think of God as increasingly remote from the world. They did not even think it right to speak of him as being in the world; that was to speak in terms which were too human; and so they took to substituting the *shechinah*, for the name of God. We read Jacob's words at Bethel: "Surely the Lord is in this place" (*Genesis* 28: 16); the Rabbis changed that to: "The *shechinah* is in this place." In *Habbakuk* we read: "The Lord is in his holy temple" (*Habbakuk* 2: 20); but the later Jews said: "God was pleased to cause his *shechinah* to dwell in the temple." In *Isaiah* we read: "My eyes have seen the King, the Lord of hosts" (*Isaiah* 6: 5); the later Jews altered it to: "Mine eyes have seen the *shechinah*, of the King of the world."

No Jew would hear the word *skēnoun* without thinking of *shechinah*; and the real meaning of the passage is that God's blessed ones would serve and live in the very sheen of his glory.

It can be so on earth. He who faithfully works and witnesses for God has always the glory of God upon his work.

## THE BLISS OF THE BLESSED

*Revelation* 7: 16, 17

> They will not hunger any more, nor will they thirst any more; the sun will not fall on them, nor any heat; because the Lamb who is in the midst of the throne will be their shepherd, and will lead them to springs of living water; and God will wipe away every tear from their eyes.

IT would be impossible to number the people who have found comfort in this passage in the house of mourning and in the hour of death.

There is spiritual promise here, the promise of the ultimate satisfying of the hunger and the thirst of the human soul. This is a promise which occurs again and again in the New Testament, and especially in the words of Jesus. "Blessed are those who hunger and thirst for righteousness, for they shall be satisfied" (*Matthew* 5: 6). Jesus said: "I am the bread of life; he who comes to me shall not hunger; and he who believes in me shall never thirst" (*John* 6: 35). "Whoever drinks of the water that I shall give him will never thirst; the water that I shall give him will become in him a spring of water welling up to eternal life" (*John* 4: 14). Jesus said: "If any one thirst, let him come to me and drink" (*John* 7: 37). God has made us for himself, as Augustine said, and our hearts are restless till they rest in him. As the hymn has it:

> O Christ, in thee my soul has found,
>   And found in thee alone,
> The peace, the joy, I sought so long,
>   The bliss till now unknown.
>
> Now none but Christ can satisfy,
>   None other name for me!
> There's love, and life, and lasting joy,
>   Lord Jesus, found in thee.

But it may well be that we should not entirely spiritualize this passage. In the early days many of the Church's members were slaves. They knew what it was to be hungry all the time; they knew what thirst was; they knew what it was for the pitiless sun to blaze down upon their backs as they toiled, forbidden to rest. Truly for them heaven would be a place where hunger was satisfied and thirst was quenched and the heat of the sun no longer tortured them. The promise of this passage is that in Christ is the end of the world's hunger, the world's pain, and the world's sorrow.

We do well to remember that John found the origin of this passage in the words of Isaiah: "They shall not hunger or thirst; neither scorching wind nor sun shall smite them; for he who has pity on them will lead them, and by springs of water will lead them" (*Isaiah* 49: 10). This is a supreme example of an Old Testament dream finding its perfect fulfilment in Jesus Christ.

## THE DIVINE SHEPHERD

*Revelation* 7: 16, 17 (*continued*)

HERE is the promise of the loving care of the Divine Shepherd for his flock.

The picture of the shepherd is something in which both the Old and New Testament delight.

"The Lord is my shepherd," begins the best loved of all the psalms (*Psalm* 23: 1). "O Shepherd of Israel," begins another (*Psalm* 80: 1). Isaiah pictures God feeding his flock like a shepherd, holding the lambs in his arms and carrying them in his bosom (*Isaiah* 40: 11). The greatest title that the prophet can give to the Messianic king is shepherd of his people (*Ezekiel* 34: 23; 37: 24).

This was the title that Jesus took for himself. "I am the good shepherd," (*John* 10: 11, 14). Peter calls Jesus the Shepherd and Bishop of our souls (1 *Peter* 2: 25), and the writer to the Hebrews speaks of him as that great shepherd of the sheep (*Hebrews* 13: 20).

This is a precious picture in any age; but it was more meaningful in Palestine than it can ever be to those who live in cities. Judaea was like a narrow plateau with dangerous country on either side. It was only a very few miles across, with on one side the grim cliffs and ravines leading down to the Dead Sea and on the other the drop to the wild country of the Shephelah. There were no fences or walls and the shepherd had to be ever on the watch for straying sheep. George Adam Smith describes the eastern shepherd. "With us sheep are often left to themselves; I do not remember to have seen in the East a flock without a shepherd. In such a landscape as Judaea, where a day's pasture is thinly scattered over an unfenced track, covered with delusive paths, still frequented by wild beasts, and rolling into the desert, the man and his character are indispensable. On some high moor, across which at night hyenas howl, when you met him sleepless, far-sighted, weather-beaten, armed, leaning on his staff, and looking out over his scattered sheep, every one on his heart, you understand why the shepherd of Judaea sprang to the front in his people's history; why they gave his name to their king, and made him the symbol of Providence; why Christ took him as the type of self-sacrifice."

Here we have the two great functions of the Divine Shepherd.

He leads to fountains of living waters. As the psalmist had it: "He leads me beside still waters" (*Psalm* 23: 2). "With thee is the fountain of life" (*Psalm* 36: 9). Without water the flock would perish; and in Palestine the wells were few and far between. That the Divine Shepherd leads to wells of water is the symbol that he gives us the things without which life cannot survive.

He wipes the tear from every eye. As he nourishes our bodies so he also comforts our hearts; without the presence and the comfort of God the sorrows of life would be unbearable, and without the strength of God there are times in life when we could never go on.

The Divine Shepherd gives us nourishment for our bodies and comfort for our hearts. With Jesus Christ as Shepherd nothing can happen to us which we cannot bear.

## THE SILENCE AND THE THUNDER OF PRAYER

*Revelation* 8: 1–5

When he opened the seventh seal, there was silence in heaven for about half an hour. And I saw the seven angels who stand in the presence of God, and seven trumpets were given to them. Another angel came and stood at the altar with a golden censer; and he was given much incense that he might add it to the prayers of the saints on the golden altar before the throne. The smoke of the incense went up with the prayers of the saints from the hand of the angel before God. And the angel took the censer and filled it with fire from the altar, and threw it on the ground. And there were crashes of thunder and loud voices and flashes of lightning and an earthquake.

BEFORE we begin to examine this passage in detail, we may note one point about its arrangement. Verse 2, which tells of the seven angels with the seven trumpets, is clearly out of place. As it stands, it interrupts the sense of the passage and it should come immediately before verse 7—probably a copyist's mistake.

The passage begins with an intensely dramatic silence in heaven for about half an hour. The sheer stillness is even more effective than the thunder and the lightning. This silence may have two meanings.

(i) It may be a kind of breathing-space in the narrative, a moment of preparation before another shattering revelation comes.

(ii) There may be something much more beautiful in it. The prayers of the saints are about to go up to God; and it may be that the idea is that everything in heaven halts so that the prayers of the saints may be heard. As R. H. Charles puts it: "The needs of the saints are more to God than all the psalmody of heaven." Even the music of heaven and even the thunder of revelation are stilled so that God's ear may catch the whispered prayer of the humblest of his trusting people.

The picture divides itself into two. In the first half an un-named angel offers the prayers of the saints to God. In Jewish thought the archangel Michael made prayer for the people of Israel and there was a nameless angel called The Angel of Peace whose duty was to see that Israel "did not fall into the extremity of Israel" and who interceded for Israel and for all the righteous.

The angel is standing at the altar. The altar in the *Revelation* frequently appears in the picture of heaven (6: 9; 9: 13; 14: 18). It cannot be the altar of burnt-offering, for there can be no animal sacrifice in heaven; it must be the altar of incense. The altar of incense stood before the Holy Place in the Temple (*Leviticus* 16: 12; *Numbers* 16: 46). Made of gold, it was eighteen inches square and three feet high. At each corner it had horns; it was hollow and was covered over with a gold plate, and round it was a little railing, like a miniature balustrade, to keep the burning coals from falling off it. In the Temple incense was burned and offered before the first and after the last sacrifices of the day. It was as if the offerings of the people went up to God wrapped in an envelope of perfumed incense.

Here we have the idea that prayer is a sacrifice to God; the prayers of the saints are offered on the altar and, like all other sacrifices, they are surrounded with the perfume of the incense as they rise to God. A man may have no other sacrifice to offer to God; but at all times he can offer his prayers and there are always angelic hands waiting to bring them to God.

There is another half of this picture. The same angel takes the censer, fills it with coals from the altar and dashes it on the ground; and this is the prelude to the thunder and the earthquake which are the introduction to more terrors. The picture comes from the vision of Ezekiel, in which the man in the linen-cloth takes coals from between the cherubim and scatters them over the city (*Ezekiel* 10: 2); and it is kin to the vision of Isaiah in which his lips are touched with a live coal from the altar (*Isaiah* 6: 6).

But this picture introduces something new. The coals from the censer introduce new woes. H. B. Swete puts it this way: "The prayers of the saints return to the earth in wrath." The idea in John's mind is that the prayers of the saints avail to bring vengeance upon those who had maltreated them.

We may feel that a prayer for vengeance is a strange prayer for a Christian, but we must remember the agony of persecution through which the Church was passing when the *Revelation* was written.

## THE SEVEN ANGELS WITH THE TRUMPETS

*Revelation* 8: 2, 6

And I saw the seven angels who stand in the presence of God, and seven trumpets were given to them; and the seven angels with the seven trumpets prepared to sound the trumpets.

THESE seven angels, known as the angels of the presence, were the same as the archangels. Their names were Uriel, Raphael, Raguel, Michael, Sariel, Gabriel and Remiel (*Tobit* 12: 15).

That they were called the angels of the presence means two things. First, they enjoyed a special honour. In an oriental court it was only the most favoured courtiers who had the right at all times to the presence of the king; to be a courtier of the presence was a special honour. Second, although to be in the presence of the king meant special honour, even more it meant immediate readiness to be despatched on service. Both Elijah and Elisha repeatedly spoke of "the Lord God of Israel before whom I stand" (1 *Kings* 17: 1; 18: 15; 2 *Kings* 3: 14; 5: 16); and the phrase really means, "The Lord God of Israel whose servant I am."

The seven angels had seven trumpets. In the visions of the Old and the New Testament the trumpet is always the symbol of the intervention of God in history. All these pictures, and there are many of them, go back to the scene at Mount Sinai, when the law was given to the people. There were on the mountain thunders and lightnings and thick cloud, and a very loud trumpet blast (*Exodus* 19: 16, 19). This trumpet blast became an unchanging part of the apparatus of the Day of the Lord. In that day the great trumpet will be blown and it will summon back the exiles from every land (*Isaiah* 27: 13). On the Day of the Lord the trumpet will be blown in Zion and the alarm sounded in the holy mountain (*Joel* 2: 1). That day will be a day of trumpet and alarm (*Zephaniah* 1: 16). The Lord will blow the trumpet and go out with the whirlwind (*Zechariah* 9: 14).

This picture passed into the New Testament visions of the last day. Paul speaks of the day when the trumpet shall sound and the corruptible will put on incorruption (1 *Corinthians* 15: 52, 53). He speaks of the trumpet of God, which is to sound when Christ comes again (1 *Thessalonians* 4: 16). Matthew speaks of the great sound of a trumpet when the elect are gathered in (*Matthew* 24: 31).

It would be wrong to expect God literally to blow the trumpet; but none the less the picture has symbolic truth in it. A trumpet blast can be three things.

(i) It can sound the alarm. It can waken from sleep or warn of danger; and God is always sounding his warnings in the ears of men.

(ii) It can be the fanfare which announces the arrival of royalty. It is a fitting symbol to express the invasion of time by the King of eternity.

(iii) It can be the summons to battle. God is always summoning men to take sides in the strife of truth with falsehood and to become soldiers of the King of kings.

## THE UNLEASHING OF THE ELEMENTS

*Revelation* 8: 7–12

The first angel sounded a blast on his trumpet, and there came hail and fire mixed with blood and launched themselves on the dry land; and a third part of the dry land was burned up, and a third part of the trees was burned up, and all green grass was burned up.

The second angel sounded a blast on his trumpet, and what I can only call a great mountain burning with fire was hurled into the sea; and a third part of the sea became blood, and a third part of the creatures in the sea who had life died, and a third part of the ships were destroyed in wreckage.

The third angel sounded a blast on his trumpet, and a great meteor blazing like a torch fell from heaven; and it fell on a third part of the rivers, and on the springs of water. And the name by which the meteor is called is Wormwood; and a third part of the waters became wormwood; and many of mankind died because of the embitterment of the waters.

The fourth angel sounded a blast on his trumpet, and a third part of the sun was smitten, and a third part of the moon, and a third part of the stars, so that a third part of their light was darkened, and so that a third part of the day did not shine, and so with the night.

HERE we have a picture of the elemental forces of nature hurled in judgment against the world. At each blast on the trumpet a different part of the world is attacked; the destruction that follows is not total for this is only the prelude to the end. First, the blast of destruction falls on the earth (verse 7); then it falls upon the sea (verses 8 and 9); then it falls upon the fresh water rivers and springs (verses 10, 11); then it falls on the heavenly bodies (verse 12). The tide of destruction is unleashed on every part of the created universe.

We have further to note where John found his imagery. For the most part the pictures find their origin in the descriptions in *Exodus* of the plagues which fell on Egypt when Pharaoh refused to allow the people to go.

In John's picture hail and fire and blood fall upon the dry land. In *Exodus* 9: 24 we read how there came upon Egypt fire mixed with a hail of unparalleled destructiveness. John to increase the terror adds blood, remembering Joel's picture of the day when the sun would be turned into darkness and the moon into blood (*Joel* 2: 10). In John's picture a third part of the sea becomes blood and the fishes in it die. In *Exodus*, when Moses lifted up his rod and smote the waters, the waters of the Nile turned to blood and the fishes in the river died (*Exodus* 7: 20, 21). In Zephaniah's picture of the Day of the Lord the threat of God is: "I will sweep away man and beast; I will sweep away the birds of the air and the fish of the sea" (*Zephaniah* 1: 3). There is no parallel for the picture of the fall of the flaming star, but there are many to the ideas of waters turning to wormwood.

Wormwood is a general name for the class of plants known as *artemisia* whose characteristic is bitterness of taste. They are not really poisonous in the sense of being fatal, although they are noxious, but the Israelites dreaded their bitterness. Wormwood was the fruit of idolatry (*Deuteronomy* 29: 17, 18). It was the threat of God through Jeremiah that God would give his people wormwood to eat and the waters of gall to drink (*Jeremiah* 9: 14, 15; 23: 15). Wormwood always stood for the bitterness of the judgment of God on the disobedient.

In John's picture there came a darkening of a third part of the lights of heaven. In *Exodus* one of the plagues was a darkness that could be felt over the whole land (*Exodus* 10: 21–23).

As we have so often seen, John is so steeped in the Old Testament that its visions come to him as the natural background of all that he has to say.

In this case it is by no means impossible that John is taking at least a part of his picture from actual events which he had seen or of which he had heard. A rain which looks like a rain of blood has more than once been reported from the Mediterranean countries. There is, for instance, a record of such a rain in Italy and all over south-east Europe in 1901. The reason for it is that fine red sand from the Sahara Desert is caught up into the upper air; and then when the rain comes it seems to be raining blood, as the rain and the fine red particles of sand fall together upon the earth. It may well be that John had seen something like this or had heard of it.

Further, he speaks of a flaming mass falling into the sea. This sounds very like a volcanic eruption. There was an eruption of Mount Vesuvius in August of A.D. 79 which decimated Naples and its bay. That would be within a very few years of the writing of the *Revelation*. The Aegean Sea has volcanic islands and volcanoes beneath the sea. Strabo, the Greek geographer, reports an eruption in the Aegean Sea, in which Patmos lay, in the year 196 B.C., which actually resulted in the formation of a new island called *Palaia Kaumenē*. Such events also may have been in John's mind.

In this picture of terror John has the vision of God using the elemental forces of nature to warn man of the final destruction to come.

## THE FLYING EAGLE

*Revelation* 8: 13

And I looked, and I heard an eagle flying in mid-heaven crying with a loud voice: "Woe! Woe! Woe! for those who dwell on the earth, because of what is going to happen when the rest of the trumpets speak, which the three angels are about to sound."

HERE we have one of the pauses in the story which the *Revelation* uses so effectively. Three fearful woes are to come upon the earth when the three angels sound the last blasts on the trumpets; but for the moment there is a pause.

In this pause the seer sees an eagle—not an angel as the Authorized Version has it. It is quite possible that the Greek could mean "one solitary eagle." The expression "mid-heaven" means the zenith of the sky, that part where the sun is at midday. Here we have a dramatic and eerie picture of an empty sky and a solitary eagle winging its way across its zenith, forewarning of the doom to come.

Again John is using an idea which is not new. We have the same picture in *Second Baruch*. When the writer of that book has seen his vision and wishes to send it to the Jews exiled in Babylon by the waters of the Euphrates, he goes on: "And I called the eagle and spake these words unto it: 'The Most High hath made thee that thou shouldest be higher than all birds. Now go, and tarry not in any place, nor enter a nest, nor settle on any tree, till thou hast passed over the breadth of the many waters of the river Euphrates, and hast gone to the people that dwell there, and cast down to them this epistle'" (2 *Baruch* 77: 21, 22).

The picture is not to be taken literally but the symbolism behind it is that God uses nature to send his messages to men.

## THE UNLOCKING OF THE ABYSS

*Revelation* 9: 1, 2

> The fifth angel sounded a blast on his trumpet, and I saw a star falling from heaven on the earth, and to him there was given the key of the shaft of the bottomless abyss; and he opened the shaft of the abyss; and smoke went up from the shaft like the smoke of a great furnace, and the sun and the air were darkened by the smoke from the abyss.

THE picture of terror mounts in its awful intensity. Now the terrors coming upon the earth are beyond nature; they are demonic; the abyss is being opened and superhuman terrors are being despatched upon the world.

The picture will become clearer if we remember that John thinks of the stars as living beings. This is common in *Enoch* where, for instance, we read of wandering and disobedient stars being bound hand and foot and cast into the abyss (*Enoch* 86: 1; 88: 1). To the Jewish mind the stars were divine beings, who by disobedience could become demonic and evil.

In the *Revelation* we read fairly often of the *abyss* or the *bottomless pit*. The abyss is the intermediate place of punishment of the fallen angels, the demons, the beast, the false prophet and of Satan (9: 1, 2, 11; 11: 7; 20: 1, 3). Their final place of punishment is the lake of burning fire and brimstone (20: 10, 14, 15). To complete the picture of these terrors we may add that Gehenna—which is not mentioned in the *Revelation*—is the place of punishment for evil men.

This idea of the abyss underwent a development. In the beginning it was the place of the imprisoned waters. In the creation story the primaeval waters surround the earth and God separates them by creating the firmament (*Genesis* 1: 6, 7). In its first idea the abyss was the place where the flood of the waters was confined by God beneath the earth, a kind of great subterranean sea, where the waters were imprisoned to make way for the dry land. The second step was that the abyss became the abode of the enemies of God, although even there they were not beyond his power and control (*Amos* 9: 3; *Isaiah* 51: 9; *Psalm* 74: 13).

Next the abyss came to be thought of as a great chasm in the earth. We see this idea in *Isaiah* 24: 21, 22, where the disobedient hosts of heaven and the kings of the earth are gathered together as prisoners in the pit.

This is the kind of picture in which inevitably horror mounts upon horror. The most detailed descriptions of the abyss are in *Enoch*, which was so influential between the Testaments. There it is the prison abode of the angels who fell, the angels who came to earth and seduced mortal women, the angels who taught men to worship demons instead of the true

God (*Genesis* 6: 1–4). There are grim descriptions of it. It has no firmament above and no firm earth beneath; it has no water; it has no birds; it is a waste and horrible place, the end of heaven and earth (*Enoch* 18: 12–16). It is chaotic. There is a fire which blazes and a cleft into the abyss whose magnitude passes all conjecture (*Enoch* 21: 1–10).

These things are not to be taken literally. The point is that in this terrible time of devastation which the seer sees coming upon the earth, the terrors are not natural but demonic; the powers of evil are being given their last chance to work their dreadful work.

## THE LOCUSTS FROM THE ABYSS

*Revelation* 9: 3–12

From the smoke locusts came forth upon the earth, and they were given power like the power of the scorpions of the earth. They were told not to harm the grass of the earth, nor any green thing, nor any tree, but only such men as had not the seal of God upon their forehead. They were not permitted to kill them, but to torture them for five months. Their torture was like the torture of a scorpion when it strikes a man; and in those days men will seek for death and not be able to find it; and they will long to die but death flees from them.

In likeness the locusts were like horses prepared for battle; on their heads were what looked like crowns of gold. Their faces were like human faces and they had hair like women's hair, and their teeth were like the teeth of lions. They had scales like iron breastplates, and the sound of their wings was like the sound of many chariots with horses running to battle. They have tails like scorpions with stings, and in their tails is their power to hurt men for five months. As king over them they have the angel of the bottomless abyss, whose name in Hebrew is Abaddon and in Greek Appolyon. The first woe has passed. Behold, there are still two woes to follow it.

FROM the smoke which emerged from the shaft of the abyss came a terrible invasion of locusts. The devastation locusts can inflict and the terror they can cause is well-nigh incredible. All through the Old Testament the locust is the symbol of destruction; and the most vivid and terrible description of them and of their destructiveness is in the first two chapters of *Joel* which are a description of an invasion of locusts; and it is from these two chapters that John takes much of his material. They laid the vine waste and stripped the bark from the trees; the field is wasted and the corn is destroyed; every tree of the field is wasted and withered; and the flocks and herds starve because there is no pasture (*Joel* 1: 7–18). They are like a great strong people who darken the very sky; they are as destructive as a flame of fire and nothing escapes them; they are like horses and they run like chariots, with a noise like flame devouring the stubble; they march in their ranks like mighty men of war; they scale the mountains, climb into houses and enter in at the windows, until the very earth shudders at them (*Joel* 2: 1–11). The two chapters of *Joel* should be read in full and set beside the description in the *Revelation*.

G. R. Driver in his commentary on *Joel* in the *Cambridge Bible for Schools and Colleges* has collected the facts about locusts in his notes and in a special appendix; and he has shown that the words of *Joel* and of the *Revelation* are no exaggeration.

The locusts breed in desert places and invade the cultivated lands for food. They may be about two inches in length, with a wing span of four to five inches. They belong to the same family as the household cricket and the grasshopper. They will travel in a column a hundred feet deep and as much as four miles long. When such a cloud of locusts appears, it is as if there had been an eclipse of the sun and even great buildings less than two hundred feet away cannot be seen.

The destruction they cause is beyond belief. When they have left an area, not a blade of grass is to be seen; the trees are stripped of their bark. Land where the locusts have settled looks as if it had been scorched with a bush fire; not one single living thing is left. Their destructiveness can best be appreciated from the fact that it is recorded that in 1866 a plague of locusts invaded Algiers and so total was the destruction which they caused that 200,000 people perished of famine in the days which followed.

The noise of the millions of their wings is variously described as like the dashing of waters in a mill-wheel or the sound of a great cataract. When the millions of them settle on the ground the sound of their eating has been described as like the crackling of a prairie fire. The sound of them on the march is like heavy rain falling on a distant forest.

It has always been noticed that the head of the locust is like the miniature head of a horse. For that reason the Italian word for locust is *cavaletta* and the German *Heupferd*.

When they move, they move inexorably on like an army with leaders. People have dug trenches, lit fires, and even fired cannon in an attempt to stop them but without success; they come on in a steady column which climbs hills, enters houses and leaves scorched earth behind.

There is no more destructive visitation in the world than a visitation of locusts, and this is the terrible devastation which John sees, although the demonic locusts from the pit are different from any earthly insect.

## THE DEMONIC LOCUSTS

*Revelation* 9: 3–12 (*continued*)

HEBREW has a number of different names for the locust which reveal its destructive power. It is called *gazam,* the *lopper* or the *shearer*, which describes how it shears all living vegetation from the earth; it is called *arbel,* the *swarmer*, which describes the immensity of its numbers; it is called *hasil,* the *finisher*, which describes the devastation it causes; it is called *solam*, the *swallower* or the *annihilator*; it is called *hargol*, the *galloper*, which describes its rapid progress over the land; it is called *tzelatzel*, the *creaker*, which describes the sound it makes.

It is not the vegetation of the earth which they are to attack; in fact they are forbidden to do that (verse 4); their attack is to be launched against the men who have not the seal of God upon their foreheads.

The ordinary locust is devastating to vegetation but not harmful to human beings; but the demonic locust is to have the sting of a scorpion, one of the scourges of Palestine. In shape the scorpion is like a small lobster, with lobster-like claws to clutch its prey. It has a long tail, which curves up over its back and over its head; at the end of the tail there is a curved claw; with this claw the scorpion strikes and it secretes poison as the blow is delivered. The scorpion can be up to six inches in length; it swarms in crannies in walls and literally under almost every stone. Campers tell us that every stone must be lifted when a tent is pitched lest a scorpion be beneath it. Its sting is worse than the sting of a hornet; it is not necessarily fatal, but it can kill. The demonic locusts have the power of scorpions added to them.

Their attack is to last for five months. The explanation of the five months is almost probably that the life-span of a locust from birth, through the larva stage, to death is five months. It is as if we might say that one generation of locusts is being launched upon the earth.

Such will be the suffering caused by the locusts that men will long for death but will not be able to die. Job speaks of the supreme misery of those who long for death and it comes not (*Job* 3: 21); and Jeremiah speaks of the day when men will choose death rather than life (*Jeremiah* 8: 3). A Latin writer, Cornelius Gallus, says: "Worse than any wound is to wish to die and yet not be able to do so."

The king of the locusts is called in Hebrew Abaddon and in Greek Apollyon. *Abaddon* is the Hebrew for *destruction*; it occurs oftenest in the phrases "death and destruction," and "hell and destruction" (*Job* 26: 6; 28: 22; 31: 12; *Psalm* 88: 11; *Proverbs* 15: 11; 27: 20). *Apollyon* is the present participle of the Greek verb *to destroy* and itself means *The Destroyer*. It is fitting that the king of the demonic locusts should be called Destruction and The Destroyer.


## THE HORSEMEN OF VENGEANCE

*Revelation* 9: 13–21

> The sixth angel sounded a blast on his trumpet and I heard a voice from the four horns of the altar saying to the sixth angel who had the trumpet: "Release the four angels who are bound at the great river Euphrates." So there came the four angels who were prepared for that hour and day and month and year, to kill a third part of the human race. The number of the armed forces of cavalry was twenty thousand times ten thousand. I heard their number, and this was how I saw in appearance the horses and those who were seated on them. They had breastplates of fiery red, and smoky blue, and sulphurous yellow. The heads of the horses were like the heads of lions, and from their mouths there issued fire and smoke and brimstone. With these three plagues they killed a third part of the human race, with the fire and the smoke and the brimstone which were issuing from their mouths. For the power of the horses is in their mouths and in their tails, for their tails are like snakes with heads, and with them they inflict their hurt.
>
> The rest of mankind, who were not killed by these plagues, even in spite of this did not repent of the deeds of their hands, so as to cease to worship demons and idols of gold and silver and bronze and stone and wood, which can neither hear nor see nor move; nor did they repent of their murders or their sorceries or their immorality or their thefts.

THE horror of the picture mounts. The demonic locusts were allowed to injure but not kill; but now come the squadrons of demonic cavalry to annihilate a third part of the human race.

This is a passage whose imagery is mysterious and whose details no one has ever been able fully to explain.

No one really knows who were the four angels bound at the river Euphrates. We can only set down what we know and what we can guess. The Euphrates was the ideal boundary of the territory of Israel. It was God's promise to Abraham: "To your descendants I give this land, from the river of Egypt to the great river, the river Euphrates" (*Genesis* 15: 18). The angels, therefore, came from the distant lands, from the alien and hostile places from which the Assyrians and the Babylonians had in time past descended with destruction upon Israel.

Further, in the *Book of Enoch* we frequently meet angels who are described as the Angels of Punishment. Their task was at the right time to unleash the avenging wrath of God upon the people. Undoubtedly these four angels were included among the Angels of Punishment.

We have to add another fact to all this. We have frequently seen how the pictures of John are coloured by actual historical circumstances. The most dreaded warriors in the world were the Parthian cavalry; and the Parthians dwelt beyond the Euphrates. It may well be that John was visualizing a terrible descent of the Parthian cavalry on mankind.

The seer adds horror to horror. The number of the hosts of this terrible cavalry is 200,000,000, which simply means that they were beyond all numbering, like the chariots of God (*Psalm* 68: 17). They seem to be armoured in flame, for their breastplates are fiery red like the glow of a blazing furnace, smoky blue like the smoke rising from a fire and sulphurous yellow like the brimstone from the pit of hell. The horses have heads like lions and tails like serpents; they breathe out destructive fire and smoke and brimstone, and their serpent-tails deal out hurt and harm. The consequence of all this is that one-third of the human race is destroyed.

It would have been only natural to think that the remainder of mankind would take warning from this dreadful fate; but they did not and continued to worship their idols and demons and in the evil of their ways. It is the conviction of the biblical writers that the worship of idols was nothing less than devil worship and that it was bound to issue in evil and immorality.

## THE UNUTTERABLE REVELATION

*Revelation* 10: 1–4

> I saw another angel, a mighty one, coming down out of heaven,
> clad in a cloud, and with a rainbow on his head. His face was as
> the sun and his feet were like pillars of fire. He had in his hand a
> little roll which was opened. He put his right foot on the sea and
> his left foot on the land, and he cried with a loud voice as a lion
> roars, and, when he cried, the seven thunders uttered their voices.
> When the seven thunders spoke, I was about to write and I heard a
> voice from heaven saying: "Set a seal on what the seven thunders
> said, and do not write it."

10: 1—11: 14 is a kind of interlude between the sounding of
the sixth and the seventh trumpets. The sixth trumpet has
already sounded, but the seventh does not sound until
11: 15, and in between there are terrible things.

The mighty angel in this passage is described in terms
which show that he came straight from the presence of God
and the Risen Christ. He is clad in a cloud and the clouds are
the chariots of God, for "God maketh the clouds his chariot"
(*Psalm* 104: 3). He has a rainbow on his head and the rainbow
is part of the glory of the throne of God (*Ezekiel* 1: 28). The
rainbow is caused by the light of the angel's face shining
through the cloud. His face is as the sun which is the
description of the face of Jesus on the Mount of Transfiguration (*Matthew* 17: 2). His voice was as the roar of a lion
which is often used as a simile of the voice of God, "the Lord
roars from Zion and utters his voice from Jerusalem" (*Joel*
3: 16; *Hosea* 11: 10; *Amos* 3: 8). Clearly this angel has come
from the very presence of God; some think that he is none
other than the glorified Christ himself.

The angel has one foot on the sea and one on the land.
This shows his size and power, for sea and land stand for
the sum total of the universe. It also shows that the power
of God stands as firm on the sea as it does on the land.
In his hand the angel has a little roll, unrolled and opened.
That is to say, he is giving John a limited revelation about a

quite small period of time. When the angel speaks, the seven thunders sound. They are most likely a reference to the seven voices of God in *Psalm* 29.

Naturally, when the seer sees the open roll and hears the angel's voice, he prepares to make a record of it; but he is ordered not to do so. That is to say, he is being given a revelation which at the moment he is not to pass on. We get exactly the same idea when Paul tells us that he was caught up to the third heaven and "heard things that cannot be told, which man may not utter" (2 *Corinthians* 12: 4). We need not even begin to speculate about what the secret revelation was. We simply know that John had experiences which he could not communicate to others. God sometimes tells a man more than that man can say or than his generation can understand.

## THE DIVINE ANNOUNCEMENT OF THE END

*Revelation* 10: 5–7

The angel whom I saw standing on the sea and on the land raised his right hand to heaven and swore by him who lives for ever and ever, who created the heaven and the things in it, and the earth and the things in it, and the sea and the things in it, that there was no time left; but that in the days of the voice of the seventh angel, when he would sound his trumpet, there would be completed the secret purpose of God, the good news of which he announced to his servants the prophets.

THE angel now makes an announcement and affirms it with an oath. Sometimes the announcement has been taken to mean that "Time shall be no more". That is to say, time as we know it is about to be ended and eternity to begin. It is more likely that the meaning is that there is no time left, that there is to be no further delay, that Antichrist is about to burst upon the scene in all his destructive terror. As the writer to the Hebrews had it: "Yet a little while and the coming one will come, and shall not tarry" (*Hebrews* 10: 37). The hour has struck when the man of sin shall be revealed (2 *Thessalonians* 2: 3). Whichever be the meaning of the phrase, certainly the message is that Antichrist is about to invade the earth; the scene is being set for the final contest.

When this happens, as the Revised Standard Version has it, the mystery of God would be fulfilled. The meaning is that the whole purpose of God in human history will stand revealed. Much in life is difficult to understand; wickedness seems to hold sway. But, as John saw it, there is going to be a final show-down. God and Antichrist, good and evil, will face each other; final and total victory will be won, the questions will find their answers and the wrongs will be righted.

Beyond all the strangeness of the picture stands the truth that history is moving towards the inevitable triumph of God and that, though evil may flourish, it cannot in the end be triumphant.

## THE JOY AND THE SORROW OF THE MESSENGER OF GOD

*Revelation* 10: 8–11

And I heard the voice which I had heard from heaven speaking again to me and saying: "Go, take the little roll which lies open in the hand of the angel who is standing on the sea and on the land." And I went away to the angel and asked him to give me the little roll. He said to me: "Take it and eat it. It will be bitter to your stomach but it will be as sweet as honey to your mouth." And I took the little roll from the hand of the angel and ate it; and it was as sweet as honey to my mouth and, when I ate it, it was bitter to my stomach. And they said to me: "You must prophesy in regard to many peoples and nations and languages and kings."

BEFORE we deal with this passage in any detail, we note how twice the seer is told to *take* the roll. It is not handed to him; even when he asks the angel to give it to him, the answer is that he must take it. The meaning is that God's revelation is never forced on any man; he must take it.

This picture comes from the experience of Ezekiel who was told to eat the roll and to fill his belly with it (*Ezekiel* 3: 1, 3). In both pictures the idea is the same. The messenger of God has to take God's message into his very life and being.

The sweetness of the roll is a recurring thought in Scripture. To the psalmist the judgments of God are sweeter than honey and the honey-comb (*Psalm* 19: 10). "How sweet are thy words to my taste! sweeter than honey to my mouth" (*Psalm* 119: 103). It may well be that behind these words lies a pleasant Jewish educational custom. When a Jewish boy was learning the alphabet, it was written on a slate in a mixture of flour and honey. He was told what the letters were and how they sounded. After the original instruction, the teacher would point at a letter and would ask: "What is that and how does it sound?" If the boy could answer correctly, he was allowed to lick the letter off the slate as a reward! When the prophet and the psalmist speak about God's words and judgments being sweeter than honey, it may well be that they were thinking of this custom.

John adds another idea to this. To him the roll was sweet and bitter at one and the same time. What he means is this. A message of God may be to a servant of God at once a sweet and bitter thing. It is sweet because it is a great thing to be chosen as the messenger of God; but the message itself may be a foretelling of doom and, therefore, a bitter thing. So for John it was an infinite privilege to be admitted to the secrets of heaven but at the same time it was bitter to have to forecast the time of terror, even if triumph lay at its end.

## ANTICHRIST

IN the passages of the *Revelation* which we are now about to approach we will on many occasions meet the figure of Antichrist. This figure has exercised a strange fascination over the minds of men and many have been the speculations and theories about him. It will, therefore, be convenient to collect the material about Antichrist at this stage and to try to piece it into a connected whole.

We may lay it down as a general principle that Antichrist stands for the power in the universe which is against God. Just as the Christ is the Holy One and the Anointed King of God, so Antichrist is the Unholy One and the King of all evil. Just as the Christ is the incarnation of God and goodness, so Antichrist is the incarnation of the Devil and of evil.

The idea of a force opposed to God was not new. Antichrist had his predecessors long before the days of the New Testament; and it will help if we look first at some of the older pictures, for they left their mark on the New Testament picture.

(i) The Babylonians had a myth in regard to the creation of the world which they shared with all the Semitic peoples and with which the Jews must have come into contact. This myth painted the picture of creation in terms of a struggle between Marduk the creator and Tiamat the dragon, who stands for primaeval chaos. There was a further belief that this struggle between God and chaos would be repeated before the world came to an end.

This old belief in the struggle between the creating God and the dragon of chaos found its way into the Old Testament and is the explanation of certain obscure passages there. Isaiah tells of the day when God will slay the leviathan and the crooked serpent and the dragon that is in the sea (*Isaiah* 27: 1). In Jewish thought this ancient dragon of chaos came to be known as Rahab. Isaiah says: "Was it not thou that didst cut Rahab in pieces, that didst pierce the dragon?" (*Isaiah* 51: 9). When the Psalmist is recounting the triumphs of God, he says: "I will mention Rahab" (*Psalm* 87: 4). "Thou didst crush Rahab like a carcass," he says (*Psalm* 89: 10). Here is one of the ancestors of the Antichrist idea and that is one of the reasons why the dragon idea reappears in the *Revelation* (12: 9).

(ii) There is the Belial—or, as it is sometimes called, Beliar—idea. The word Belial frequently occurs in the Old Testament as a synonym for evil. An evil man or woman is called a son or daughter of Belial. Eli's wicked sons are sons of Belial (1 *Samuel* 2: 12). When Hannah was silently praying for a child in the Temple, Eli thought that she was drunk but Hannah says that she is not a daughter of Belial (1 *Samuel* 1: 16). The wicked Nabal is called a son of Belial (1 *Samuel* 25: 17, 25). One of Shimei's insults was to call David a son of Belial (2 *Samuel* 16: 7). The false witnesses produced by Jezebel against Naboth are sons of Belial (1 *Kings* 21: 10, 13), as are Jeroboam's revolutionary followers (2 *Chronicles* 13: 7). The exact meaning of the word is in doubt. It has been taken to mean prince of the air, hopeless ruin, worthlessness. Between the Testaments Belial came to be regarded as the chief of the demons. In the New Testament the word occurs only once: "What accord has Christ with Belial?" (2 *Corinthians* 6: 15). There it is used as the antithesis of Christ. It may well be that this idea came in part at least from the Persian religion with which the Jews came into contact. Persian religion, Zoroastrianism, conceived of the whole universe as the battleground in which the struggle was fought out between Ormuzd, the god of light, and Ahriman, the god of darkness. Here again we have the conception of a force in the world opposed to God and fighting against him.

(iii) There is a sense in which the obvious Antichrist is Satan, the Devil. Sometimes Satan is identified with Lucifer, the son of the morning, the angel who in heaven rebelled against God and was cast down to hell. "How you are fallen from heaven, O Day Star, son of Dawn!" (*Isaiah* 14: 12). It is easy to find instances in which Satan—the very name means the Adversary—acted in such a way as to overturn the purpose of God, for it is his very nature to do so. Such an instance was when Satan persuaded David to number the people in direct contravention of the command of God (1 *Chronicles* 21: 1). But though Satan is the direct opponent of God, he remains an angel, whereas Antichrist is a visible figure upon earth in which the very essence of evil has become incarnate.

(iv) There is a sense in which the development of the idea of the Messiah made the development of the idea of Antichrist inevitable. The Messiah, God's Anointed One, is bound to meet with opposition; and that opposition is entirely likely to crystallize into one supreme figure of evil. We must remember that *Messiah* and *Christ* mean the same thing, being the Hebrew and the Greek respectively for *The Anointed One*. Where there is the Christ, there will of necessity be the Antichrist, for so long as there is sin there will be opposition to God.

(v) In the Old Testament there is more than one picture of the divine battle with the assembled opposition to God. We find such a picture in the struggle with Gog and Magog (*Ezekiel* 38), and in the destruction of the destroyers of Jerusalem (*Zechariah* 14).

But, so far as the later Jews were concerned, the peak of the manifestation of evil was connected with one terrible episode in their history. This is commemorated in *Daniel's* picture of the little horn, which waxed great even against heaven, which stopped the daily sacrifice, which cast down the sanctuary (*Daniel* 8: 9–12). The little horn stands for Antiochus Epiphanes of Syria. He determined to introduce Greek ways, language and Greek worship into Palestine, for he regarded himself as the missionary of Greek culture. The Jews resisted. Antiochus Epiphanes invaded Palestine and captured Jerusalem. It was said that eighty thousand Jews were either slaughtered or sold into slavery. To circumcise a child or to possess a copy of the Law was a crime punishable by death. History has seldom, or never, seen so deliberate an attempt to wipe out the religion of a whole people. He desecrated the Temple. He erected an altar to Olympian Zeus in the Holy Place and on it sacrificed swine's flesh; and he turned the rooms of the Temple into public brothels. In the end the gallantry of the Maccabees restored the Temple and conquered Antiochus; but to the Jews Antiochus was the incarnation of all evil.

It can be seen that the figure of Antichrist was taking shape already in the Old Testament; the incarnation of evil is an idea that is already there.

We now turn to the idea of Antichrist in the New Testament.

(i) There is very little mention of the Antichrist idea in the Synoptic Gospels. The only real occurrence is in the chapters which deal with the end and the signs of the end. There Jesus is represented as saying: "Then if any one says to you, 'Lo, here is the Christ!' or 'There he is!' do not believe it. For false Christs and false prophets will arise and show great signs and wonders, so as to lead astray, if possible, even the elect" (*Matthew* 24: 23, 44; *Mark* 13: 6, 22; *Luke* 21: 8). In the Fourth Gospel Jesus is represented as saying: "I have come in my Father's name, and you do not receive me; if another comes in his own name, him you will receive" (*John* 5: 43). There the idea of Antichrist is rather that of false teaching, leading men away from true loyalty to Jesus Christ, a line of thought which, as we shall see, occurs again in the New Testament.

(ii) One of the main pictures of Antichrist is that of the Man of Sin in *Second Thessalonians* 2. Paul is reminding the Thessalonians of that which he had already taught them by word of mouth and of that which was an essential part of his teaching. He says: "Do you not remember that when I was still with you I told you this?" (2 *Thessalonians* 2: 5). In this picture there is first to be a general falling away; then the man of sin will come who will exalt himself above God and claim the worship which belongs to God by right, and work lying signs and wonders which will deceive many. At the moment when Paul is writing there is something which restrains this final manifestation of evil (2 *Thessalonians* 2: 7). In all probability Paul means the Roman Empire, seen by him as keeping the world from disintegrating into the chaos of the last time. Here Antichrist is concentrated into one person who is the very essence of evil. This rather connects itself with the Beliar idea of the Old Testament and with the conflict of light and darkness in the Persian world view.

(iii) The idea of Antichrist occurs in the Letters of John. It is, in fact, only there that the actual word occurs. In the last time Antichrist is to come; in the times in which John writes many Antichrists have come; therefore, says John, they know that they are living in the last time (1 *John* 2: 18). He who denies the Father and the Son is Antichrist (1 *John* 2: 22). In particular he who denies that Jesus Christ is come in the flesh is Antichrist (1 *John* 4: 3; 2 *John* 7). The supreme characteristic of Antichrist is the denial of the reality of the Incarnation.

Here again the main connection of Antichrist is with heresy. Antichrist is the spirit of falsehood which seduces men from the truth and leads them into mistaken ideas which are the ruin of the Christian faith.

(iv) It is in the *Revelation* that the fullest picture of Antichrist is painted and it occurs in more than one form.

(*a*) In 11: 7 there is the picture of the beast from the abyss, who is to slay the two witnesses in Jerusalem and who is to reign for forty-two months. This gives us the picture of Antichrist as coming, as it were, from hell, to have a terrible and destructive, but limited, time of power. In this picture there is at least some connection with the *Daniel* picture of Antiochus Epiphanes as the little horn. That is certainly where the period of forty-two months comes from, for that was the period during which the terror of Antiochus and the desecration of the Temple lasted.

(*b*) In 12 there is the picture of the great red dragon, who persecutes the woman clothed with the sun, the woman who begets the man child. This dragon is ultimately defeated and cast out of heaven. The dragon is definitely identified with the old serpent the devil (12: 9). This has clearly some kind of connection with the old myth of the dragon of chaos who was the enemy of God.

(*c*) In 13 there is the picture of the beast with the seven

heads and the ten horns, which comes from the sea, and
the other beast with the two horns, which comes from the
land. There is no doubt that what is in John's mind is the
terror and the savagery of Caesar worship; and in this case
Antichrist is the great begetter of persecution of the
Christian Church. Here the idea is of cruel, persecuting
power, bent on the utter destruction of Christ and his
Church.

(*d*) In 17: 3 we have the picture of the scarlet coloured
beast, with the seven heads and the ten horns, on which the
woman called Babylon is seated. We are told that the seven
heads are seven mountains on which the woman sits. In the
*Revelation* Babylon symbolizes Rome and Rome was built
on seven hills. Clearly this picture stands for Rome and
Antichrist is Rome's persecuting power unleashed upon the
Church.

It is of great interest to note the change here. As we have
seen, to Paul, when he wrote *Second Thessalonians,* Rome
was the one power which restrained the coming of Antichrist.
In *Romans* 13: 1–7 Paul writes of the state as divinely
appointed and urges all Christians to be loyal citizens. In
1 *Peter* 2: 13–17 the order to Christians is willingly to
submit themselves to the government of the state, to fear God
and to honour the king. In the *Revelation* there is a world of
difference; times had changed; the full fury of persecution
had broken out; and Rome had become to John the Antichrist.

(v) We note one last element in the picture of Antichrist.
With the old Jewish idea of this anti-God power and with
the Christian idea of a power who was the incarnation of
evil, there combined an idea from the Graeco-Roman world.
The worst of the Roman Emperors in the early days was
Nero who was regarded as the supreme monster of iniquity,
not only by the Christians, but also by the Romans
themselves. Nero died by suicide in A.D. 68, and there went
up a sigh of relief. But almost immediately there arose the
belief that he was not dead and that he was waiting in
Parthia to descend on the world with the terrible hordes of the

Parthians to let loose destruction and terror. This idea is called the *Nero redivivus*, the Nero resurrected, myth. In the ancient world it was widespread more than twenty years after Nero was dead. To the Christians, Nero was a figure of concentrated evil. It was he who had put the blame of the great fire of Rome on to the Christians; it was he who had initiated persecution; it was he who had found the most savage methods of torture. Many Christians believed in the *Nero redivivus* myth; and frequently—as in certain parts of the *Revelation—Nero redivivus* and Antichrist were identified and the Christians thought of the coming of Antichrist in terms of the return of Nero.

## THE VISION OF THINGS TO COME

*Revelation* 11

A measuring rod like a staff was given to me, with the instructions: "Rise and measure the Temple of God, and the altar and those who worship there. But leave out of the reckoning the outer Court which is outside the Temple and do not measure it, for it has been given to the Gentiles, and they will trample on the Holy City for forty-two months.

And I will give the task of prophesying to my two witnesses and they will prophesy for twelve hundred and sixty days, clothed in sackcloth. These witnesses are the two olive trees and the two lampstands who stand before the Lord of all the earth. If anyone tries to harm them, fire comes out of their mouth and devours their enemies; and whoever tries to hurt them must be thus killed.

These have the authority to shut up the heaven so that rain may not fall during the period for which they prophesied a drought; and they have authority over the waters to turn them into blood and to smite the earth with every plague as often as they wish.

When they shall have completed their witness, the beast which comes up from the abyss will make war with them and will overcome them and will kill them. Their corpses shall lie in the street of the great city, whose spiritual name is Sodom and Egypt, and where their Lord also was crucified. There are those of the peoples and tribes and tongues and nations who are to see their bodies for three and a half days, and they will not allow their bodies to be placed in a tomb. Those who inhabit the land will rejoice over them and will make merry and will send gifts to each other, because these two prophets tortured those who inhabit the land."

After the three and a half days a breath of life from God entered into them, and they stood on their feet, and great fear fell upon all who saw them. They heard a great voice from heaven saying to them: "Come up here." And they went up to heaven in the cloud, and their enemies saw them. At that hour there was a great earthquake, and the tenth of the city collapsed and seven thousand persons were killed, and the rest of the people were in fear and gave glory to the God of heaven.

The second woe is gone and, behold, the third is coming quickly.

The seventh angel sounded a blast on his trumpet and there came great voices in heaven saying: "The kingdom of this world has become the kingdom of our Lord and of his Anointed One, and he will reign for ever and ever."

The twenty-four elders, who sat upon their thrones in the presence of God, fell down upon their faces, and worshipped God saying: "We give you thanks, O Lord God, the Almighty, who are and who were, that you have taken your supreme authority and that you have entered upon your reign. The nations have raged, and your wrath has come, and there has come the time to judge the dead, and to give their reward to your servants the prophets and to God's dedicated people and to those who fear your name, both small and great, and to destroy those who are the destroyers of the earth."

And the Temple of God was opened in heaven, and in the Temple there was seen the Ark of the Covenant, and there were lightnings and voices and thunders and an earthquake and a great storm of hail.

IT is better to see this chapter as a whole, before we make any attempt to deal with it in detail. It has been said that it is at one and the same time the most difficult and the most important chapter in the *Revelation*. Its difficulty is obvious and it contains problems of interpretation about whose solution there can be no real certainty. Its importance lies in the fact that it contains a deliberate summary of the rest of the book. The seer has eaten the little roll and taken into his mind the message of God; and now he sets it down, not yet in detail but in the broad lines of its development. So certain is he of the course of events that from verse 11 he alters the tense of his narrative and speaks of things still in the future as if they were past. Let us then set out the scheme of this chapter which is also the scheme of the rest of the book.

(i) Verses 1 and 2. Here is the picture of the measuring of the Temple. As we shall see, the measuring is closely parallel to the sealing and is for the purposes of protection when the demonic terrors descend upon the world.

(ii) Verses 3–6. Here is the preaching of the two witnesses who are heralds of the end.

(iii) Verses 7–10. Here is the first emergence of Antichrist in the form of the beast from the abyss, and the temporary triumph of Antichrist which results in the death of the two witnesses.

(iv) Verses 11–13. Here follows the restoration to life of the witnesses and the consequent repentance and conversion of the Jews.

(v) Verses 14–19. Finally, here is the first sketch of the final triumph of Christ, the thousand years of his initial reign, the rising of the nations, the defeat of the nations and the judgment of the dead, and the establishment of the Kingdom of God and of his Anointed One.

We now proceed to examine the chapter in detail.


## THE MEASURING OF THE TEMPLE

*Revelation* 11: 1, 2

To the seer is given a measuring rod like a staff. The word for *measuring rod* is literally *reed*. There were certain grasses which grew with stalks like bamboo canes as much as six or eight feet high; these stalks were used as measuring rods. The word *rod* actually stands for a Jewish unit of measurement, equal to six cubits. The cubit was originally the space from the tip of the elbow to the tip of the middle finger and was reckoned as seventeen or eighteen inches; so the rod is equal to about nine feet.

The picture of measuring is common in the visions of the prophets. We find it in *Ezekiel, Zechariah* and *Amos* (*Ezekiel* 40: 3, 6; *Zechariah* 2: 1; *Amos* 7: 7–9); and no doubt these previous visions were in John's mind.

We find the idea of measuring used in more than one way. It is used as a preparation for building or for restoration and also as a preparation for destruction. But here the meaning lies in preservation. The measuring is like the sealing which is described in 7: 2, 3; the sealing and the measuring are both for the protection of God's faithful ones in the demonic terrors to descend upon the earth.

The seer has to measure the Temple, but he must omit from his measurement the outer court which has been given over to the Gentiles. The Temple in Jerusalem was divided into four courts, converging, as it were, upon the Holy of Holies. There was the Court of the Gentiles, into which Gentiles might come but beyond which they might not pass under penalty of death. Between it and the next court was a balustrade, into which were set tablets warning any Gentile that to come further was to be liable to instant death. Next came the Court of the Women beyond which women could not come; then the Court of the Israelites beyond which ordinary men could not come. Lastly, there was the Court of the Priests, which contained the Altar of the Burnt-Offering, made of brass, the Altar of Incense, made of gold, and the Holy Place; and into this court only the priests might come.

The seer is to measure the Temple. But the date of the *Revelation*, as we have seen, is somewhere about A.D. 90; and the Temple in Jerusalem had been destroyed in A.D. 70. How, then, could the Temple be measured?

The solution lies in this. Almost certainly John is taking over a picture which had already been used. Almost certainly this passage was *originally* spoken or written in A.D. 70, during the last siege of Jerusalem. During that siege the party of the Jews who would never admit defeat were the Zealots; they would rather die to a man, as indeed they ultimately did. When who would never admit defeat were the Zealots; they would rather die to a man, as indeed they ultimately did. When the walls of the city were breached, these Zealots retired into the Temple to make a last desperate resistance there. It is practically certain that some of their prophets said: "Never fear. The Gentile invaders may reach the outer Court of the Gentiles and defile it; but they will never penetrate into the inner Temple. God would never allow that." That confidence was disappointed; the Zealots perished and the Temple was destroyed; but *originally* the measuring of the inner courts and the abandoning of the outer court stood for the Zealot hope in those last terrible days.

John takes this picture and completely spiritualizes it. When he speaks of the Temple, he is not thinking of the Temple building at all which had been blasted out of existence more than twenty years before. For him the Temple is the Christian Church, the people of God. This picture meets us repeatedly in the New Testament. The Christians are living stones, built into a spiritual house (1 *Peter* 2: 5). The Church is founded on the apostles and the prophets; Jesus is the corner stone; the whole Church is growing into a holy temple in the Lord (*Ephesians* 2: 20, 21). "Do you not know," says Paul, "that you are God's temple?" (1 *Corinthians* 3: 16; cp, 2 *Corinthians* 6: 16).

The measuring of the Temple is the sealing of the people of God; they are to be preserved in the terrible time of trial; but the rest are doomed to destruction.

## THE LENGTH OF THE TERROR

*Revelation* 11: 1, 2 (*continued*)

THE length of the terror is to be forty-two months; the time of the preaching of the witnesses is to be twelve hundred and sixty days; their corpses are to lie on the street for three and a half days. Here is something which occurs again and again (cp. 13: 5; 12: 6); and occurs in still another form in 12: 14 where the period is *a time, times and half a time*. This is the famous phrase which goes back to *Daniel* (7: 25; 12: 7). We have to enquire, first, into the meaning of the phrase and, second, into its origin.

Its meaning is three and a half years. That is what forty-two months, and twelve hundred and sixty days—by Jewish reckoning—are. A time, times and half a time is equal to one year plus two years plus half a year.

The origin of the phrase comes from that most terrible time in Jewish history when Antiochus Epiphanes, King of Syria, tried to force Greek language, culture and worship upon the Jews and was met with the most violent and stubborn resistance. The roll of the martyrs was immense but the dreadful process was finally halted by the rising of Judas Maccabaeus.

Judas and his heroic followers waged guerrilla warfare and won the most amazing victories. Finally Antiochus and his forces were driven out and the Temple was restored and cleansed. The point is that this dreadful period lasted from June 168 B.C. to December 165 B.C. (To this day the Jews celebrate in December the Festival of Hanukah which commemorates the restoration and the cleansing of the Temple.) That is to say this dreadful time lasted almost exactly three and a half years. It was during that time that *Daniel* was written and the phrase was coined which ever afterwards was stamped on the Jewish mind as indicating a period of terror and suffering and martyrdom.

## THE TWO WITNESSES

*Revelation* 11: 3–6

IT was always part of Jewish belief that God would send his special messenger to men before the final coming of the Day of the Lord. In *Malachi* we hear God say: "Behold, I send my messenger to prepare the way before me" (*Malachi* 3: 1). *Malachi* actually identifies the messenger as Elijah: "Behold, I will send you Elijah the prophet before the great and dreadful Day of the Lord comes" (*Malachi* 4: 5). So, then, in our passage we have the coming of the messengers of God before the final contest.

These messengers have the task of prophesying; they will prophesy for 1,260 days, that is for three and a half years, which, as we have seen, is the period always connected with terror and destruction to come. Their message will be sombre, for they are clothed in sackcloth. It will be a message of condemnation; to listen to it will be like a torture and the people will be glad when the two witnesses are killed (verse 10).

(i) Some scholars have entirely allegorized this passage. They see in the two witnesses the Law and the Prophets, or the Law and the Gospel, or the Old Testament and the New Testament. Or, they see in the two witnesses a picture of the Church. Jesus had told his followers that they must be witnesses to him in Jerusalem, in Judaea, in Samaria, and to the uttermost parts of the earth (*Acts* 1: 8). Those who explain the two witnesses by the witness of the Church explain the number *two* by referring to *Deuteronomy* 19: 15, where it is said that if a charge is brought against anyone it must be confirmed by the evidence of two witnesses. But the picture of the two witnesses is so definite that it seems to refer to definite persons.

(ii) The two witnesses have been taken to be Enoch and Elijah. Neither Enoch nor Elijah was said to die. "Enoch walked with God; and he was not; for God took him" (*Genesis* 5: 24); Elijah was taken up in a whirlwind and in a chariot of fire to heaven (2 *Kings* 2: 11); and Tertullian (*Concerning the Soul*, 50) refers to a belief that they were being kept by God in heaven to bring death to Antichrist.

(iii) Much more likely the witnesses are Elijah and Moses. Elijah was held to be the greatest of the prophets, just as Moses was the supreme law-giver; and it was fitting that the two outstanding figures in the religious history of Israel should be God's messengers at the last time. It was these two who appeared to Jesus on the Mount of Transfiguration (*Mark* 9: 4). Further, the things said of them fit Moses and Elijah as they fit no one else. It is said (verse 6) that they have power to turn the water into blood and to smite the earth with all plagues, and that is what Moses did (cp. specially *Exodus* 7: 14–18). It is said that fire proceeds out of their mouth and burns up their enemies, and that they can shut up the heavens so that the rain is withheld. That is what Elijah did with the company of soldiers sent to take him (2 *Kings* 1: 9, 10) and when he prophesied to Ahab that there would be no rain upon the earth (1 *Kings* 17: 1). We have already seen that Elijah was expected to return to herald the end; and it would not be difficult to regard God's promise that he would raise up a prophet like Moses (*Deuteronomy* 18: 18) as a prophecy that Moses himself would return.

## THE SAVING DEATH OF THE TWO WITNESSES

*Revelation* 11: 7–13

THE witnesses are to preach for their allotted time and then will come Antichrist in the form of the beast from the abyss; and the two witnesses will be cruelly slain.

This is to happen in Jerusalem; but Jerusalem is called by the terrible names of Sodom and Egypt. Long before this Isaiah had addressed the rulers of Jerusalem as the rulers of Sodom and the people of Jerusalem as the people of Gomorrah (*Isaiah* 1: 9, 10). Sodom and Gomorrah stand as the types of sin, the symbols of those who had not received strangers (cp. the story in *Genesis* 19: 4–11) and who had turned their benefactors into slaves (*Wisdom* 19: 14, 15). The wickedness of Jerusalem had already crucified Jesus Christ and in the days to come it is to regard the death of his witnesses with joy.

So will the people of Jerusalem hate the two witnesses that they will leave their bodies unburied in the street. In Jewish thought it was a terrible thing that a body should not be buried. When the heathen attacked God's people, to the Psalmist it was the greatest tragedy of all that there was none to bury them (*Psalm* 79: 3); the threat to the disobedient prophet, a threat which came true, was that his carcase would not come to the sepulchre of his fathers (1 *Kings* 13: 22). Even worse, such will be the hatred of the people for the witnesses of God that they will regard their death as a reason for festival.

But that is not the end. After three and a half days— here we have the same period—the breath of life entered again into the two slain witnesses and they stood upon their feet. Still more startling things were to happen. In sight of all, the two witnesses were summoned up into heaven, re-enacting, as it were, Elijah's first departure to heaven in the whirlwind and the chariot of fire (2 *Kings* 2: 11).

To add to the terror came a destructive earthquake which wrecked a tenth of the city and brought death to seven thousand of its inhabitants. The result was that those who had seen these terrifying events and were spared, gave glory to God. That is to say, they repented, for that is the only real way to give glory to God.

The great interest of this passage lies in the fact that the unbelievers were won by the sacrificial death of the witnesses and by God's vindication of them. Here is the story of the Cross and of the Resurrection all over again. Evil must be conquered and men won, not by force but by the acceptance of suffering for the name of Christ.


## THE FORECAST OF THINGS TO COME

*Revelation* 11: 14–19

WHAT makes this passage difficult is that it seems to indicate

that things have come to an end in final victory, while there
is still half the book to go. The explanation, as we have
seen, is that this passage is a summary of what is still to
come. The events foreshadowed here are as follows.

(i) There is the victory in which the kingdoms of the
world become the kingdoms of the Lord and of his Anointed
One. This is really a quotation of *Psalm* 2: 2, and is
another way of saying that the Messianic reign has begun.
In view of this victory the twenty-four elders, that is, the
whole Church, break out in thanksgiving.

(ii) This victory leads to the time when God takes his
supreme authority (verse 17). That is to say, it leads to the
thousand year reign of God, the Millenium, a thousand year
period of peace and prosperity.

(iii) At the end of the Millenium there is to come the final
attack of all the hostile powers (verse 18); they will be finally
defeated and then will follow the last judgment.

In verse 19 we come back, as it were, to the present.
There is a vision of the heavenly Temple opened and of the
Ark of the Covenant. Two things are involved in this vision.

(i) The Ark of the Covenant was in the Holy of Holies,
the inside of which no ordinary person had ever seen, and
into which even the High Priest went only on the Day of
Atonement. This must mean that now the glory of God is
going to be fully displayed.

(ii) The reference to the Ark of the Covenant is as a
reminder of God's special covenant with his people. Originally
that covenant had been with the people Israel; but the new
covenant is with all of every nation who love and believe in
Jesus. Whatever the terror to come, God will not be false to
his promises.

This is a picture of the coming of the full glory of God,
a terrifying threat to his enemies but an uplifting promise to the
people of his covenant.

## THE WOMAN AND THE BEAST

*Revelation* 12

IT is necessary to read this chapter as a whole before we examine it in detail.

A great sign appeared in the sky—a woman clothed with the sun, and with the moon beneath her feet, and with a crown of twelve stars on her head; and she was with child, and she cried aloud in her labour and in her agony to bear the child.

And another sign appeared in heaven—lo! a great flame-coloured dragon, with seven heads and ten horns, and with seven royal diadems upon its heads. Its tail swept a third part of the stars from the sky and cast them on to the earth. The dragon stood in front of the woman who was about to bear the child so that it might devour the child as soon as she bore him.

She bore a man child who is destined to rule the nations with a rod of iron; and her child was snatched away to God, even to his throne.

The woman fled to the desert where she had a place prepared for her by God, that they might care for her there for one thousand two hundred and sixty days.

There was war in heaven, in which Michael and his angels fought with the dragon and the dragon and his angels fought with them. The dragon was powerless to prevail and there was no longer any place for him in heaven. The great dragon, the ancient serpent, who is called the Devil and Satan, the deceiver of all mankind, was thrown down to earth, and his angels were thrown down with him. And I heard a great voice in heaven saying:

"Now have come the salvation and the power and the kingdom of our God, and the authority of his Anointed One, because there has been cast down the accuser of our brothers, who night and day accuses them before God. They have overcome him through the blood of the Lamb and through the word of their witness, and they did not love their soul to death. Rejoice, therefore, you heavens and you who dwell in them. Alas for the earth and the sea! because the Devil has come down to you with great wrath and well aware that he has only a little time left."

When the Devil saw that he was cast down into the earth, he pursued the woman who bore the man-child. The two wings of the great eagle were given to the woman, that she might fly to the desert to her place, where she is cared for for a time and times and half a time away from the serpent. And after the woman the serpent hurled water from his mouth like a river, that he might cause her to be carried away by the river of water; but the earth helped the woman and opened its mouth and swallowed the river which the dragon hurled from his mouth.

The dragon was enraged because of the woman and went away to make war with the rest of her family, those who keep the commandments of God and who bear their witness to Jesus. And he stood on the sand of the sea.


# THE WOMAN WITH CHILD

*Revelation* 12: 1, 2

JOHN saw an amazing vision, like a tableau in the sky, whose details he draws from many sources. The woman is clothed with the sun; the moon is her footstool; and she has a crown of twelve stars. The Psalmist says of God that he covers himself with light as with a garment (*Psalm* 104: 2). In the *Song of Solomon* the poet describes his loved one as being fair as the moon and clear as the sun (*Song of Solomon* 6: 10). So John got part of his picture from the Old Testament. But he added something which the pagans of Asia Minor would well recognize as part of the old Babylonian picture of the divine. They frequently depicted their goddesses as crowned with the twelve signs of the zodiac and this also is in John's mind. It is as if he took all the signs of divinity and beauty which he could find and added them together.

This woman is in labour to bear a child who is undoubtedly the Messiah, Christ, cp. verse 5 where he is said to be destined to rule the nations with a rod of iron. That is a quotation from *Psalm* 2: 9 and was an accepted description of the Messiah. The woman, then, is the mother of the Messiah.

(i) If the woman is the "mother" of the Messiah, an obvious suggestion is that she should be identified with Mary; but she is so clearly a superhuman figure that she can hardly be identified with any single human being.

(ii) The persecution of the woman by the dragon suggests that she might be identified with the Christian Church. The objection is that the Christian Church could hardly be called the mother of the Messiah.

(iii) In the Old Testament the chosen people, the ideal Israel, the community of the people of God, is often called the Bride of God. "Your Maker is your husband" (*Isaiah* 54: 5). It is Jeremiah's sad complaint that Israel has played the harlot in disloyalty to God (*Jeremiah* 3: 6–10). Hosea hears God say: "I will betroth you to me for ever" (*Hosea* 2: 19, 20). In the *Revelation* itself we hear of the marriage feast of the Lamb and the Bride of the Lamb (*Revelation* 19: 7; 21: 9). "I betrothed you to Christ," writes Paul to the Corinthian Church, "to present you as a pure bride to her one husband" (2 *Corinthians* 11: 2).

This will give us a line of approach. It was from the chosen people that Jesus Christ sprang in his human lineage. It is for the ideal community of the chosen ones of God that the woman stands. Out of that community Christ came and it was that community which underwent such terrible suffering at the hands of the hostile world. We may indeed call this the Church, if we remember that the Church is the community of God's people in *every* age.

From this picture we learn three great things about this community of God. First, it was out of it that Christ came; and out of it Christ has still to come for those who have never known him. Second, there are forces of evil, spiritual and human, which are set on the destruction of the community of God. Third, however strong the opposition against it and however sore its sufferings, the community of God is under the protection of God and, therefore, it can never be ultimately destroyed.

## THE HATRED OF THE DRAGON

*Revelation* 12: 3, 4

HERE we have the picture of the great, flame-coloured dragon. In our study of the antecedents of Antichrist we saw that the eastern peoples regarded creation in the light of the struggle between the dragon of chaos and the creating God of order. In the Temple of Marduk, the creating god, in Babylon there was a great image of a "red-gleaming serpent" who stood for the defeated dragon of chaos. There can be little doubt that that is where John got his picture. This dragon appears in many forms in the Old Testament.

It appears as *Rahab*. "Was it not thou that didst cut Rahab in pieces, that didst pierce the dragon?" (*Isaiah* 51: 9). It appears as *leviathan*. "Thou didst break the heads of the dragons in the waters. Thou didst crush the heads of leviathan" (*Psalm* 74: 12–14). In the day of the Lord, God with his sore and great and strong sword will punish leviathan (*Isaiah* 27: 1). It appears in the dramatic picture of *behemoth* in *Job* 40: 15–24. The dragon which is the arch-enemy of God is a common and terrible figure in the thought of the east. It is the connection of the dragon and the sea which explains the rivers of water which the dragon emits to overcome the woman (verse 15).

The dragon has seven heads and ten horns. This signifies its mighty power. It has seven royal diadems. This signifies its complete power over the kingdoms of this world as opposed to the kingdom of God. The picture of the dragon sweeping the stars from the sky with its tail comes from the picture in *Daniel* of the little horn who cast the stars to the ground and trampled on them (*Daniel* 8: 10). The picture of the dragon waiting to devour the child comes from *Jeremiah*, in which it is said of Nebuchadnezzar that "he has swallowed me like a monster" (*Jeremiah* 51: 34).

H. B. Swete finds in this picture the symbolism of an eternal truth about the human situation. In the human situation, as Christian history sees it, there are two figures who occupy the centre of the scene. There is man, fallen, always under the attack of the powers of evil but always struggling towards the birth of a higher life. And there is the power of evil, ever watching for its opportunity to frustrate the upward reach of man. That struggle had its culmination on the Cross.

## THE SNATCHING AWAY OF THE CHILD

*Revelation* 12: 5

THE child which the woman bore was destined to rule the nations with a rod of iron. As we have seen, this quotation from *Psalm* 2: 9 indicates that the child was the Messiah.

When the child was born, he was rescued from the dragon by being snatched up to heaven, even to the throne of God. The word used here for the child being *snatched up* is the same as is used in 1 *Thessalonians* 4: 17 to describe the Christian being *caught up* to meet the Lord in the air (cp. 2 *Corinthians* 12: 2 where Paul uses it to tell of himself being caught up into the third heaven).

In a sense this is a puzzling passage. As we have seen, the reference is to Jesus Christ as Messiah, and, as John tells it, the story goes straight from his Birth to his Ascension; the snatching up must refer to the Ascension. As the *Acts* has it: "He was lifted up" (*Acts* 1: 9). The strange thing is the total omission of the earthly life of Jesus. This is due to two things.

It is due to the fact that John is not at the moment interested in anything other than the fact that Jesus Christ was delivered by the direct action of God from the hostile powers which continually attacked him.

It is due also to the fact that all through the *Revelation* John's interest is not in the human Jesus but in the exalted Christ, who is able to rescue his people in the time of their distresses.

## THE FLIGHT TO THE DESERT

*Revelation* 12: 6

HERE we read of the woman escaping into the desert from the attack of the dragon. By the help of God she escaped into a place where she was nourished and which had been prepared for her.

There is no doubt that there are many pictures in John's mind. There is the picture of the escape of Elijah to the brook Cherith, where he was nourished by the ravens (1 *Kings* 17: 1–7); and of his flight into the desert, when he was nourished by the angelic messenger (1 *Kings* 19: 1–8). There is the picture of the flight of Mary and Joseph with the baby Jesus into Egypt to escape the murderous intent of Herod (*Matthew* 2: 13). But two incidents are specially in John's mind.

(i) In the time of Antiochus Epiphanes, when it was death to keep the law and to worship the true God, many "who sought after justice and judgment went down to the wilderness to dwell there" (1 *Maccabees* 2: 29).

(ii) Jerusalem was destroyed by the Romans in A.D. 70. The years immediately before that were terrible years of bloodshed and of revolution in which anyone with eyes to see and a mind to understand could forecast what was about to happen. Eusebius, the Christian historian, tells us that, before the final disaster came, the Christians in Jerusalem had been warned by a revelation given to approved men to leave Jerusalem and to cross the Jordan into Perea and to dwell there in a town called Pella (Eusebius: *The Ecclesiastical History* 3: 5). This is actually referred to in the account of Jesus's words to the disciples about the last times. When they saw the last terrors coming they were to flee to the mountains (*Mark* 13: 14); this is exactly what they did.

H. B. Swete again sees something symbolic here. The Church had to flee into the wilderness and the wilderness is lonely. For the early Christians life was lonely; they were isolated in a pagan world. There are times when Christian witness is bound to be a lonely thing—but even in human loneliness there is divine companionship.

The one thousand two hundred and sixty days are once again the standard period of distress.


## SATAN, THE ENEMY OF GOD

*Revelation* 12: 7–9

HERE we have the picture of war in heaven between the Dragon, the Ancient Serpent, the Devil, Satan—all these names describe the one evil being—and Michael and all his angels. The idea seems to be that, such was his hatred, the dragon pursued the Messiah even to heaven, where he was met by Michael with his heavenly legions and finally cast out. It will be convenient to gather together here what Scripture has to say about Satan; it presents a complicated picture.

(i) There is the echo of the ancient story of a primaeval war in heaven. Satan was an angel who conceived "the impossible thought" of placing his throne higher than that of God (2 *Enoch* 29: 4, 5) and was cast out of heaven. The Babylonians had a similar story of Ishtar, the god of the morning star. He, too, rebelled against God and was cast down from heaven. There is one definite reference to this old story in the Old Testament. In *Isaiah* we read: "How you are fallen from heaven, O Day Star, son of Dawn!" (*Isaiah* 14: 12). The sin which caused the fall from heaven was pride. There may be a reference to this in 1 *Timothy* 3: 6, where it is urged that the Christian preacher must be kept from pride lest he fall into the same condemnation as the devil did. When Satan was cast out of heaven, his dwelling-place became the air in which he had to wander; that is why he is sometimes called The Prince of the Air (*Ephesians* 2: 2).

(ii) There is a strong line of thought in the Old Testament in which Satan is still an angel under God's command and with access to his presence. In *Job* we find Satan numbered amongst the sons of God and possessing access to his presence (*Job* 1: 6–9; 2: 1–6); and in *Zechariah* we also find Satan in the presence of God (*Zechariah* 3: 1, 2).

To understand this conception of Satan we must first understand what the word *Satan* means. *Satan* originally meant simply an *adversary*. Even the angel of the Lord who stood in the path of Balaam to stop him from his sinful intentions can be called a *satan* against him (*Numbers* 22: 22). The Philistines feared that David would be their *satan* (1 *Samuel* 29: 4). When Solomon entered upon his kingdom, he was so blessed by God that he had no *satan* left (1 *Kings* 5: 4). But later the foreign kings, Hadad and Rezon, were both to become his *satans* (1 *Kings* 11: 14, 23).

In the Old Testament Satan was the angel who was the counsel for the prosecution against men in the presence of God, their Adversary. Thus he is the counsel for the prosecution against Job, cynically suggesting that Job serves God for what he can get out of it and that, if he is involved in disaster, his loyalty will soon cease (*Job* 1: 11, 12), and he is given permission by God to use every weapon short of death to test Job (*Job* 2: 1–6). So in *Zechariah* Satan is the accuser of Joshua the High Priest (*Zechariah* 3: 1, 2). In *Psalm* 109: 6 the Authorized Version actually uses the word *Satan* in this sense: "Let Satan stand at the right hand of the wicked." The Revised Standard Version rightly alters the translation to: "Let an *accuser* bring him to trial."

So, in the Old Testament Satan was the angel who is the counsel for the prosecution when a man was on trial before God; while Michael was the counsel for the defence. Between the Testaments there seems to have been a belief that there was more than one Satan engaged in the task of bringing accusations against men and we read of the archangel whose duty it was to fend off the Satans (1 *Enoch* 40: 6).

For the most part in the Old Testament Satan was very much under the jurisdiction of God.

(iii) In the Old Testament we never read of the Devil, although sometimes we come across devils; but in the New

Testament Satan becomes the Devil. The Greek is *Diabolos*,
literally a *slanderer*. There is not a very great dividing line
between being a prosecuting counsel who brings charges
against men and inventing such charges and tempting men
into actions where such charges will be forthcoming. So, then,
in the New Testament Satan becomes the seducer of men.
We find that in the story of the temptations of Jesus the
three names are indiscriminately used. This power of evil is
Satan (*Matthew* 4: 10; *Mark* 1: 13); the Devil (*Matthew*
4: 1, 5, 8, 11; *Luke* 4: 2, 3, 5, 13); and the Tempter
(*Matthew* 4: 3).

Since this is so, we find Satan engaged in certain nefarious
purposes in the New Testament story. He seeks to seduce
Jesus in his temptations. He puts the terrible scheme of
betrayal into Judas's mind (*John* 13: 2; 13: 27; *Luke* 22: 3).
He is out to make Peter fall (*Luke* 22: 31). He persuades
Ananias to keep back part of the price of the possession he
had sold (*Acts* 5: 3). He uses every wile (*Ephesians* 6: 11) and
every device (2 *Corinthians* 2: 11) to achieve his seducing
purposes. He is the cause of illness and pain (*Luke* 13: 16;
*Acts* 10: 38; 2 *Corinthians* 12: 7). He hinders the work of the
gospel by sowing the tares which choke the good seed
(*Matthew* 13: 39), and by snatching away the seed of the
word from the human heart before it can gain an entry
(*Mark* 4: 15; *Luke* 8: 12).

Thus Satan becomes the enemy of God and man, the
Evil One *par excellence*, for we should probably translate
in the Lord's Prayer: "Deliver us from the Evil One"
(*Matthew* 6: 13).

He can be called the Ruler of this World (*John* 12: 31;
14: 30; 16: 11), for, having been cast out of heaven, he has
to exert his evil influence among men. He comes to be
identified with the serpent because of the story of the Fall in
*Genesis* 3.

(iv) The strange thing is that the history of Satan is a
tragedy, whatever version of the story we use. In one version,
Satan is the angel of light, once the greatest of the angels,

whose pride caused him to seek to be higher than God and who was cast out of heaven. In the other version, Satan was a real servant of God and perverted his service into an opportunity for sinning. Satan is the supreme example of that tragedy in which the best becomes the worst.

## THE SONG OF THE MARTYRS IN GLORY

*Revelation* 12: 10–12

IN these verses we have the song of the glorified martyrs when Satan is cast out of heaven.

(i) Satan appears as the Accuser *par excellence*; Satan, as H. B. Swete put it, is "the cyncial libeller of all that God has made." According to Renan he is "the malevolent critic of creation." Satan stands for the sleepless vigilance of evil against good.

The historical background of the age in which the *Revelation* was written lends sharpness to this picture of Satan. This was the great age of the informer, the *delator*. People were constantly being arrested, tortured, killed because someone had informed against them. Tacitus, writing some years before, had said: "He who had no foe was betrayed by his friend." That ancient world knew only too well what malevolent, cynical, venal accusers were like.

(ii) This picture, then, shows us what we might call the cleansing of heaven. Satan, the malevolent Accuser, is cast out for ever. It is for this reason that the martyrs in glory sing their song of triumph.

The martyrs are those who have overcome Satan.

(*a*) Martyrdom is itself a conquest of Satan. The martyr, has proved superior to every seduction and to every threat and even to the violence of Satan. Here is a dramatic truth for life—every time we choose to suffer rather than to be disloyal is the defeat of Satan.

(*b*) The victory of the martyrs is won through the blood of the Lamb. There are two meanings here. First, on his Cross and through his Resurrection Jesus overcame forever the worst that evil could do to him; and those who have entrusted their lives to him share in that victory. Second, through the sacrifice of Jesus Christ on the Cross sin is forgiven; when a man accepts in faith what Christ has done for him, his sins are wiped out. *And when he is forgiven, there is nothing for which he can possibly be accused.* As Charles Wesley put it:

> No condemnation now I dread;
>     Jesus, and all in him is mine!
> Alive in him, my living Head,
>     And clothed in righteousness divine,
> Bold I approach the eternal throne,
> And claim the crown, through Christ my own.

(*c*) The martyrs are victorious, because they lived the great principle of the gospel. They did not consider life more important than loyalty. "He who loves his life loses it; and he who hates his life in this world will keep it for eternal life" (*John* 12: 25). This principle runs all through the gospel (*Matthew* 10: 39; 16: 25; *Mark* 8: 35; *Luke* 9: 24; 17: 33). For us this is not necessarily a matter of dying for the faith but of setting loyalty to Jesus Christ before the comfortable way.

(iii) This passage finishes with the idea that Satan is cast out of heaven and has come down to earth. His power in heaven is broken, but he has still power on earth; and he rages ferociously because he knows that all that he has left is a short time upon this earth before he is finally destroyed.


## THE ATTACK OF THE DRAGON

*Revelation* 12: 13–17

THE dragon, that is the Devil, on being cast out of heaven and descending to earth, attacked the woman who was the mother of the man child. We have seen that the woman stands for the Church in its widest sense of God's Chosen People from the midst of whom God's Anointed One came.

Here, then, is a certain symbolism. The dragon can injure the child by injuring the mother; that is to say, to injure the Church is to injure Jesus Christ. The words of the Risen Christ to Paul on the Damascus road were: "Saul, Saul, why do you persecute *me*?" (*Acts* 9: 4). Paul's persecution had been directed against the *Church*; but the Risen Christ makes it clear that persecution of his Church is persecution of himself. When we despoil the Church of the help we might have given it, we despoil Jesus of the help we might have given him; and when we serve the Church, we serve Jesus himself.

We have already seen (verse 6) that the escape of the woman to the desert place comes from the escape of the Church to Pella on the other side of Jordan before the final destruction of Jerusalem. But in the escape of the woman and in the attack of the dragon John uses two pictures very familiar to those who knew the Old Testament.

The woman escaped on the two wings of the great eagle. Again and again in the Old Testament the eagle's wings are the symbol of the upbearing arms of God. "You have seen," God said to Israel, "what I did to the Egyptians, and how I bore you on eagles' wings, and brought you to myself" (*Exodus* 19: 4). "Like an eagle that stirs up its nest, that flutters over its young, spreading out its wings, catching them, bearing them on its pinions, the Lord alone did lead him (the people of Israel)" (*Deuteronomy* 32: 11, 12). As the Scots paraphrase has it of *Isaiah* 40: 31:

> On eagles' wings they mount, they soar,
>   their wings are faith and love,
> Till, past the cloudy regions here,
>   they rise to heav'n above.

We may note that, when men came to allegorize Scripture, Hippolytus saw in the eagles' wings the symbol of "the two holy arms of Christ outstretched upon the Cross."

The second picture is of the floods of water cast out by the serpent. We have seen how the old dragon of chaos was a sea dragon and, therefore, to connect the floods with him is quite natural. But again here we have an Old Testament picture. Again and again in the Old Testament tribulation and persecution are likened to an overwhelming flood. "All thy waves and thy billows have gone over me" (*Psalm* 42: 7). It is God's promise to the Psalmist that "the rush of great waters" shall not come near him (*Psalm* 32: 6). If the Lord had not helped him, the waters would have overwhelmed him and the streams would have gone over his soul (*Psalm* 124: 4). When he passes through the waters, God will be with him (*Isaiah* 43: 2).

The chapter finishes with two further pictures.

When the dragon ejected the floods of waters, the earth swallowed them up and so the woman was saved. It is not difficult to see where John got this picture. It quite often happened in Asia Minor that rivers were swallowed up in the sand only to reappear after travelling a distance underground. There was, for instance, a case of this near Colossae, an area which John must have known well.

But it is not so easy to see what the picture means. The symbolism is very likely this. Nature itself is on the side of the man who is faithful to Jesus Christ. As Froude the historian pointed out, in the world there is a moral order and in the long run it is well with the good and ill with the wicked.

Finally John has the picture of the dragon going to war with the rest of the family of the woman, with the rest of the Church. This tells of the coming spread of persecution all over the Church.

As John saw it, Satan cast down to earth is in his last terrible convulsion and that convulsion is going to involve the whole family of the Church in the agony of persecution.

## THE POWER OF THE BEAST

*Revelation* 13

I saw a beast coming up from the sea. It had ten horns and seven heads; and it had ten royal crowns on its horns; and on its heads I saw blasphemous names.

The beast which I saw was like a leopard; its feet were like a bear's feet; its mouth was like a lion's mouth; and to it the dragon delegated its power and its throne and its great authority.

I saw that one of its heads looked as if it had been wounded to death; and its deadly wound had been healed.

The whole earth was drawn in wonder after the beast; and they worshipped the dragon, because it had delegated its authority to the beast; and they worshipped the beast. "Who," they said, "is like the beast? Who is able to make war with it?" To it there was given a mouth which made arrogant and blasphemous claims; and it was given authority to go on doing so for forty-two months. It opened its mouth to launch blasphemies against God, to insult his name and his dwelling-place and those who dwell in the heavens.

It was given power to make war with the dedicated people of God and to overcome them; and it was given authority over every tribe and people and tongue and race. All who dwell upon the earth will worship it, everyone whose name has not been written from the foundation of the world in the Book of Life of the Lamb who was slain.

Whoever has an ear, let him hear.

If anyone is to be taken into captivity, into captivity let him go. If anyone slays with the sword, he himself will be slain with the sword. Here is the summons to steadfastness and to loyalty from the dedicated people of God.

I saw another beast coming up from the land, and it had two horns like a lamb and it spoke like a dragon. It exercises before it all the power of the first beast. It causes the earth and those who dwell in it to worship the first beast, the beast whose deadly wound has been healed. It works such great miracles that it causes even fire to come down from heaven in the sight of men. It deceives those who dwell on the earth, because of the miracles which it has the power to do in the presence of the beast. It tells those who dwell upon the earth to make an image of the beast, who has the wound of the sword, and who lived again. It was given power to give the breath of life to the image of the beast, so that the image of the beast should even speak and so that it should bring it about that all who do not worship the beast should be killed. It causes all, small and great, rich and poor, free men and slaves, to take to themselves a mark on their right hand or on their forehead. It so arranges things that no one can buy or sell, unless he has the mark, which consists of the name of the beast or the number of his name.

Here there is need of wisdom. Let him who has understanding reckon the number of the beast, for the number is the number of a man; and his number is six hundred and sixty-six.

IT will be much easier if we treat this chapter as a whole before we undertake any detailed study of it. That is all the more necessary because this chapter is the essence of the whole book.

The general meaning is this. Satan, cast out of heaven, knows that his time is short and is determined to do as much damage as he can. To cause that damage on earth he delegates his power to the two beasts who are the central figures in this chapter.

The beast from the sea stands for the Roman Empire, to John the incarnation of evil and is described in terms which come from *Daniel*. In *Daniel* 7: 3–7 there is a vision of four great beasts who come out of the sea; they are the symbols of the great empires which have held world power and of an empire which, when *Daniel* was written, was holding world sway. The beast like a lion with an eagle's wings stands for Babylon; the one like a bear stands for Media; the one like a leopard with four wings stands for Persia; and the fourth stands for the empire of Alexander the Great. As the writer of *Daniel* saw these world powers, they were so savage and inhuman that they could be symbolized by nothing but bestial figures. It was only natural for a Jew to go back to this picture of the beastly empires when he wished to find a picture of another satanic empire threatening God's people in his own day.

John's picture in the *Revelation* puts together in the one beast the features of all four. It is like a leopard with bear's feet and a lion's mouth. That is to say, for John the Roman Empire was so satanic that it included all the terrors of the evil empires which had gone before.

This beast has *seven heads* and *ten horns*. These stand for the rulers and the emperors of Rome. Since Augustus, the first Roman Emperor, there had been seven emperors; Tiberius, A.D. 14–37; Caligula, A.D. 37–41; Claudius, A.D. 41–54; Nero, A.D. 55–68; Vespasian, A.D. 69–79; Titus, A.D. 79–81; Domitian, A.D. 81–96. These seven emperors are the seven heads of the beast. But in addition it is said that the beast had *ten* horns. The explanation of this second figure lies in this. After the death of Nero there was a short period of almost complete chaos. In eighteen months three different men briefly occupied the imperial power, Galba, Otho and Vitellius. They are not included in John's list of the seven heads but are included in the list of the ten horns.

John says that on the heads of the beast there were *blasphemous names*. These are the titles which the emperors took to themselves. Every emperor was called *divus* or *sebastos*, which means *divine*. Frequently the very name *God* or *Son of God* was given to the emperors; and Nero on his coins called himself *The Saviour of the World*. For any man to call himself divine was a blasphemous insult to God. Further, the later emperors took as their title the Latin word *dominus*, or its Greek equivalent *kurios*, both of which mean *lord* and in the Old Testament are the special title of God and in the New Testament the special title of Jesus Christ.

The second beast which figures in this chapter, the beast from the land, is the whole provincial organisation of magistrates and priesthoods designed to enforce Caesar worship, which confronted the Christians with the choice either of saying, "Caesar is Lord," or of dying.

So, then, our picture falls into place. These two savage beasts, the might of Rome and the organisation of Caesar worship, launched their combined attack on the Christians—and no nation had ever withstood the might of Rome. What hope had the Christians—poor, defenceless, outlaws?

### THE HEAD WOUNDED AND RESTORED

There is another recurring theme in this chapter. Among the

seven heads there is one which has been mortally wounded and restored to life (verse 3); that head above all is to be worshipped (verses 12 and 14); it is the supreme evil, the supreme enemy of Christ.

We have seen that the seven heads stand for the seven Roman emperors. A head wounded and restored to life will, therefore, stand for an emperor who died and came to life again. Here is symbolized the *Nero redivivus*, or Nero resurrected, legend which the Christians fused with the idea of Antichrist. In the *Sibylline Oracles* we read of the expectation in the last terrible days of the coming of a king from Babylon whom all men hate, a king fearful and shameless and of abominable parentage (5: 143–148). A matricide shall come from the east and bring ruin on the world (5: 361–364). One who dared the pollution of a mother's murder will come from the east (4: 119–122). An exile from Rome with a myriad of swords shall come from beyond the Euphrates (4: 137–139).

It is only when we realize what Nero was that we see how his return might well seem the coming of Antichrist.

No man ever started life with a worse heritage than Nero. His father was Cnaeus Domitius Ahenobarbus, who was notorious for wickedness. He had killed a freedman for no other crime than refusing to drink more wine; he had deliberately run over a child in his chariot on the Appian Way; in a brawl in the Forum he had gouged out the eye of a Roman knight; and he finally died of dropsy brought on by his debauchery. His mother was Agrippina, one of the most terrible women in history. When Ahenobarbus knew that he and Agrippina were to have a child he cynically said that nothing but a monstrous abomination could come from himself and her. When Nero was three, Agrippina was banished by the Emperor Caligula. Nero was handed over to the care of his aunt Lepida who entrusted his education to two wretched slaves, one a barber and the other a dancer.

Under the Emperor Claudius, Agrippina was recalled from exile. She had now only one ambition—somehow to make her son emperor. She was warned by fortune-tellers that, if ever

Nero became emperor, the result for her would be disaster. Her answer was: "Let him kill me, so long as he reigns."

Agrippina set to work with all the passion and the intrigue of her stormy nature. Claudius already had two children, Octavia and Britannicus, but Agrippina badgered him into adopting Nero as his son, when Nero was eleven years of age, and persuaded him to marry her although he was her uncle. Agrippina then summoned the famous philosopher, Seneca, and the great soldier, Afranius Burrus, to be Nero's tutors. Steadily Britannicus, the heir to the throne, was pushed into the background and Nero was given the limelight.

For five years the marriage lasted and then Agrippina arranged for Claudius's poisoning by a dish of poisoned mushrooms. When Claudius lay in a coma, she hastened his end by brushing his throat with a poisoned feather. No sooner had Claudius died, than Nero was led forth as emperor, the army having been bribed to support him.

A curious situation ensued. For the next five years Rome was never better governed. Nero was busy playing at painting, sculpture, music, theatricals; he was the complete dilettante; and the wise Seneca and the upright Burrus governed the empire.

Then Nero stopped being the cultured dilettante and embarked on a career of vicious crime. At night with other gilded youths he would roam the streets attacking all whom he could find. Worse was to come. He murdered Britannicus as a possible rival.

No young man or woman was safe from his lust. He was a blatant homosexual. He publicly married a youth named Sporus in a state wedding; and he took Sporus with him on a bridal tour of Greece. He was "married" to a freedman called Doryphorus. He took Poppaea Sabina the wife of Otho, his closest friend, as his paramour, and kicked her to death when she was with child.

He had a passion for wild extravagance and extracted money from all and sundry. The imperial court was a welter of murder, immorality and crime.

One of Nero's passions was building. In A.D. 64 came the great fire of Rome which burned for a week. There is not the slightest doubt that Nero began it or that he hindered every attempt to extinguish it, so that he might have the glory of rebuilding the city. The people well knew who was responsible for the fire but Nero diverted the blame on to the Christians and the most deliberately sadistic of all persecutions broke out. He had the Christians sown up in the skins of wild animals and set his savage hunting dogs upon them. He had them enclosed in sacks with stones and flung into the Tiber. He had them coated with pitch and set alight as living torches to light the gardens of his palace.

The insanity of evil grew wilder and wilder. Seneca was forced to commit suicide; Burrus was murdered by a poisoned draught which Nero sent him as a cure for a sore throat; anyone who incurred Nero's slightest displeasure was killed.

Agrippina made some attempt to control him and finally he turned against her. He made repeated attempts to murder her—by poison, by causing the roof of her house to collapse, by sending her to sea in a boat designed to break up. Finally, he sent his freedman Anicetus to stab her to death. When Agrippina saw the dagger, she bared her body. "Strike my womb," she said, "because it bore a Nero."

It could not last. First Julius Vindex rebelled in Gaul, then Galba in Spain. Finally the senate took its courage in its hands and declared Nero a public enemy. In the end he died by suicide in the wretched villa of a freedman called Phaon.

This is the head of the beast, wounded and restored; the Antichrist whom John expected was the resurrected Nero.

We must now look at this chapter section by section in more detail. This may involve a certain amount of repetition, but in a chapter so central and so difficult the repetition will make for clarity.

## THE DEVIL AND THE BEAST

*Revelation* 13: 1–5

WE begin by summarizing the facts already set out in the

introductory material to this chapter. The beast is the Roman Empire; the seven heads are the seven emperors in whose time Caesar worship became a power in the empire—Tiberius, Caligula, Claudius, Nero, Vespasian, Titus and Domitian. The ten heads are these seven emperors together with the three other rulers whose total reigns lasted for only eighteen months in the time of chaos which followed the death of Nero—Galba, Otho and Vitellius. The head which was wounded and restored to life again symbolizes the *Nero redivivus* idea.

In this picture the Roman Empire is symbolized by a beast which was like a leopard, with a bear's feet and a lion's mouth.

This indicates a completely changed attitude to Rome. Paul had received nothing but help from the Roman government. Time and again the intervention of the Roman authorities and the fact that he was a Roman citizen had saved him from the fury of the Jews. It had been so in Philippi (*Acts* 16); in Corinth (*Acts* 18); in Ephesus (*Acts* 19); and in Jerusalem (*Acts* 21 and 22). It had been Paul's view that the powers that be were ordained of God and that all Christians must render a conscientious obedience to them (*Romans* 13: 1–6). In the Pastoral Epistles prayer is to be made for kings and for all who are in authority (1 *Timothy* 2: 1). In *First Peter* the injunction is to be a good citizen; to be subject to governors; to fear God, and to honour the emperor (1 *Peter* 2: 13–17). In 2 *Thessalonians* 2: 6, 7 the most probable explanation is that it is the Roman Empire which is the restraining force which keeps the world from disintegrating into chaos and the man of sin from beginning his reign.

In the *Revelation* things are changed. Caesar worship has emerged. The emperors call themselves by blasphemous names—divine, Son of God, Saviour, Lord. The might of Rome is arrayed to crush the Christian faith; and Rome has become the agent of the devil.

In the description of the beast, H. B. Swete sees a symbol of the power of Rome. The empire has the vigilance, craft and cruelty of the leopard, ever ready to spring upon its prey; it has the crushing strength of the bear; it is like the lion whose roar terrifies the flock.

"Who is like the beast?" is a grim parody of the great question: "Who is like thee, O Lord, among the gods?" (*Exodus* 15: 11). H. B. Swete points out that the beast's claim to pre-eminence lies not in any moral greatness but in sheer brute force. Any empire founded on brute force and not on moral greatness is anti-God. The description of the beast as speaking haughty things (verse 5) comes from the description in *Daniel* of the little horn (*Daniel* 7: 8, 20).

One great truth stands out in this section. In this world a man and a nation have the choice between being the instrument of Satan and the instrument of God.

## INSULT TO GOD

*Revelation* 13: 6–9

VERSE 6 is difficult. It says of the beast that it opened its mouth to launch blasphemies against God and his dwelling-place and those who dwell in the heavens.

(i) This may be taken quite generally. It may mean that the power of the empire and the institution of Caesar worship are a blasphemy against God, and heaven, and the angels. If we like to take this a little further, we can take more out of the word used for God's *dwelling-place*; the Greek is *skēnē*, which means a *tent* or a *tabernacle* or a *place to dwell*. Although it has really no connection with it, *skēnē* always reminded a Jew of the Hebrew word *shechinah*, *the glory of God*. So it may be that John is saying that the whole conduct of the Roman Empire, and particularly the institution of Caesar worship, is an insult to the glory of God.

(ii) But it is possible to take this passage in a more particular sense. The beast is the Roman Empire. It may be that John is thinking of *all* the ways—not just those in his own time—in which Rome had insulted God and his dwelling-place.

Most Roman Emperors were embarrassed by Caesar worship; but not Caligula, A.D. 37–41, who was an epileptic and more than a little mad. He took his divinity very seriously and insisted that he should be universally worshipped.

The Jews had always been exempt from Caesar worship because the Romans were well aware of their immovable allegiance to the worship of one God. This is closely parallel to the fact that of all peoples in the empire the Jews alone were exempt from military service, because of their strict observance of food laws and their absolute observance of the Sabbath. But Caligula insisted that an image of himself should be set up within the Holy of Holies in the Temple in Jerusalem. The Jews would have suffered extermination rather than submit to such desecration of the Holy Place but Caligula had actually collected an army to enforce his demand (Josephus: *Antiquities of the Jews* 18: 8) when by great good fortune he died.

If ever there was an insult to the dwelling-place of God, this action of Caligula was one. And it may well be that this notorious incident is in John's mind when he speaks of the insults which the beast launched against the dwelling-place of God.

## EARTHLY DANGER AND DIVINE SAFETY

*Revelation* 13: 6–9 *(continued)*

IT was given to the beast to overcome those whose names were not written in the Book of Life. The Book of Life is mentioned frequently in the *Revelation* (3: 5; 13: 8; 17: 8; 20: 12; 20: 15; 21: 27). In the ancient world rulers kept registers of those who were citizens of their realms; only when a man died or lost his rights as a citizen, was his name removed. The Book of Life is the register of those who belong to God.

In verse 8 there is a question of translation. So far as the

Greek goes, there are two equally possible translations, either: "Those whose names have been written before the foundation of the world in the Book of Life of the Lamb that was slain," or, "Those whose names have been written in the Book of Life of the Lamb who was slain from the foundation of the world."

(i) The first is undoubtedly the translation in the parallel passage in *Revelation* 17: 8. A close parallel would be in *Ephesians* 1: 4 where Paul says that God has chosen us in Jesus Christ before the foundation of the world. The meaning would then be that God has chosen his own from before the beginning of time, and nothing in life or in death, nothing in time or eternity, nothing that the Devil or the Roman Empire can ever do can pluck them from his hand. This is the rendering of the Revised Standard Version and the newer translations.

(ii) The second translation speaks of Jesus Christ as the Lamb slain from the foundation of the world. A close parallel to this would be in 1 *Peter* 1: 19, 20 where Peter speaks of Jesus and his sacrifice as being foreordained before the foundation of the world. The Jews held the belief that Michael, the archangel, was created before the foundation of the world to be the mediator between Israel and God; and that Moses was created before the foundation of the world to be the mediator of the covenant between God and Israel. There would, therefore, be nothing unfamiliar to Jewish thought in saying that Jesus was created before the beginning of the world to be the Redeemer of mankind.

We have in these two translations two equally precious truths. But, if we must choose, we must choose the first, because there is no doubt that is the way in which John uses the phrase when he repeats it in *Revelation* 17: 8.

## THE CHRISTIAN'S ONLY WEAPONS

*Revelation* 13: 10

AT first sight this is a difficult verse.

If anyone is to be taken into captivity, into captivity let him go.

If anyone slays with the sword, he himself will be slain with the sword. Here is the summons to steadfastness and to loyalty from the dedicated people of God.

The verse is made up of two quotations. It begins by quoting from *Jeremiah* 15: 2, where Jeremiah is told to tell the people that such as are for death will go forth to death; such as are for the sword will go forth to the sword; such as are for famine will go forth to famine; and such as are for captivity will go forth to captivity. The idea there is that there is no escaping the decree of God. The verse then goes to quote the saying of Jesus in *Matthew* 26: 52. In the Garden of Gethsemane, when the mob has come to arrest Jesus and Peter draws his sword to defend him, Jesus says: "Put your sword back into its place: for all who take the sword will perish by the sword." There are three things here.

(i) If the Christian faith means imprisonment, the Christian must unmurmuringly accept it. Whatever is involved in following Christ, the Christian must accept.

(ii) Christianity can never be defended by force; the man who takes the sword perishes with the sword. When the Roman government began persecuting, the Christians could be numbered perhaps by the hundred thousand; and yet it never occurred to them to use force to resist. It is an intolerable paradox to defend the gospel of the love of God by using the violence of man.

(iii) There are weapons which the Christian can use and these are steadfastness and loyalty. The word for *steadfastness* is *hupomonē*, which does not simply mean passively enduring but courageously accepting the worst that life can do and turning it into glory. The word for loyalty is *pistis*, which means that fidelity which will never waver in its devotion to its Master.

## THE POWER OF THE SECOND BEAST

*Revelation* 13: 11–17

THIS passage deals with the power of the second beast, the

organization set up to enforce Caesar worship throughout the empire. Certain things are said about this power.

(i) It produces signs and wonders, such as fire from heaven; it brings it about that the image of the beast should speak. Everywhere there were statues of the emperor in the presence of which the official act of worship was carried out. In all ancient religions the priests knew how to produce signs and wonders; they knew well how to produce the effect of a speaking image. Pharaoh had had his magicians in the time of Moses, and the imperial priesthood had its experts in conjuring tricks and ventriloquism and the like.

In verse 11 there is a curious phrase. This beast from the land is said to have two horns like a lamb; that is, it is a grim parody of the Lamb in the Christian sense of the term. But it is also said to speak *like a dragon*. It is just possible that that last phrase should be that it spoke *like the serpent*. The reference would then be to the serpent who seduced Eve in the Garden of Eden. The imperial priesthood could easily use seductive appeals: "Look what Rome has done for you; look at the peace and the prosperity you enjoy; have you ever known a greater benefactor than the emperor? Surely in simple gratitude you can give him this formal act of worship." There are always excellent arguments why the Church should compromise with the world; but the fact remains that, when it does, Christ is betrayed again.

(ii) This beast brings it about that those who will not worship will be killed. That was, in fact, the law. If a Christian refused to make the act of worship to Caesar, he was liable to death. The death penalty was not always carried out; but, if a Christian had not the mark of the beast, he could not buy or sell. That is to say, if a man refused to worship the emperor, even if his life was spared, he would be economically ruined. It remains true that the world knows how to bring pressure to bear on those who will not accept its standards. Often still a man has to choose between material success and loyalty to Jesus Christ.

## THE MARK OF THE BEAST

*Revelation* 13 : 11–17 (*continued*)

THOSE who had given the worship to Caesar which was demanded had on them *the mark of the beast* on their right hand and on their forehead. This mark is another of the grim parodies which occur in this chapter; it is a parody of a sacred Jewish custom. When a Jew prayed, he wore *phylacteries* on his left arm and on his forehead. They were little leather boxes with little scrolls of parchment inside them on which the following passages were written— *Exodus* 13 : 1–10; 13 : 11–16; *Deuteronomy* 6 : 4–9; 11 : 13–21.

The word for the mark of the beast is *charagma*, and it could come from more than one ancient custom.

(i) Sometimes domestic slaves were branded with the mark of their owner. But usually they were branded only if they had run away or had been guilty of some grave misdemeanour. Such a mark was called a *stigma*; we still use the word in English. If the mark is connected with this, it means that those who worship the beast are his property.

(ii) Sometimes soldiers branded themselves with the name of their general, if they were very devoted to him. This, to some extent, corresponds to the modern custom of tattooing upon one's person the name of someone specially dear. If the mark is connected with this, it means that those who worship the beast are his devoted followers.

(iii) On every contract of buying or selling there was a *charagma*, a seal, and on the seal the name of the emperor and the date. If the mark is connected with this, it means that those who worship the beast accept his authority.

(iv) All coinage had the head and inscription of the emperor stamped upon it, to show that it was his property. If the mark is connected with this, it again means that those who bear it are the property of the beast.

(v) When a man had burned his pinch of incense to Caesar, he was given a certificate to say that he had done so. The mark of the beast may be the certificate of worship, which a Christian could obtain only at the cost of denying his faith.

## THE NUMBER OF THE BEAST

*Revelation* 13 : 18

In this verse we are told that the number of the beast is six hundred and sixty-six; and it is almost certainly true that more ingenuity has been expended on this verse than on any other verse in Scripture. Who is this satanic beast so symbolized? It must be remembered that the ancient peoples had no figures and the letters of the alphabet did duty for numbers as well. This is as if in English we used A for 1, B for 2, C for 3, D for 4, and so on. Every word, therefore, and in particular every proper name, can also be a number. One charming and romantic way in which use was made of this fact is quoted by Deissmann. On the walls of Pompeii a lover wrote: "I love her whose number is 545," and thereby he at one and the same time identified and concealed his loved one!

The suggestions as to the meaning of 666 are endless. Since it is the number of the beast, everyone has twisted it to fit his own arch-enemy; and so 666 has been taken to mean the Pope, John Knox, Martin Luther, Napoleon and many another. Dr. Kepler provides us with an example of what ingenuity produced during the Second World War. Let $A = 100$; $B = 101$; $C = 102$; $D = 103$ and so on. Then we can make this addition:

$$
\begin{array}{rcl}
H & = & 107 \\
I & = & 108 \\
T & = & 119 \\
L & = & 111 \\
E & = & 104 \\
R & = & 117 \\
\end{array}
$$

and the sum is 666!

Very early we saw that the *Revelation* is written in code; it is clear that nowhere will the code be more closely guarded than in regard to this number which stands for the arch-enemy of the Church. The strange thing is that the key must have been lost very early; for even so great a Christian scholar as Irenaeus in the second century did not know what the number stood for.

We set down four of the very early guesses.

Irenaeus suggested that it might stand for Euanthas. In Greek numbers E = 5; U = 400; A = 1; N = 50; TH (the Greek letter *theta*) = 9; A = 1; S = 200; and the sum is 666. But as to what Euanthas meant Irenaeus had no suggestion to make; so he had simply substituted one riddle for another.

Another suggestion was that the word in question was *Lateinos*. L = 30; A = 1; T = 300; E = 5; I = 10; N = 50; O = 70; S = 200; and the sum is 666. *Lateinos* could be taken to mean Latin and, therefore, could stand for the Roman Empire.

A third suggestion was *Teitan*. T = 300; E = 5; I = 10; T = 300; A = 1; N = 50; and the sum is 666. *Teitan* could be made to yield two meanings. First, in Greek mythology the Titans were the great rebels against God. Second, the family name of Vespasian and Titus and Domitian was Titus, and possibly they could be called the Titans.

A fourth suggestion was *arnoume*. A = 1; R = 100; N = 50; O = 70; U = 400; M = 40; E = 5; and the sum is 666. It is just possible that *arnoume* could be a form of the Greek word *arnoumai*, "I deny." In this case the number would stand for the denial of the name of Christ.

None of these suggestions is convincing. The chapter itself gives us by far the best clue. There recurs again and again the mention of the head that was wounded to death and then restored. We have already seen that that head symbolizes the Nero redivivus legend. We might well, therefore, act on the assumption that the number has something to do with Nero. Many ancient manuscripts give the number as 616. If we take Nero in *Latin* and give it its numerical equivalent, we get:

$$N = 50$$
$$E = 6$$
$$R = 500$$
$$O = 60$$
$$N = 50$$

The total is 666; and the name can equally well be spelled without the final N which would give the number 616. In Hebrew the letters of Nero Caesar also add up to 666.

There is little doubt that the number of the beast stands for Nero; and that John is forecasting the coming of Antichrist in the form of Nero, the incarnation of all evil, returning to this world.

## THE FATHER'S OWN

*Revelation* 14: 1

I saw, and behold the Lamb stood on Mount Sion, and there were with him one hundred and forty-four thousand who had his name, and the name of his Father written on their foreheads.

JOHN'S next vision opens with the Lamb standing in triumph on Mount Sion and with him the one hundred and forty-four thousand of whom we read in chapter 7. They are marked with his name and with the name of his Father on their foreheads. We have already thought about the meaning of the marking but we must look at it again. In the ancient world a mark upon a person could stand for at least five different things.

(i) It could stand for *ownership*. Often the slave was branded with his owner's mark, as sheep and cattle are branded. The company with the Lamb belong to God.

(ii) It could stand for *loyalty*. The soldier would sometimes brand his hand with the name of the general whom he loved and would follow into any battle. The company of the Lamb are the veterans who have proved their loyalty.

(iii) It could stand for *security*. There is a curious third or

fourth century papyrus letter from a son to his father Apollo.
Times are dangerous, and the son and the father are separated.
The son sends his greetings and good wishes, and then goes
on: "I have indeed told you before of my grief at your
absence from among us, and my fear that something dreadful
might happen to you, and that we may not find your body.
Indeed, I often wished to tell you that, having regard to the
insecurity, I wanted *to stamp a mark* upon you" (*P. Oxy.* 680).
The son wished to put a mark upon his father's body in
order to keep it safe. The company of the Lamb are those
marked for security in life and in death.

(iv) It could stand for *dependence*. Robertson Smith quotes
a curious example of this. The great Arab chieftains had
their humble clients who were absolutely dependent on them.
Often the sheik would brand them with the same mark as he
used to brand his camels to show that they were dependent
on him. The company of the Lamb are those who are utterly
dependent on his love and grace.

(v) It could stand for *safety*. It was common for those who
were the devotees of a god to be stamped with his sign. Sometimes that worked very cruelly. Plutarch tells us that after the
disastrous defeat of the Athenians under Nicias in Sicily,
the Sicilians took the captives and branded them on the
forehead with a galloping horse, the emblem of Sicily
(Plutarch: *Nicias* 29). 3 *Maccabees* tells us that Ptolemy the
Fourth of Egypt ordered that "all Jews should be degraded
to the lowest rank and to the condition of slaves; and that
those who spoke against it should be taken by force and put
to death; and that these when they were registered should
be marked with a brand on their bodies, with the ivy leaf,
the emblem of Bacchus" (3 *Maccabees* 2: 28, 29).

These instances involve degradation and cruelty. But there
were others. The Syrians were regularly tattooed on the
wrist or the neck with the mark of their god. But there is a
more relevant instance than any of these. Herodotus (2: 113)
tells us that there was a temple of Heracles at the Canopic
mouth of the Nile which possessed the right of asylum. Any

criminal, slave or free man, was safe there from pursuing vengeance. When such a fugitive reached that temple, he was branded with certain sacred marks in token that he had delivered himself to the god and that none could touch him any more. They were the marks of absolute security. The company of the Lamb are those who have cast themselves on the mercy of God in Jesus Christ and are for ever safe.

## THE SONG WHICH ONLY GOD'S OWN CAN LEARN

*Revelation* 14: 2, 3

> And I heard a voice from heaven like the sound of many waters and like the voice of great thunder, and the voice I heard was like the sound of harpers playing on their harps. And they were singing a new song before the throne and before the four living creatures and before the elders, and no one was able to learn the song except the one hundred and forty-four thousand who had been purchased for God from the earth.

THIS passage begins with a wonderful description of the voice of God.

(i) It was like the sound of many waters. Here we are reminded of the *power* of the voice of God, for there is no power like the crash of the mountainous waves upon the beaches and the cliffs.

(ii) It was like the voice of great thunder. Here we are reminded of the *unmistakableness* of the voice of God. No one can fail to hear the thunder-clap.

(iii) It was like the sound of many harpers playing on their harps. Here we are reminded of the *melody* of the voice of God. There is in that voice the gentle graciousness of sweet music to calm the troubled heart.

The Lamb's company were singing a song which only they could learn. Here there is a truth which runs through all life. To learn certain things a man must be a certain kind of person. The Lamb's company were able to learn the new song because they had passed through certain experiences.

(*a*) They had suffered. There are certain things which only sorrow can teach. As someone made the poets say: "We learned in suffering what we teach in song." Sorrow can produce resentment but it can also produce faith and peace and a new song.

(*b*) They had lived in loyalty. It is clear that, as the years pass on, the leader will draw closer to his loyal followers and they to him; then he will be able to teach them things the unfaithful or spasmodic follower can never learn.

(*c*) That is another way of saying that the company of the Lamb had made steady progress in spiritual growth. A teacher can teach deeper things to a mature student than to an immature beginner. And Jesus Christ can reveal more treasures of wisdom to those who day by day grow up into him. The tragedy of so many is static Christianity.

## THE FINEST FLOWER

*Revelation* 14: 4a

These are they who have not defiled themselves with women, for they are virgins.

WE take this half verse by itself, for it is one of the most difficult sayings in the whole of the *Revelation*, and it is of the utmost importance to get its meaning clear. It describes the unsullied purity of those who are in the company of the Lamb, but in what does that purity consist?

(i) Does it describe those who in sexual relationships have been pure? That can hardly be the case, for the people in question are described, not simply as *pure,* but as *virgins*, that is, as those who have never known sexual relations at all.

(ii) Does it describe those who have kept themselves free from spiritual adultery, that is, from all disloyalty to Jesus

Christ? Again and again in the Old Testament we find it said of the people of Israel that they went awhoring after strange gods (*Exodus* 34: 15; *Deuteronomy* 31: 16; *Judges* 2: 17; 8: 27, 33; *Hosea* 9: 1). But this passage does not read as if it was metaphorical.

(iii) Does it describe those who have remained celibate? The days soon came when the Church glorified virginity and held that the highest Christian life was possible only for those who renounced marriage altogether. The Gnostics held that "marriage and generation are from Satan." Tatian held that "marriage is corruption and fornication." Marcion set up churches for those who were celibates and from which all others were barred. One of the greatest of the early fathers, Origen, voluntarily castrated himself to ensure perpetual virginity. In the *Acts of Paul and Thecla* (11) it is the charge of Demas against Paul that "he deprives young men of wives and maidens of husbands by saying that in no other way shall there be a resurrection for you save by remaining chaste and keeping the flesh chaste." There is a record of a Roman trial (Ruinart: *Acts of the Martyrs*, 27th April, 304) in which the Christians are described as "the people who impose upon silly women and tell them that they must not marry and persuade them to adopt a fanciful chastity." This is precisely the spirit which was to beget the monasteries and the convents, and the implication that everything to do with sex and the body is wrong.

This is far from the teaching of the New Testament. Jesus glorified marriage, saying that for this cause a man left his own family and was so closely united to his wife that they were one flesh, and warning that what God has joined no man may put asunder (*Matthew* 19: 4–6). In his highest teaching Paul glorified marriage, likening the relationship of Christ to his Church to the relationship between man and wife (*Ephesians* 5: 22–33). The writer to the Hebrews lays it down: "Let marriage be held in honour among all" (*Hebrews* 13: 4).

What, then, are we to say of our present passage? If we are

to treat it honestly, we cannot avoid the conclusion that it praises celibacy and virginity and belittles marriage. There are two possible explanations.

(*a*) It is possible that the writer of the *Revelation* did mean to exalt celibacy and virginity; the likelihood is that he was writing about A.D. 90 when this tendency was already in the Church. If that is so we will have to lay this passage on one side, because, tested by the rest of the New Testament, it is not a correct statement of the Christian ethic.

(*b*) There is another possible interpretation. When scribes were copying New Testament books they often added notes and comments in the margin, to explain the text. It may well be that some scribe in later days, copying this passage wished to give *his* opinion as to who the one hundred and forty thousand were; and added in the margin: "This means those who never defiled themselves with women and who remained virgins." This is all the more likely since many of the later scribes were monks. When the manuscript was recopied, the comment in the margin may well have been included in the text as very commonly happened. This would then mean that the first half of verse 4 is not the words of John at all but the comment of a scribe.

## THE IMITATION OF CHRIST

*Revelation* 14: 4b, 5

> These are they who follow the Lamb wherever he goes. They were bought from amongst men, a sacrifice to God and to the Lamb, and no falsehood was found in their mouth, for they are without blemish.

THE company of the Lamb are those who follow the Lamb wherever he goes. The simplest definition of a Christian is simply one who follows Jesus Christ. "Follow me!" Jesus said to Philip (*John* 1: 43), and to Matthew (*Mark* 2: 14). "Follow me!" he said to the rich young ruler (*Mark* 10: 21), and to the unnamed disciple (*Luke* 9: 59). When Peter asked what was to happen to John, Jesus told him not to bother about what would happen to others but to concentrate on following him (*John* 21: 19–22). He left us an example, said Peter, that we should follow in his steps (1 *Peter* 2: 21).

John calls the company of the Lamb three things.

(i) They are a sacrifice to God and to the Lamb. The word for *sacrifice* is *aparchē*. This really means the sacrifice of the first-fruits. The first-fruits were the best of the crop; they were a symbol of the harvest to come; and they were a symbolic dedication of the whole harvest to God. So the Christian is the best that can be offered to God; each Christian is a foretaste of the time when all the world will be dedicated to God; and the Christian is the man who has consecrated his life to God.

(ii) No falsehood was found in their mouth. This is a favourite thought in Scripture. "Blessed is the man," says the Psalmist, "in whose spirit there is no deceit" (*Psalm* 32, 2). Isaiah said of the servant of the Lord: "And there was no deceit in his mouth" (*Isaiah* 53: 9). Zephaniah said of the chosen remnant of the people: "Nor shall there be found in their mouth a deceitful tongue" (*Zephaniah* 3: 13). Peter took the words about the servant and applied them to Jesus: "No guile was found on his lips" (1 *Peter* 2: 22). There is something here which we can well understand. Just as we desire friends who are sincere, so does Jesus Christ.

(iii) They are without blemish. The word is *amōmos* and is characteristically a sacrificial word. It describes the animal which is without flaw and so fit for an offering to God. It is interesting to note how often this word is used of the Christian. God has chosen us that we should be holy and *without blame* before him (*Ephesians* 1: 4; cp. *Colossians* 1: 22). The Church must be glorious, *not having spot,* or wrinkle or any such thing (*Ephesians* 5: 27). Peter speaks of Jesus as a Lamb *without blemish* and without spot (1 *Peter* 1: 19). We received life to make of it a sacrifice to God; and that which is offered to God must be without blemish.

There follows the vision of the three angels, the angel with the summons to worship the true God (verses 6 and 7), the angel who foretells the doom of Rome (verse 8), and the angel who foretells the judgment and destruction of those who have denied their faith and worshipped the beast (verses 9–12).

## THE SUMMONS TO THE WORSHIP OF GOD

*Revelation* 14: 6, 7

> And I saw another angel flying in the midst of the sky with an everlasting gospel to preach to those who dwell upon the earth and to every race and tribe and tongue and people. And he was saying with a great voice: "Fear God and give him glory, because the hour of his judgment has come, and worship him who made the heaven and the earth and the sea and the springs of waters."

ONE of the signs which were to precede the end was that the gospel would be preached in all the world for a witness to all nations (*Matthew* 24: 14). Here is the fulfilment of that prophecy. The angel comes with the message of the gospel to all races and tribes and tongues and peoples.

The angel comes with an *everlasting* gospel. *Everlasting* could mean that the gospel is eternally valid, that even in a world which is crashing to its doom its truth still stands. It could mean that the gospel has existed from all eternity. Paul in the great doxology in *Romans* speaks of Jesus Christ as the revelation of the mystery which was kept secret since the world began (*Romans* 16 : 25). It could mean that the gospel is the eternal purpose of God for man. It could mean that it deals with the eternal things.

It may seem strange that the angel with the gospel is followed immediately by the angels of doom. But the gospel has of necessity a double-edged quality. It is good news for those who receive it but it is judgment to those who reject it.

And the condemnation of those who reject it is all the greater because they were given the chance to accept it.

The words of the angel are interesting. They are a summons to worship the God who is the Creator of all things. This message is not specifically Christian but the basis of all religion. It corresponds exactly to the message which Paul and Barnabas brought to the people of Lystra, when they told them that they must "turn from these vain things to a living God who made the heaven, and the earth, and the sea, and all that is in them" (*Acts* 14: 15). H. B. Swete called this "an appeal to the conscience of untaught heathenism, incapable as yet of apprehending any other."

## THE FALL OF BABYLON

*Revelation* 14: 8

And another angel, a second angel, followed him saying: "Fallen, fallen is the great Babylon, who made all the nations to drink of the wine of the wrath of her fornication."

HERE is prophesied the doom of Rome. Throughout the *Revelation* Rome is described as Babylon, a description which was common between the Testaments. The writer of 2 *Baruch* begins his pronouncement against Rome: "I, Baruch, say this against thee, Babylon" (2 *Baruch* 11: 1). When the *Sibylline Oracles* describe the imagined flight of Nero from Rome, they say: "Then shall flee from Babylon a king shameless and fearless, whom all mortals and the best men loathe" (*Sibylline Oracles* 5: 143). In the ancient days Babylon to the prophets had been the very incarnation of power and lust and luxury and sin; and to the early Jewish Christians Babylon seemed to have been reborn in the lust and luxury and immorality of Rome.

The fall of Babylon to Cyrus the Persian had been one of the shattering events of ancient history. The very words which the *Revelation* uses are echoes of those in which the ancient prophets had foretold that fall. "Fallen, fallen is Babylon," said Isaiah, "and all the images of her gods he has shattered to the ground" (*Isaiah* 21: 9). "Suddenly Babylon has fallen," said Jeremiah, "and been broken" (*Jeremiah* 51: 8).

Babylon is said to have made all the nations drink of the wine of the wrath of her fornication. In this phrase two Old Testament conceptions have been fused into one. In *Jeremiah* 51: 7 it is said of Babylon: "Babylon was a golden cup in the Lord's hand, making all the earth drunken; the nations drank of her wine; therefore, the nations went mad." The idea is that Babylon had been a corrupting force which had lured the nations into a kind of insane immorality. The background is the picture of a prostitute persuading a man into immorality by filling him full of wine, so that he could no longer resist her wiles. Rome has been like that, like some glittering prostitute seducing the world. The other picture is of the cup of the wrath of God. Job says of the wicked man: "Let him drink of the wrath of the Almighty" (*Job* 21: 20). The Psalmist speaks of the wicked having to drink the dregs of the red cup in the hand of God (*Psalm* 75: 8). Isaiah speaks of Jerusalem having drunk the cup of God's fury (*Isaiah* 51: 17). God instructs Jeremiah to take the wine cup of his fury and to give it to the nations to drink (*Jeremiah* 25: 15).

We might paraphrase by saying that Babylon made the nations drink of the wine which seduces men to fornication and which brings as its consequence the wrath of God.

Behind all this remains the eternal truth that the nation or the man whose influence is to evil will not escape the avenging wrath of God.

## THE DOOM OF THE MAN WHO DENIES HIS LORD

*Revelation* 14: 9–12

And another angel, a third angel, followed them saying with a great voice: "If anyone worships the beast and his image, and receives a mark upon his forehead or upon his hand, he too shall drink of the wine of the wrath of God, mingled undiluted in the cup of his wrath, and he will be tortured with fire and brimstone in the presence of the holy angels and of the Lamb. The smoke of their torture ascends for ever and ever, and those who worship the beast and his image have no rest by day or night, nor has anyone who receives the mark of his name.

Here is the summons to steadfastness on the part of God's dedicated ones, who keep the commandments of God and maintain their loyalty to him.

WARNING has already been given of the power of the beast and of the mark that the beast will seek to set upon all men (chapter 13). Now there is warning to those who fail in that time of trial.

It is significant that this is the fiercest warning of all. Of all dooms, as the *Revelation* sees it, the doom of the apostate is worst. The reason is that the Church was battling for its very existence. If it was to continue the individual Christian must be prepared to face suffering and trial, imprisonment and death. If the individual Christian yielded, the Church died. In our day the individual Christian is still of paramount importance, but his function now is not usually to protect the faith by being ready to die for it, but to commend it by being diligent to live for it.

The doom of the apostate is thought of in pictures of the most terrible judgment that ever fell on this earth—that of Sodom and Gomorrah. "Lo, the smoke of the land went up like the smoke of a furnace" (*Genesis* 19: 28). John echoes the words of Isaiah describing the day of the Lord's vengeance: "And the streams of Edom shall be turned into pitch, and her soil into brimstone; her land shall become burning pitch. Night and day it shall not be quenched; its smoke shall go up for ever. From generation to generation it shall lie waste; none shall pass through it for ever and ever" (*Isaiah* 34: 8–10).

The wicked will be destroyed in the presence of the holy angels and of the Lamb. As we have seen before, part of the blessedness of heaven was to see the suffering of the sinner in hell. As 2 *Esdras* has it: "There shall be shewn the furnace of hell, and opposite to it the paradise of delight" (2 *Esdras* 7: 36). We have the same idea in the *Book of Enoch*: "I will give them over (the wicked) into the hands of mine elect: as straw in the fire, so shall they burn before the face of the holy: as lead in the water shall they sink before the face of the righteous, and no trace of them shall be found any more" (*Enoch* 48: 9). A feature of the last days will be "the spectacle of righteous judgment in the presence of the righteous" (*Enoch* 27: 2, 3). When Chrysostom was encouraging Olympias to steadfastness, he encouraged her by promising that in due time she would see the divine torture of the persecutors, just as Lazarus saw Dives tormented in flames.

We may dislike this line of thought; we may condemn it as subchristian—and indeed it is. But we have no real right to speak until we have gone through the same sufferings as the early Christians did. Many a time the heathen had looked down from the crowded seats of the arena on the sufferings of the Christians; and the early Christians were sustained by the thought that some day the divine justice of heaven would adjust the balance of earth's injustices.

## THE REST OF THE FAITHFUL SOUL

*Revelation* 14: 13

And I heard a voice from heaven saying: "Blessed are the dead who die in the Lord from now on. Yes, says the Spirit, they are blessed, because they rest from their labours, for their deeds follow with them."

AFTER the terrible prophecies of the terrors to come and the terrible warnings to those who are false, there comes the gracious promise.

Blessed are the dead who die in the Lord—the idea of dying in the Lord occurs more than once in the New Testament.

Paul speaks of the dead in Christ (1 *Thessalonians* 4: 16)
and of those who have fallen asleep in Christ (1 *Corinthians*
15: 18). The meaning of all these phrases is *those who come
to the end still one with Christ*. Everything was trying to separate
men from Christ; but the supreme happiness was for those
who came to the end still inseparable from the Master whom
they loved.

The promise is of rest. They will rest from their labours.
Rest is never so sweet as after the most strenuous toil. As
Spenser had it:

> Sleep after toil, port after stormy seas,
> Ease after war, death after life does greatly please.

Their works follow with them—at first this sounds as if the
*Revelation* is preaching salvation by works. But we have to be
careful what John means by works. He speaks of the works
of the Ephesians—their labour and their patience (2: 2); he
speaks of the works of the Thyatirans—their charity and their
service and their faith (2: 19). By works he means *character*.
He is in effect saying: "When you leave this earth, all that you
can take with you is yourself. If you come to the end of this
life still one with Christ, you will take with you a character
tried and tested like gold, which has something of his reflection
in it; and, if you take with you to the world beyond a
character like that, blessed are you."

## THE HARVEST OF JUDGMENT

*Revelation* 14: 14–20

> And I saw and behold a white cloud, and seated on the cloud
> one like a son of man. On his head he had a victor's crown of
> gold, and in his hand he had a sharp sickle. And another angel
> came forth from the temple, saying with a great voice to him who
> was seated on the cloud: "Put in your sickle, and begin to reap,
> because the hour to reap has come, because the harvest of the
> earth is ripe and more than ripe." And he who was seated on the

cloud put in his sickle upon the earth, and the earth was reaped. And another angel came from the temple which is in heaven and he too had a sharp sickle, and there came forth from the altar another angel, the angel who controls the fire, and he called with a great voice to him who had the sharp sickle saying: "Put in your sharp sickle and gather the clusters of the vine of the earth, because the grapes are ripe." So the angel put his sickle into the earth, and gathered the vintage of the earth, and cast it into the great winepress of the wrath of God. And the winepress was trodden outside the city, and blood came out of the winepress, as high as the horses' bridles, for sixteen hundred stades.

THE final vision of this chapter is of judgment depicted in pictures which were very familiar to Jewish thought.

It begins with the picture of the victorious figure of one like a son of man. This comes from *Daniel* 7: 13, 14: "And I saw in the night visions, and, behold with the clouds of heaven, there came one like a son of man and he came to the ancient of days, and was presented before him. And to him was given dominion and glory and kingdom, that all peoples, nations and languages should serve him."

This picture goes on to depict judgment in two metaphors familiar to Scripture.

It depicts judgment in terms of *harvesting*. When Joel wished to say that judgment was near, he said: "Put in the sickle, for the harvest is ripe" (*Joel* 3: 13). "When the grain is ripe," said Jesus, "at once he puts in the sickle, because the harvest has come" (*Mark* 4: 29); and in the parable of the wheat and the tares he uses the harvest as a picture of judgment (*Matthew* 13: 24–30; 37–43).

It depicts judgment in terms of the winepress, which consisted of an upper and a lower trough connected by a channel. The troughs might be hollowed out in the rock or they might be built of brick. The grapes were put into the upper trough which was on a slightly higher level. They were then trampled with the feet and the juice flowed down the connecting channel into the lower trough. Often in the Old Testament, God's judgment is likened to the trampling of the grapes. "The Lord flouted all my mighty men in the midst of me . . . the Lord has trodden as in a winepress the virgin daughter of Judah" (*Lamentations* 1: 15). "I have trodden the winepress alone; and from the peoples no one was with me; I trod them in my anger, and trampled them in my wrath; their lifeblood is sprinkled upon my garments" (*Isaiah* 63: 3).

Here, then, we have judgment depicted in the two familiar figures of the harvest and of the winepress. To this is added another familiar picture. The wine press is to be trodden outside the city, that is, Jerusalem. Both in the Old Testament and in the books between the Testaments there was a line of thought which held that the Gentiles would be brought to Jerusalem and judged there. Joel has a picture of all the nations gathered into the valley of Jehoshaphat and judged there (*Joel* 3: 2, 12). Zechariah has a picture of a last attack of the Gentiles on Jerusalem and of their judgment there (*Zechariah* 14: 1–4).

There are two difficult things in this passage. First, there is the fact that the one like a son of man reaps and also an angel reaps. We may regard the one like the son of man, the risen and victorious Lord, reaping the harvest of his own people, while the angel with the sharp sickle reaps the harvest of those destined for judgment.

Second, it is said that the blood came up to the horses' bridles and spread for a distance of sixteen hundred stades or furlongs. No one has ever discovered a really satisfying explanation of this. The least unsatisfactory explanation is that sixteen hundred stades is almost exactly the length of Palestine from north to south; and this would mean that the tide of judgment would flow over and include the whole land. In that case the figure would symbolically describe the completeness of the judgment.

## THE VICTORS OF CHRIST

*Revelation* 15: 1, 2

And I saw another sign in heaven, great and wonderful—it was seven angels, with seven plagues which are the final ones, because in them the wrath of God reaches its climax. And I saw what I can only call a sea of glass intermingled with fire; and I saw standing beside the sea of glass, with the harps of God, those who had emerged victorious from their struggle with the beast and with his image and with the number of his name.

It might have been thought that John could have conveniently stopped when he had told of the reaping of judgment; but he has still much to tell—the final horrors, of the thousand year reign of the saints, of the final battle and of the final blessedness.

He has told of the opening of the seven seals; he has told of the sounding of the seven trumpets; and now he must tell of the pouring out of the seven bowls of the wrath of God. His arrangement is typical of the way the apocalyptic writers tended to arrange their material in groups of seven and of three and would regard three groups of seven as standing for perfection.

The scene is in heaven. Before John tells of the seven angels with the seven bowls of wrath, he has a picture of those who came through martyrdom for Christ. They are standing beside the sea which looked as if it was of glass. We have already seen this sea in 4: 6. This time the glass is intermingled with fire, a natural addition in the circumstances. This is a passage of judgment and fire in Scripture is often the symbol of judgment. There comes upon Egypt hail mingled with fire (*Exodus* 9: 24); the chaff is to be consumed in the fire (*Matthew* 3: 12); our God is a consuming fire (*Hebrews* 12: 29). The whole scene is grimly illuminated with the lurid light of the fire of judgment which is to descend upon the earth.

We are shortly to hear of the song of Moses. This is the song which Moses sang when the children of Israel had come triumphantly through the dangers of the crossing of the Red Sea. Even so, as H. B. Swete puts it, the martyrs have come safely through the sea of martyrdom and have arrived at the shore of heaven.

It is said that the martyrs have emerged victorious from their contest with the forces of Antichrist. There is something very significant here. The martyrs died the most savage deaths *and yet they are said to have emerged victorious.* It was the very fact that they had died that made them victors; if they had remained alive by being false to their faith, they would have been the defeated. Again and again the records of the early church describe a day of martyrdom as a day of victory. In the record of the martyrdom of Saint Perpetua we read: "The day of their victory dawned, and they walked from prison to the amphitheatre as if they were walking to heaven, happy and serene in countenance." Jesus said: "Whoever would save his life will lose it, and whoever loses his life for my sake will find it" (*Matthew* 16: 25). The real victory is not prudently to preserve life but to face the worst that evil can do and if need be to be faithful to death. "May God deny you peace," said Unamuno the Spanish mystic, "and give you glory."

## THE SONG OF THE VICTORS OF CHRIST

*Revelation* 15: 3, 4

And they sing the song of Moses, the servant of God, and the song of the Lamb:
    Great and wonderful are your works,
      O Lord, God the Almighty;
    Just and true are your ways,
      King of the nations.
    Who shall not fear and glorify your name, O Lord?
      Because you alone are holy;
      Because all the nations will come and worship before you;
      Because your righteous judgments have been made plain
        for all to see.

THE victorious martyrs sing two songs. They sing the song of the Lamb which, as we have seen, is the song which they alone could learn (14: 3). They sing the song of Moses, the servant of God. This was the song which Moses sang in triumph to God after the safe crossing of the Red Sea. It is in *Exodus* 15: 1–19. "The Lord is my strength and my song, and he has become my salvation. . . . Who is like thee, O Lord, among the gods, who is like thee, majestic in holiness, terrible in glorious deeds, doing wonders? . . . The Lord will reign for ever and ever." This song was stamped upon the memory of the Jews. It was sung at every Sabbath evening service in the synagogue. At every Jewish service the recital of the *Shema*, the creed of Israel, was followed by two prayers—it still is—and one of these prayers refers to this song: "True it is that thou art Jehovah our God, and the God of our fathers, our King, and the King of our fathers, our Saviour, and the Saviour of our fathers, our Creator, the Rock of our Salvation, our Help and our Deliverer. Thy name is from everlasting, and there is no God beside thee. A new song did they that were delivered sing to thy name by the sea-shore; together did all praise and own thee King, and say, Jehovah shall reign, world without end! Blessed be the Lord who saveth Israel." The song of Moses commemorated the greatest deliverance in the history of God's people Israel, and the victorious martyrs, brought through the sea of persecution to the promised land of heaven, sing that song.

But the martyrs have their own song. Two things stand out about it.

(i) It is almost entirely composed of quotations from the Old Testament. We set down first the words in the song and below them the Old Testament passages of which they remind us.

> *Great and wonderful are your works.*

O Lord, how great are thy works! (*Psalm* 92: 5); The works of the Lord are great (*Psalm* 111: 2); he has done marvellous (wonderful) things (*Psalm* 98: 1); Wonderful are thy works (*Psalm* 139: 14).

> *Just and true are your ways.*

The Lord is just in all his ways, and kind in all his doings (*Psalm* 145: 17).

> *Who shall not fear and glorify your name, O Lord?*

All the nations thou hast made shall come and bow down before Thee, O Lord; and shall glorify thy name (*Psalm* 86: 9).

> *You alone are holy.*

There is none holy like the Lord (1 *Samuel* 2: 2); Let them praise thy great and terrible name! Holy is he! (*Psalm* 99: 3); Holy and terrible is his name (*Psalm* 111: 9).

> *All the nations will come and worship before you.*

All the nations thou hast made shall come and bow down before thee, O Lord (*Psalm* 86: 9).

> *Your righteous judgments are made manifest.*

The Lord has made known his victory, he has revealed his vindication in the sight of the nations (*Psalm* 98: 2).

A passage like this lets us see how steeped in the Old Testament John was.

(ii) There is another thing which must strike anyone about the song of the triumphant martyrs. There is not one single word in it about their own achievement; from beginning to end the song is a lyric outburst on the greatness of God.

Heaven is a place where men forget themselves and remember only God. As R. H. Charles finely puts it: "In the perfect vision of God self is wholly forgotten." H. B. Swete puts it this way: "In the presence of God the martyrs forget themselves; their thoughts are absorbed by the new wonders that surround them; the glory of God and the mighty scheme of things in which their own sufferings form an infinitesimal part are opening before them; they begin to see the great issue of the world-drama, and we hear the doxology with which they greet their first unclouded vision of God and his works."

## THE AVENGING ANGELS

*Revelation* 15: 5–7

And after this I saw, and the temple of the tent of witness in heaven was opened, and there came out of the temple the seven angels who have the seven plagues; and they were clothed in shining white linen, and they were girt about the breasts with golden girdles. And one of the four living creatures gave to the seven angels seven golden bowls filled with the wrath of God who lives for ever and ever.

*The tent of witness,* or *the tent of testimony,* is a common title in the Old Testament for the tabernacle in the wilderness (*Numbers* 9: 15; 17: 7; 18: 2). It is, therefore, clear that John is seeing this picture, not in terms of the Jerusalem temple, but in terms of the ancient tabernacle.

It is from within the tabernacle that the seven avenging angels come forth. In the centre of the Holy Place within the tabernacle lay the Ark of the Covenant, the chest in which were contained the tables of the ten commandments, the essence of the Law. That is to say, these angels come out from the place where the Law of God rests and come to show that no man or nation can with impunity defy the Law of God.

They are clothed in a shining white robe and are girt about the breasts with a golden girdle. The robes of the angels are symbolic of three things. (*a*) Their dress is priestly dress. The robe of white fine linen and the gold embroidered girdle about the breast is the dress of the High Priest. The High Priest might well be called God's representative among men; and these angels come forth as the avenging representatives of God. (*b*) Their dress is royal dress. The white linen and the high girdle are the garments of princes and of kings; and these angels come forth with the royalty of the King of kings upon them. (*c*) Their dress is heavenly dress. The young man at the empty tomb of Christ was clothed in a long white garment (*Mark* 16: 5; *Matthew* 28: 3); and the angels are the inhabitants of heaven, come to execute God's decrees upon earth.

It is one of the four living creatures who hands them the bowls of the wrath of God. When we were thinking about the four living creatures when they first emerged on the scene (4: 7) we saw that the first was like a lion, the second like an ox, the third like a man, and the fourth like an eagle; and that, they may well symbolize all that is strongest and bravest and wisest and swiftest in nature. If that be so, it is fitting that one of them should hand the bowls of wrath to the seven angels. The bowls of wrath are to bring disasters in nature to the world; and the symbolism may well be that nature is handing itself to God to serve his purposes.

## THE UNAPPROACHABLE GLORY

*Revelation* 15: 8

> And the temple was filled with smoke from the glory of God and from his power, and no one could enter into the temple until the seven plagues of the seven angels had been completed.

THE idea of the glory of God being symbolized as smoke is common in the Old Testament. In the vision of Isaiah the whole house was filled with smoke (*Isaiah* 6: 4).

Further, the idea that no one could approach while the smoke was there is also common in the Old Testament. This was true both of the tabernacle and of the temple. Of the tabernacle it is said: "Then the cloud covered the tent of meeting, and the glory of the Lord filled the tabernacle. And Moses was not able to enter the tent of meeting, because the cloud abode upon it, and the glory of the Lord filled the tabernacle" (*Exodus* 40: 34, 35). Of the dedication of Solomon's temple it is said: "And when the priests came out of the holy place, a cloud filled the house of the Lord, so that the priests could not stand to minister because of the cloud, for the glory of the Lord filled the house of the Lord" (1 *Kings* 8: 10, 11).

There is a double idea here. There is the idea that the

purposes of God will often be clouded to men, for no man can see into the mind of God; and there is the idea that the holiness and the glory of God are such that man in his own right can never approach God.

But R. H. Charles sees more in this passage. No man could come into the temple until the seven plagues of the seven angels have been completed. Charles sees in that a symbolic statement that no approach of man to God can halt the coming judgment.

## THE SEVEN BOWLS OF THE WRATH OF GOD

*Revelation* 16

IT will be better to read through the whole chapter before we study it in detail.

1 And I heard a great voice out of heaven saying to the seven angels: Go, and pour out the seven bowls of the wrath of God
2 upon the earth. The first angel went away and poured out his bowl upon the earth, and there came an outbreak of evil and malignant ulcerous sores on the men who had the mark of the beast and who worshipped his image.
3 The second poured out his bowl upon the sea; and it became blood, like the blood of a dead man, and every living thing died of the things in the sea.
4 The third poured out his bowl upon the rivers and the
5 springs of waters, and they became blood. And I heard the angel of the waters saying: You are just, you who are and who were, O Holy One, because you have delivered this
6 judgment. Because they poured out the blood of God's dedicated ones and of the prophets, you have given them blood to drink. They well deserved it.
7 And I heard the altar saying: Yes, O Lord, the Almighty, true and just are your judgments.
8 The fourth poured out his bowl upon the sun, and it was given
9 power to scorch men with fire; and men were scorched with a great scorching. And men flung their insults at the name of the God who had authority over the plagues, but they did not repent to give him glory.

10   The fifth poured out his bowl upon the throne of the beast, and his kingdom was wrapped in darkness, and men gnawed their tongues in anguish.

11   And men flung their insults at the God of heaven for their pains and their sores, but they did not repent from their deeds.

12   The sixth poured out his bowl on the great river Euphrates, and its water was dried up, that the way for the kings from the east might be prepared.

13   I saw three unclean spirits, like frogs, come from the mouth of the dragon, and the mouth of the beast, and the mouth

14   of the false prophet, for they are demonic spirits who perform signs, which go out to the kings of the whole inhabited world, to bring them together for war on the great day of God, the Almighty.

15   (Behold, I come like a thief. Blessed is he who is awake, and who keeps his garments so that he may not walk naked and so that his shame may not be exposed to the gaze of men.)

16   And they gathered them to the place that is called in Hebrew Har Maggedon.

17   The seventh poured out his bowl upon the air and there came a great voice from the Temple, from the throne, saying: It is done!

18   And there came flashes of lightning and voices and peals of thunder, and a great earthquake such as never happened since mankind was upon the earth, so great was the earthquake.

19   And the great city was split into three parts, and the cities of the nations collapsed. And the great Babylon was remembered before God, to give her the cup of the wine of the wrath of

20   his anger. Every island fled and the mountains were not to be

21   found. Great hailstones, weighing as much as a hundredweight, descended from heaven upon men. And men hurled their insults at God for the plague of the hail, because the plague was exceedingly great.

Here we have the last terrible plagues. They have a certain connection with two things, the ten plagues in Egypt and the terrors which followed the sounding of the seven trumpets in *Revelation* 8–11. It is worth while to set out the three lists in order to see the resemblances.

First, we set out the ten plagues when Moses confronted Pharaoh with the wrath of God.

   (i) The water made into blood (*Exodus* 7: 20–25).
  (ii) The frogs (8: 5–14).
 (iii) The lice (8: 16–18).
 (iv) The flies (8: 20–24).
  (v) The plague on the cattle (9: 3–6).
 (vi) The boils and sores (9: 8–11).
(vii) The thunder and the hail (9: 22–26).
(viii) The locusts (10: 12–19).
 (ix) The darkness (10: 21–23).
  (x) The slaying of the first-born (12: 29, 30).

Second, we set out the terrors which followed the sounding of the seven trumpets.

   (i) The coming of hail, fire and blood, through which a third part of the trees and all the green grass are withered (*Revelation* 8: 7).
  (ii) The flaming mountain cast into the sea, whereby one third of the sea becomes blood (8: 8).
 (iii) The fall of the star Wormwood into the waters, whereby the waters become bitter and poisonous (8: 10, 11).
 (iv) The smiting of one third of the sun and the moon and the stars, whereby all is darkened (8: 12).
  (v) The coming of the star who unlocks the pit of the abyss, from which comes the smoke out of which come the demonic locusts (9: 1–12).
 (vi) The loosing of the four angels bound in the Euphrates and the coming of the demonic cavalry from the east (9: 13–21).
(vii) The announcement of the final victory of God and of the rebellious anger of the nations (11: 15).

Third, we set out the terrors of this chapter.

   (i) The coming of the ulcerous sores upon men (*Revelation* 16: 2).

(ii) The sea becoming like the blood of a dead man (16: 3).

(iii) The rivers and fountains becoming blood (16: 4).

(iv) The sun becoming scorchingly hot (16: 8).

(v) The darkness over the kingdom of the beast, and its agony (16: 10).

(vi) The drying up of the Euphrates to open a way for the hordes of the kings of the east (16: 12).

(vii) The pollution of the air and the accompanying terrors in nature, the thunder, the earthquake, the lightning and the hail (16: 17–21).

It is easy to see how many things these lists have in common—the hail, the darkness, the blood in the waters, the ulcerous sores, the coming of the terrible hordes from beyond the Euphrates. But in the *Revelation* there is this difference between the terrors which follow the trumpets and the terrors which follow the pouring out of the bowls. In the former the destruction is always limited, for instance, to one third of the earth; but in the latter the destruction is complete on the enemies of God.

In this final series of terrors John seems to have gathered together the horrors from all the stories of the avenging wrath of God and to have hurled them on the unbelieving world in one last terrible deluge of disaster.

## THE TERRORS OF GOD

*Revelation* 16: 1–11

THE voice from the temple is the voice of God who is despatching his angelic messengers with their terrors upon men.

The first terror is a plague of malignant and ulcerous sores. The word is the same as is used to describe the boils and the sores in the plague in Egypt (*Exodus* 9: 8–11); the pains which will follow disobedience to God (*Deuteronomy* 28: 35); the sores of the tortured Job (*Job* 2: 7).

The second terror is the turning of the waters of the sea into blood; this and the following terror, the turning of the rivers and the springs into blood, is reminiscent of the turning of the waters of the Nile into blood in the days of the plagues in Egypt (*Exodus* 7: 17–21). It may be that the thought of a sea of blood came to John in Patmos; often there he must have seen the sea like blood in the dying splendour of the sunset.

In Hebrew thought every natural force—the wind, the sun, the rain, the waters—had its directing angel. These angels were the ministering servants of God, placed in charge of various departments of nature. It might have been thought that the angel of the waters would have been angry to see the waters turned into blood; but even he admits the justice of God's action. In verse 6 the reference is to actual persecution in the Roman Empire. God's dedicated ones are the members of the Christian Church; the prophets are not the Old Testament prophets but the prophets of the Christian Church (1 *Corinthians* 12: 28; *Acts* 13: 1; *Ephesians* 4: 11), who, being the leaders of the Church, were always the first to suffer in any time of persecution. The grim punishment of those who have shed the blood of the leaders and of the rank and file of the Church is that the waters will be gone from the earth and there will be nothing but blood to drink.

In verse 7 the voice of the altar praises the justice of the judgments of God. This may be the voice of the angel of the altar, for the altar, too, had its angel; or the idea may be this. The altar in heaven is the place where both the prayers of his people and the lives of his martyrs are offered as a sacrifice to God; and the voice of the altar may be, so to speak, the voice of Christ's praying and suffering Church praising the justice of God when his wrath falls upon their persecutors.

The fourth terror is the scorching of the world by the sun; the fifth is the coming of the thick darkness, reminiscent of the darkness which came upon Egypt (*Exodus* 10: 21–23).

In verses 9, 11 and 21 we have a kind of refrain which runs

through this chapter. The men on whom these terrors fell cursed God—but they did not repent, impervious alike to the goodness and to the severity of God (*Romans* 11: 22). It is the picture of men who had no doubt of the existence of God and even saw his hand in events—and who still went their own way.

We are bound to ask ourselves whether we are so very different. We do not doubt the existence of God; we know that God is interested in us and in the world which he has made; we are well aware of God's laws; we know his goodness and we know that sin has its punishment; and yet time and time again we go our own way.


## THE HORDES FROM THE EAST

*Revelation* 16: 12

THIS gives us a picture of the drying up of the Euphrates and the opening of a way for the hordes of the east to descend upon the world.

One of the curious features of the Old Testament is the number of times when the drying up of the waters is a sign of the power of God. It was so at the Red Sea. "The Lord drove the sea back . . . and made the sea dry land" (*Exodus* 14: 21). It was so at Jordan, when the people under Joshua passed through the river. "All the Israelites passed over on dry ground" (*Joshua* 3: 17). In *Isaiah* the act of the power of God is that he will enable men to pass through the Egyptian sea dry-shod (*Isaiah* 11: 16). The threat of God's vengeance in *Jeremiah* is: "I will dry up her sea, and make her fountain dry" (*Jeremiah* 51: 36). "All the depths of the Nile," says Zechariah, "shall dry up" (*Zechariah* 10: 11).

It may well be that here John is actually remembering a famous incident in history. Herodotus tells us (1: 191) that when Cyrus the Persian captured Babylon he did so by drying up the Euphrates. The river flows right through the centre of

Babylon. When Cyrus came to Babylon her defences seemed so strong that her capture seemed impossible. Cyrus formed a brilliant plan. He left one section of his army at Babylon and another he took up the river. By a magnificent engineering feat he temporarily deflected the course of the river into a lake. The level of the river dropped and in the end the channel of the river through Babylon became a dry road; along that road there was a breach in the defences and by that road the Persians gained an entry into Babylon, and the city fell.

John is using a picture which was engraved in the minds of all in his generation. The greatest enemies of Rome, the one nation she could not subjugate, were the Parthians who lived beyond the Euphrates. Their cavalry was the most dreaded force of fighting men in the world. For the cavalry of the Parthians to come sweeping across the Euphrates was a thought to strike terror into the bravest heart. Further, as we have already seen, it was to Parthia that Nero was said to have gone; and it was from Parthia that *Nero redivivus* was expected to come back; in other words, it was from across the Euphrates that the invasion of Antichrist was expected.


## THE UNCLEAN SPIRITS LIKE FROGS

*Revelation* 16: 13–16

THESE four verses are full of problems which must be solved if their meaning is to become reasonably clear.

Three unclean spirits, like frogs, came out of the mouth of the dragon, the beast, and the false prophet.

In the Greek there is a kind of play on words. The unclean spirits came out of the mouths of the evil forces. The mouth is the organ of speech and speech is one of the most influential forces in the world. Now the word for *spirit* is *pneuma* which is also the word for *breath*. To say, therefore, that an evil spirit came out of a man's mouth is the same as to say that an evil breath came out of his mouth. As H. B. Swete puts it, the dragon, the beast, and the false prophet "breathed forth evil influences."

It is said that the unclean spirits were like frogs.

(i) Frogs are connected with plagues. One of the plagues in Egypt was a plague of frogs (*Exodus* 8: 5–11). "He sent frogs . . . which destroyed them," says the Psalmist (*Psalm* 78: 45). "Their land swarmed with frogs even in the chambers of their kings" (*Psalm* 105: 30).

(ii) Frogs are unclean animals. Although not mentioned by name, they are included by definition in the list of unclean things in the water and the sea which begins in *Leviticus* 11: 10. The frog stands for an unclean influence.

(iii) Frogs are famous for their empty and continuous croaking—*brekekekex coax coax*, as Aristophanes transliterated it. "The frog," said Augustine, "is the most loquacious of vanities (*Homily on Psalm* 77: 27). The sound the frog makes is the symbol of meaningless speech.

(iv) In Zoroastrianism, the Persian religion, frogs are the bringer of plagues and the agent of Ahriman, the power of darkness, in his struggle against Ormuzd, the power of light. It is fairly certain that John would know this bit of Persian lore.

So, then, to say that frogs came out of the mouth of the dragon, the beast, and the false prophet is to say that their words were like plagues, were unclean, were empty futilities, and were the allies of the power of the dark.


## THE FALSE PROPHET

*Revelation* 16: 13–16 (*continued*)

OUR next problem is to identify the false prophet. The dragon is identified as Satan (12: 3, 9). The beast, the Roman

Empire with its Caesar worship, has already appeared in 13: 1. But this is the first time the false prophet has appeared upon the scene. Since he appears without any explanation, we must assume that John believes that the reader already has the key to his identity.

The false prophet was a figure whom God's people were well warned to expect both in the Old and in the New Testament. In the Old Testament men are forbidden to listen to the false prophet, however impressive his signs may be, and it is laid down that the punishment for the false prophet is death (*Deuteronomy* 13: 1–5). It was part of the regular duty of the Sanhedrin to deal with the false prophet and to condemn him to death. The Christian Church was warned that false Christs and false prophets would arise to seduce Christ's people (*Mark* 13: 22). H. B. Swete says of these false prophets that the name covers a whole class—"magic-vendors, religious impostors, fanatics, whether deceivers or deceived, regarded as persons who falsely interpret the mind of God. True religion has no worse enemies and Satan no better allies."

The false prophet is mentioned here and in 19: 20 and 20: 10; if we place two passages together, we will find a clue to his identity. 19: 20 tells us that in the end the false prophet was captured along with the beast and he is described as the person who worked miracles before the beast, and deceived those who had the mark of the beast and worshipped its image. In 13: 13, 14 we have a description of the second beast, the beast from the land; it is said that this second beast does great wonders . . . and that he deceives those who dwell on the earth by means of those miracles which he was allowed to do in the presence of the beast. That is to say, the works of the false prophet and the works of the second beast are identical; so, then, the false prophet and the beast from the land are to be identified. We have already seen that that beast is to be identified with the provincial organisation for the enforcement of emperor worship. The false prophet, then, stands for the organization which seeks to make men worship the emperor and abandon the worship of Jesus Christ.

A man who tries to introduce the worship of other gods, who tries to make men compromise with the state or with the world, who tries to seduce other men from the exclusive worship of God is always a false prophet.

## ARMAGEDDON

*Revelation* 16: 13–16 (*continued*)

WE have still another problem to solve in this passage. The evil spirits went out and stirred up the kings of all the earth to bring them to battle. The idea of a final conflict between God and the forces of evil is an old one. We find it in *Psalm* 2: 2: "The kings of the earth set themselves, and the rulers take counsel together, against the Lord, and his anointed."

This battle was to take place at what the Authorized and Revised Standard Versions call *Armageddon*. Moffatt has *Harmagedon*. The Revised Version has *Har-Magedon*. Even the name is uncertain.

*Magedon* or *Maggedon* may well be connected with the name Megiddo. Megiddo is in the Plain of Esdraelon, which was part of the great highway from Egypt to Damascus. From the most ancient times to the time of Napoleon it was one of the great battle-grounds of the world. This was the plain where Barak and Deborah overthrew Sisera and his chariots (*Judges* 5: 19–21); where Ahaziah died by the arrows of Jehu (2 *Kings* 9: 27); where the good Josiah perished in battle with Pharaoh Necho (2 *Kings* 23: 29, 30), a tragedy which burned itself into the Jewish mind and which the Jews never forgot (*Zechariah* 12: 11). It was a battle-ground, as H. B. Swete says, "familiar to a student of Hebrew history."

*Armageddon* would mean *the city of Megiddo*; *Harmagedon* would mean *the mountain of Megiddo*. It is most likely that the latter form is right, and yet the plain seems a much more likely battle-ground than the mountains. But there is another strand to add to this. When Ezekiel was describing the last struggle with Gog and Magog, he said that the final victory would be won in *the mountains of Israel* (*Ezekiel* 38: 8, 21; 39: 2, 4, 17). It may well be that John spoke of the Mount of Megiddo to bring his story into line with the ancient prophecy.

By far the most likely view is that the word is Har-Magedon, and that it describes the region near Megiddo in the Plain of Esdraelon which was perhaps the most storied of all battle-grounds in Jewish history.

We must mention two other views of this strange word. Gunkel thought that it went back to the old Babylonian story of the struggle between Marduk, the creator, and Tiamat, the ancient power of chaos. But it is less than likely that John knew that story.

Another view connects it with *Isaiah* 14: 13 where Lucifer is made to say: "Above the stars of God I will set my throne on high; I will sit on the *mount of assembly.*" The Babylonians believed that there was a mountain called Aralu in the north country, which, rather like Olympus in Greece, was the home of the gods. Lucifer is going to take his seat among the gods; it has been suggested that the Mount of Mageddon is this mountain, and that the picture is of a last battle against the assembled gods in their own dwelling-place.

## NATURE AT WAR

*Revelation* 16: 17–21

THE seventh bowl was poured out upon the air. H. B. Swete speaks of "the air that all men breathe." If the air was polluted, the very life of man was attacked at its source. Nature became at war with man. That was what happened.

There came lightning and thunder and earthquake. The first century was notable for earthquakes, but John says that, whatever horror the world has known from the shaking earth, the earthquake to come will far surpass them all.

The great Babylon, that is Rome, is split into three. Rome had thought that she could do as she liked with impunity—but now her sin was remembered and her fate was on the way. The mills of God may grind slowly but in the end there is no escape for sin.

The earthquake sank the islands and levelled the mountains. The last of the terrible features was a deadly hail in which the hailstones weighed as much as a hundredweight. Here is another recurring feature of the manifestations of the wrath of God. A devastating hail was part of the plagues of Egypt (*Exodus* 9: 24). In the battle with the five Amorite kings at Beth-horon, under Joshua, there came a great hail upon the enemies of Israel so that more died by the hailstones than died by the sword (*Joshua* 10: 11). Isaiah speaks of the tempest of hail and the destroying storm which God in his judgment will send (*Isaiah* 28: 2). Ezekiel speaks of God pleading with men with pestilence and blood, and sending an overflowing rain, and great hailstones, fire, and brimstone (*Ezekiel* 38: 22).

The emptying of the seven bowls of wrath upon the earth ends with the chorus which has run all through the chapter. The men to whom these things happened remained impervious to any appeal of God's love or God's anger. God has given men the terrible responsibility of being able to lock their hearts against him.

Chapters 17 and 18 tell of the fall of Babylon. Chapter 17 is one of the most difficult in the *Revelation*. The best way in which to study it is first to read it as a whole; then to make certain general identifications and so to see the general line of thought in it; and finally to study it in some detail. This will involve a certain amount of repetition, but in a section like this repetition is necessary.

## THE FALL OF ROME

*Revelation* 17

1  One of the seven angels, who had the seven bowls, came and spoke with me. "Come here," he said, "and I will show you the judgment of the great harlot, who sits upon many waters,

2  with whom the kings of the earth committed fornication and with the wine of whose adultery those who inhabit the earth have become drunken."

3  He carried me away in the Spirit to a desert place, and I saw a woman, seated upon a scarlet beast, which was full of names which were insults to God, and which had seven heads and ten horns.

4  The woman was clothed in purple and scarlet and bedizened with gold and jewellery and pearls. She had in her hand a golden cup, full of abominations and the unclean things of her fornication.

5  And on her forehead there was written a name with a meaning which was secret except to those who knew its meaning: "Babylon, the great, the mother of the harlots and the abominations of the earth." I saw the woman, drunk

6  with the blood of God's dedicated people and with the blood of the martyrs of Jesus. When I saw her I was stricken

7  with a great wonder. The angel said to me: "Why are you moved to wonder? I will tell you the secret meaning of the woman and of the beast who bears her and has the seven

8  heads and the ten horns. The beast, which you saw, was and is not, and is about to come up from the abyss, and is on the way to destruction; and the inhabitants of the earth, whose names are not written in the Book of Life from the foundation of the world will be stricken with wonder, when they see the beast, because it was, and is not, and

9  will come. Here there is need for a mind with wisdom. The seven heads are seven hills on which the woman sits. They

10  are also seven kings. Five have fallen; one at present exists; another has not yet come, and, when he shall come, he

11  must remain for a short time. The beast, which was and is not, is itself the eighth. It proceeds from the series of the seven and it is on the way to destruction.

12  The ten heads you saw are ten kings, who have not yet received

13 their royal authority, but they are to receive authority as kings for one hour in the company of the beast. They have one mind in common and they hand over power and authority to the beast.

14 These shall make war with the Lamb, and the Lamb will conquer them, because he is the Lord of lords and the King of kings, and the called, the chosen and the loyal will share his victory."

15 And he went on to say to me: "The waters which you saw, on which the harlot is seated, are peoples and crowds and nations and tongues.

16 The ten horns, which you saw, and the beast will hate the harlot, and will make her desolate and naked, and will devour her flesh, and will burn her in the fire; for it is God who

17 has put it into their minds to perform his purpose, and to be of one mind to give their royal power to the beast, until the words of God shall be fulfilled.

18 And the woman which you saw is the great city which has dominion over the kings of the earth."

## 1. THE WOMAN ON THE BEAST

The woman is Babylon, that is to say, Rome. The woman is said (verse 1) to sit upon many waters. In this picture of Rome, John was using many of the things said by the prophets about ancient Babylon. In *Jeremiah* 51: 13 Babylon is addressed as: "O you who dwell by many waters." The river Euphrates actually ran through the midst of Babylon; and she was also the centre of a system of irrigation canals, spreading out in every direction. When this description is applied to Rome, it does not make sense. Later in verse 15, John realizes this and gives the waters a symbolic interpretation as the many nations and peoples and tongues over whom Rome rules. For this way of speaking, also, we must look to the Old Testament. When Isaiah is forecasting the invasion of Palestine by Assyria, he writes: "Therefore, behold, the Lord is bringing up against them the waters of the River, mighty and many, the king of Assyria and all his glory; and it will rise over all its channels and go over all its banks; and it will sweep on into Judah, it will overflow and pass on, reaching even to the neck" (*Isaiah* 8: 7, 8). Again, when Jeremiah is prophesying the coming invasion, he uses the same picture: "Behold, waters are rising out of the north, and shall become an overflowing torrent; they shall overflow the land, and all that fills it" (*Jeremiah* 47: 2).

*In verse 4 the woman is said to* be clothed in purple and scarlet and decked with all kinds of ornaments. This is symbolic of the luxury of Rome and of the meretricious and lustful way in which it was used, the picture of a wealthy courtesan, decked out in all her finery to seduce men.

*The woman is said to* have in her hand a golden cup, full of abominations. Here we have another picture of Babylon taken direct from the prophetic condemnation of the Old Testament. Jeremiah said: "Babylon was a golden cup in the Lord's hand, making all the earth drunken; the nations drank of her wine; therefore the nations went mad" (*Jeremiah* 51: 7). So Rome is said to hold the golden cup in which is that power of seduction which has spread immorality over all the earth.

*The woman is said to* have a name on her forehead (verse 5). In Rome the prostitutes in the public brothels wore upon their foreheads a frontlet giving their names. This is another vivid detail in the picture of Rome as the great corrupting prostitute among the nations.

*In verse 6 the woman is said to* be drunk with the blood of God's dedicated people and with the blood of the martyrs. This is a reference to the persecution of the Christians in the Roman Empire. But it does more than simply stamp Rome as the great persecutor. She is glutted with slaughter; and she has revelled in that slaughter as a drunken man revels in wine.

In verse 16 she is to be destroyed by the invasion of the ten kings. This we shall discuss more fully when we come to discuss the symbolism of the beast. It is sufficient to say just now that it foretells the destruction of Rome by the rising against her of her subject nations. It is as if to say that the great prostitute will in the end be destroyed by her lovers turning against her.

## 2. THE BEAST

It is much harder to fix the meaning of the beast than of the woman, mainly because the meaning of the beast does not stay steady. The beast has a series of interconnected meanings, whose point of union is that they are all closely connected with Rome and with her empire.

(i) The woman sits on the beast and the beast is filled with blasphemous names which are all insults to God (verse 3). If the woman is Rome, clearly the beast is the Roman Empire. It is full of blasphemous names. This includes two things. First, it is a reference to the many gods of which the Roman Empire was full. All these names are insults to God, for they are all infringements of his supreme and unique authority. No one has the right to the name of god save only the true God. Second, it is a reference to many of the titles of the emperor. The emperor was *Sebastos*, or *Augustus*, which means *to be reverenced*; and reverence belongs to God alone. The emperor was *divus* or *theios*, which, the first in Latin and the second in Greek, mean *divine*; and to God alone belongs that adjective. Many of the emperors were called *sōtēr*, *saviour*, which is uniquely the title of Jesus Christ. Most common of all, the emperor was in Latin *dominus* and in Greek *kurios*, *lord,* which is the very name of God.

(ii) The beast has seven heads and ten horns (verse 3). This is a repetition of what is said of the beast in 13: 1, and we shall very soon return to its meaning here.

(iii) The beast was, and is not, and is about to come (verse 8). This goes back to 13: 3, 12, 14 and is a clear reference to the *Nero redivivus* legend, which is never far from the mind of John. We have already seen that the ideas of Nero resurrected and of Antichrist had become inseparably connected. Therefore, in this passage the beast stands for Antichrist.

(iv) The beast has seven heads. These are doubly explained.

(*a*) In verse 9 the seven heads are seven hills. Here we have an easy identification. Rome was the city upon seven hills; this once again identifies the beast with Rome.

(*b*) The second identification is one of the riddles of the *Revelation* (verses 10 and 11).

> They (the heads) are also seven kings. Five have fallen; one at present exists; another has not yet come, and, when he shall come, he must remain for a short time. The beast, which was and is not, is itself the eighth. It proceeds from the series of the seven, and it is on its way to destruction.

*Five have fallen.* The Roman Empire began with Augustus; and the first five emperors were Augustus, Tiberius, Caligula, Claudius, and Nero. These, then, are the five who have fallen. We have already seen that after the death of Nero there were two years of chaos in which Galba, Otho and Vitellius followed each other in quick succession. They were not in any real sense emperors and cannot be included in any list.

*One at present exists.* This must be Vespasian, the first emperor to bring back stability to the empire, after the chaos following the death of Nero; he reigned from A.D. 69–79.

*Another has not yet come, and, when he shall come, he must remain for a short time.* Vespasian was succeeded by Titus, whose reign lasted for only two years from 79–81.

*The beast which was, and is not, is itself the eighth. It proceeds from the series of the seven, and is on its way to destruction.* This can only mean that the emperor who followed Titus is being identified with Nero redivivus and Antichrist; and the emperor who followed Titus was Domitian.

Can Domitian reasonably be identified with the evil force which Nero redivivus personified? We turn to the life of Domitian written by Suetonius the Roman biographer, remembering that Suetonius was not a Christian. Domitian, as Suetonius tells, was an object of terror and hatred to all.

We get a grim picture of him at the beginning of his reign. "He used to spend hours in seclusion every day, doing nothing but catch flies and stab them with a keenly-sharpened stylus." Any psychologist would find that a curiously revealing picture. He was insanely jealous and insanely suspicious. He formed a homosexual attachment for a famous actor called Paris. One of the pupils of Paris so much resembled his teacher that it was not unreasonable to suppose that he was his son; the lad was promptly murdered. Hermogenes, the historian, wrote things which Domitian did not like; he was executed, and the scribe who had copied the manuscript was crucified. Senators were slaughtered right and left. Sallustius Lucullus, governor of Britain, was executed because he allowed a new type of lance to be called Lucullan. Domitian revived the old punishment of having his victims stripped naked, fixed by the neck in a fork of wood and beaten to death with rods. He put down a civil war that broke out in the provinces. Suetonius goes on: "After his victory in the civil war he became even more cruel, and, to discover any conspirators who were in hiding, tortured many of the opposite party by a new form of inquisition, inserting fire in their privates; and he cut off the hands of some of them."

Early in his reign he appeared wearing a golden crown with the figures of Jupiter, Juno and Minerva in it, while the priest of Jupiter sat by his side. When he received back his divorced wife, he announced that she had returned to the divine couch. When he entered the amphitheatre, he loved to be greeted with the cry: "Good fortune attend our lord and his lady." He began his official edicts: "Our lord and god bids this to be done." Soon that was the only way in which he might be addressed.

He was so suspicious that he never gave prisoners a hearing in private, and, even when he heard them with his guards present, they were chained. He so feared for his own life that he had the passages and colonnades through which he moved tiled with phlengite stone, which is like a mirror, so that he could see anyone who was moving behind him.

Finally, on 18 September, A.D. 96, he was murdered in the bloodiest circumstances.

To all this we may add a final fact; it was Domitian who first made Caesar worship compulsory and who was, therefore, responsible for unloosing the flood-tides of persecution on the Christian Church.

It might well be that John saw in Domitian the reincarnation of Nero. Others did precisely the same. Juvenal spoke of Rome being "enslaved to a bald-headed Nero" (Domitian was bald) and was exiled and finally murdered for his temerity. Tertullian called Domitian "a man of Nero's type of cruelty," and "a sub-Nero," a verdict which Eusebius repeated.

The one difficulty is that it makes it look as if John wrote in the reign of Vespasian; and we know that John in fact wrote under Domitian. Two possibilities may explain this. John may have written this particular vision years before in the time of Vespasian, lived to see it come terribly true and incorporated it in his final draft of the *Revelation*. Or he may have written it all in the reign of Domitian, and, projected himself back into the time of Vespasian to trace in retrospect the terrible lines that history had taken.

However we explain it, the picture is satisfied if we hold that John saw in Domitian the reincarnation of Nero, the supreme embodiment of Roman wickedness and defiance of God; we need not go on to say that he identified Domitian with Antichrist.

There remains one problem in identification and it is less susceptible of definite solution than the others. In verses 12–17 it is said that the ten horns are ten kings who have not yet received their power. They will receive it, and when they do, two things will happen. They will unanimously agree to hand over their own power to the beast; and with him they will rise against the harlot and make war with the Lamb and finally be defeated.

By far the likeliest interpretation of this is that the ten kings are the satraps of the Parthian hosts, who will make common cause with Nero redivivus and under him fight the last battle in which Rome will be destroyed and the Lamb will subdue every hostile force in the universe.

### THE CITY WHICH BECAME A HARLOT

*Revelation* 17: 1, 2

IN these two verses Rome is described as the great harlot. More than once in the Old Testament heathen and disobedient cities are described as harlots. It is thus that Nahum describes Nineveh, when he speaks of the multitude of the whoredoms of the well-favoured harlot (*Nahum* 3: 4). It is thus that Isaiah describes Tyre (*Isaiah* 23: 16, 17). Even Jerusalem can be so described. "How the faithful city has become a harlot!" mourns Isaiah (*Isaiah* 1: 21). And the charge of Ezekiel is: "You trusted in your beauty and played the harlot" (*Ezekiel* 16: 15).

It is a way of speaking which is strange to modern ears; but there is great symbolism behind it.

(i) Behind it is the idea of God as the lover of the souls of his people. Primasius, the old Latin commentator, says that Rome is called a harlot, because "she left her Creator and prostituted herself with devils." When we turn our backs upon God, it is not so much a sin against law as a sin against love.

(ii) There is another idea behind this. Beckwith suggests that Rome is called the great harlot, because she is "an allurement to godlessness and immorality." The sin of the harlot is not only that she sins herself, but also that she deliberately persuades others into sin. God will never hold guiltless the man who seduces others into sin.

### THE VISION IN THE WILDERNESS

*Revelation* 17: 3

JOHN says that he was carried away in the Spirit to a desert place.

The prophet is a man who lives in the Spirit. "The Spirit," said Ezekiel, "lifted me up and took me away" (*Ezekiel* 3: 14). "The Spirit lifted me up between earth and heaven, and brought me in visions of God to Jerusalem" (*Ezekiel* 8: 3). "And the Spirit lifted me up, and brought me in the vision by the Spirit of God into Chaldea to the exiles" (*Ezekiel* 11: 24). It is not that the Spirit physically moves a man about from place to place; but, when a man lives in the Spirit, his horizons are widened; he may live in time, but he becomes a spectator of eternity. The prophets could see the trends of history ahead because they lived in the Spirit.

One of the ever-recurring features of the Bible story is that it was in the desert that the great men of God saw their visions. It was in the wilderness that Moses met God (*Exodus* 3: 1). It was when he had gone a day's journey into the wilderness that Elijah met God and regained his courage and his faith (1 *Kings* 19: 4). It was in the wilderness that John the Baptist grew to manhood and it was there that he received his message from God (*Luke* 1: 80). It was to the wilderness that Jesus went to settle the way he would take before he set out to preach and teach and die for men and for God (*Matthew* 4: 1).

It may well be that there is not enough quietness in our lives for us to receive the message which God is eager to give.

## THE GREAT HARLOT

*Revelation* 17: 4, 5

THESE verses give us a vivid picture of the great harlot. She is clothed in purple and scarlet, the royal colours, the colours of luxury and splendour. She is bedecked with gold and precious stones and pearls. She has the golden cup with which she makes her lovers drunk. She has the harlot's frontlet on her forehead with her name. The name is a *mystery*. In Greek a *mustērion* is not necessarily something abstruse; it is something quite unintelligible to the uninitiated but crystal clear to the initiated. The *mystery* in this case is that Babylon means Rome; the thing which the stranger does not know, but which the Christian reader does know, is that while the story is told under the name of Babylon everything relates to Rome.

(i) John may have got this picture from the temple prostitutes of Asia Minor. One of the strange features of ancient religion was that to many temples there were attached sacred prostitutes; there were, for instance, a thousand of them attached to the Temple of Aphrodite at Corinth. To have intercourse with them was an act of worship which paid homage to the life force.

(ii) John possibly had in mind the most notorious of all the Roman Empresses, Messalina. She was the wife of the weak and almost imbecile Claudius; and it is related of her that at nights she would go down to the public brothels and serve there like any common prostitute. Juvenal paints the picture in vivid terms (*Satire* 6: 114–132): "Hear what Claudius endured. As soon as his wife perceived that her husband was asleep, this august harlot was shameless enough to prefer a common mat to the imperial couch. Assuming a night-cowl, and attended by a single maid she issued forth; then, having concealed her raven locks under a light-coloured peruque, she took her place in a brothel reeking with long-used coverlets. Entering an empty cell reserved for herself, she there took her stand, under the feigned name of Lycisca, her nipples bare and gilded, and exposed to view the womb that bore thee, O nobly-born Britannicus. Here she graciously received all comers, asking from each his fee; and when at length the keeper dismissed the girls, she remained to the very last before closing her cell, and with passion still raging hot within her went sorrowfully away. Then, exhausted by men but unsatisfied, with soiled cheeks, and begrimed by the smoke of the lamps, she took back to the imperial pillow all the odours of the stews."

When even an empress stooped to this, is there any wonder that John thought of Rome as a harlot?

The cup of the harlot Rome is full of unclean things. Lest it be thought that this is the verdict of some narrow-minded Christian, let it be remembered that Tacitus called Rome "the place into which from all over the world all atrocious and shameful things flow and where they are most popular," and Seneca called her "a filthy sewer." John's picture of Rome is actually restrained in comparison with some of the pictures which the Romans themselves drew. This was the civilization into which Christianity came; and it was out of this that men were converted to chastity. We may well speak of the miracles of the Cross.

## DRUNK WITH THE BLOOD OF THE SAINTS AND THE MARTYRS

*Revelation* 17: 6

As we have already pointed out in the general introduction to this chapter, the way in which John describes Roman persecution is very significant. He says that Rome is drunk with the blood of the saints and the martyrs. The implication is that Rome did not simply persecute the Christians as a legal necessity but took fiendish delight in hounding Christians to death.

No doubt John is thinking of the persecution which took place under Nero. The Neronic persecution sprang from the great fire in A.D. 64 which burned for a week and devastated Rome. The people of Rome were convinced that the fire was no accident; they were also convinced that those who tried to extinguish it were hindered and that when it died down, it was deliberately rekindled; and they were also convinced that the instigator of the fire was Nero. Nero had a passion for building, and the people believed that he had deliberately burned down the city in order to rebuild it.

Nero had to find a scapegoat to divert suspicion from himself; and he fixed on the Christians. This was the first great persecution and in many ways the most savage of all. We quote Tacitus's description in full because it is one of the few passages in pagan literature where the name of Christ occurs (Tacitus: *Annals* 15: 44):

> All human efforts, all the lavish gifts of the emperor (Nero), and the propitations of the gods, did not banish the sinister belief that the conflagration was the result of an order. Consequently to get rid of the report, Nero fastened the guilt and inflicted the most exquisite tortures on a class hated for their abominations, called Christians by the populace. Christus, from whom the name had its origin, suffered the extreme penalty during the reign of Tiberius, at the hands of one of our procurators, Pontius Pilatus, and a most mischievous superstition, thus checked for the moment, again broke out not only in Judaea, the first source of the evil, but even in Rome, where all things hideous and shameful from every part of the world find their centre and become popular. Accordingly, an arrest was first made of all who pleaded guilty; then, upon their information, an immense multitude was convicted, not so much of the crime of firing the city, as of hatred of mankind. Mockery of every sort was added to their deaths. Covered with the skins of beasts, they were torn by dogs, and perished, or were nailed to crosses, or were doomed to the flames and burned, to serve as a nightly illumination when daylight had expired. . . . Hence, even for criminals who deserved extreme and exemplary punishment, there arose a feeling of compassion, for it was not, as it seemed for the public good, but to glut one man's cruelty that they were being destroyed.

## THE REINCARNATION OF EVIL

*Revelation* 17: 7–11

In the introduction to this chapter we have already seen that the likeliest explanation is that John is projecting himself backwards into the reign of Vespasian. The five who have been are Augustus, Tiberius, Caligula, Claudius, Nero; the one who is is Vespasian; the one who is to come and who is to last for only a very short time is Titus; the one who is to be the equivalent of the head wounded and restored, who is to be Nero all over again, is Domitian, the man of savage cruelty. Lying behind all this imagery are three permanent truths.

(i) Even when Nero died, his wickedness lived on and John sees it re-emerging in Domitian, the new Nero. Everyone leaves something behind in this world. It may be a memory which is a helper of all that is fine and good; it may be an evil influence which lays a trail of trouble for many generations to come. Every man's life points somewhere; he must see that it points to goodness and to God.

(ii) In verse 8 we read that those whose names have not been written in the Book of Life will be dazzled at the coming of the evil one. There are always those who can be dazzled by evil. The one way to avoid its fascination is to keep our eyes on Jesus Christ. Then evil is seen for what it is.

(iii) In verse 11 we read that the beast is on his way to destruction. However great the success of evil may be, it has in it the seeds of self-destruction. He who allies himself with evil has chosen the losing side.

## THE PURPOSES OF MAN AND THE PURPOSES OF GOD

*Revelation* 17: 12–18

THIS passage speaks of the ten kings whom the ten horns represent. It is likely that the ten kings are the satraps of the East and of Parthia whom the resurrected Nero, the Antichrist, is to lead against Rome. Or they may simply stand for all the world powers which in the end will turn against Rome and destroy her. We note certain things in this passage.

(i) In verse 14 we read that these world powers war with the Lamb but the Lamb destroys them; and the called, the chosen and the loyal share in the victory of the Lamb. One of the great conceptions of Jewish thought was that the saints and the martyrs would share in God's final triumph.

"Sinners," says *Enoch*, "shall be delivered into the hands of the righteous" (*Enoch* 91: 12). "Be hopeful, ye righteous," says *Enoch* again, "for suddenly shall the sinners perish before you, and ye shall have lordship over them according to your desires" (*Enoch* 96: 1). In a grim passage the same book says: "Woe to you who love the deeds of unrighteousness. . . . Know that you shall be delivered into the hands of the righteous, and they shall cut off your necks and slay you, and have no mercy upon you" (*Enoch* 98: 12). In the *Wisdom of Solomon* there is the same promise to those who have lived and suffered and died for God. "Having borne a little chastening, they shall receive great good, because God made trial of them and found them worthy of himself. As gold in the furnace he proved them, and as a whole burnt-offering he accepted them. And in the time of their visitation they shall shine forth, and as sparks among the stubble they shall run to and fro. They shall judge nations and have dominion over peoples" (*Wisdom* 3: 5–8). It is no doubt this belief that was in the minds of James and John when they came and asked Jesus for the places on his right and his left when he entered into his kingdom (*Matthew* 20: 21; *Mark* 10: 37).

This Jewish thought has two aspects, one noble and one subchristian. The subchristian one is that there were times when this became nothing other than a thirst for vengeance; but who shall blame the persecuted for longing for the day when the world's roles will be reversed in eternity? The noble idea is that the saints and martyrs will aid Christ to win his triumph and share in the glory. It is an affirmation that for us, too, after the Cross comes the crown.

(ii) Verse 16 gives a picture of the ten horns rising violently against the harlot who had been their mistress. They will devour her flesh. In the Old Testament that is the action of a most savage and powerful enemy. It is the complaint of the Psalmist that the wicked ate up his flesh (*Psalm* 27: 2; A.V.). The wicked in Israel, with their grasping oppression, eat the flesh of the people of God (*Micah* 3: 3). This is a picture of terrible vengeance. They will burn her in the fire. This is the punishment for the most heinous sin (*Leviticus* 20: 14), and above all the punishment for the daughter of a priest who has been guilty of sexual immorality (*Leviticus* 21: 9).

It is to be noted that the harlot's previous lovers turned against her. Evil has in it a divisive power.

(iii) In verses 12 and 13 we read of the ten kings making common purpose with the beast; and in verse 17 we read that God put this into their hearts that his purposes might be carried out and his words fulfilled. Here is a strange thing. These evil powers thought they were working out their own purposes but they were, in fact, working out the purposes of God. R. H. Charles says: "Even the wrath of men is made to praise God." The truth behind this is that God never loses control of human affairs. In the last analysis God is always working things together for good.

## THE DOOM OF ROME

*Revelation* 18: 1–3

> After these things I saw another angel coming down from heaven. He had great authority and the earth was lit up by his glory. He cried with a loud voice saying: "Fallen, fallen is Babylon the great. She has become a dwelling-place of demons, and a stronghold of every unclean spirit, and a stronghold of every unclean and hated bird, because the nations have drunk of the wine of the wrath of her fornication, and the kings of the earth have committed fornication with her, and the merchants of the earth have grown rich with the wealth of her wantonness."

IN this chapter we have a form of prophetic literature common in the prophetic books of the Old Testament. This is what is called "A Doom Song," the doom song of the city of Rome.

We quote certain Old Testament parallels. In *Isaiah* 13: 19–22 we have the doom song of ancient Babylon:

> And Babylon, the glory of kingdoms, the splendour and pride of the Chaldeans, will be like Sodom and Gomorrah when God overthrew them. It will never be inhabited or dwelt in for all

generations; no Arab will pitch his tent there, no shepherds will make their flocks lie down there. But wild beasts will lie down there, and its houses will be full of howling creatures; there ostriches will dwell, and there satyrs will dance. Hyenas will cry in its towers, and jackals in the pleasant palaces; its time is close at hand and its days will not be prolonged.

In *Isaiah* 34: 11–15 we have the doom song of Edom:

But the hawk and the porcupine shall possess it, the owl and the raven shall dwell in it. He shall stretch the line of confusion over it, and the plummet of chaos over its nobles. . . . Thorns shall grow over its strongholds, nettles and thistles in its fortresses. It shall be the haunt of jackals, an abode for ostriches. And wild beasts shall meet with hyenas, the satyr shall cry to his fellow; yea, there shall the night hag alight, and find for herself a resting place. There shall the owl nest and lay and hatch and gather her young in her shadow; yea, there shall the kites be gathered, each one with her mate.

*Jeremiah* 50: 39 and 51: 37 are part of doom songs of Babylon:

Therefore wild beasts shall dwell with hyenas in Babylon, and ostriches shall dwell in her; she shall be peopled no more for ever, nor inhabited for all generations. And Babylon shall become a heap of ruins, the haunt of jackals, a horror and a hissing without inhabitant.

In *Zephaniah* 2: 13–15 we have the doom song of Nineveh:

And he will make Nineveh a desolation, a dry waste like the desert. Herds shall lie down in the midst of her, all the beasts of the field; the vulture and the hedgehog shall lodge in her capitals; the owl shall hoot in the window, the raven croak on the threshold; for her cedar work will be laid bare. This is the exultant city that dwelt secure, that said to herself, "I am and there is none else." What a desolation she has become, a lair for wild beasts! Every one who passes by her hisses and shakes his fist.

In spite of their grim foretelling of ruin these passages are all great poetry of passion. It may be that here we are far from the Christian doctrine of forgiveness; but we are very close to the beating of the human heart.

In our passage the angel charged with the message of doom comes with the very light of God upon him. No doubt John was thinking of *Ezekiel* 43: 1, 2: "He brought me to the gate, the gate facing east; and behold the glory of the God of Israel came from the east; and the sound of his coming was like the sound of many waters; and the earth shone with his glory." H. B. Swete writes of this angel: "So recently he has come from the Presence that in passing he brings a broad belt of light across the dark earth."

So certain is John of the doom of Rome, that he speaks of it as if it had already happened.

We note one other point. Surely the most dramatic part of the picture is the demons haunting the ruins. The pagan gods banished from their reign disconsolately haunt the ruins of the temples where once their power had been supreme.

## COME YE OUT!

*Revelation* 18: 4, 5

> I heard another voice from heaven saying: "Come out, my people, from her, lest you become partners in her sins, and lest you share in her plagues, because her sins are piled as high as heaven, and God has remembered her unrighteous deeds."

THE Christians are bidden come out of Rome before the day of destruction comes, lest, sharing in her sins, they also share in her doom. H. B. Swete says that this call to come out rings through Hebrew history. God is always calling upon his people to cut their connection with sin and to stand with him and for him.

It was the call which came to Abraham: "Now the Lord said to Abraham, Go from your country, and your kindred, and your father's house, to the land that I will show you" (*Genesis* 12: 1). It was the call that came to Lot, before the destruction of Sodom and Gomorrah: "Up, get out of this place, for the Lord is about to destroy the city" (*Genesis* 19: 12–14). It was the call that came to Moses in the days of the wickedness of Korah, Dathan and Abiram: "Get away from about the dwelling of Korah, Dathan and Abiram. . . . Depart, I pray you, from the tents of these wicked men" (*Numbers* 16: 23–26). "Go forth from Babylon," said Isaiah, "flee from Chaldea" (*Isaiah* 48: 20). "Flee from the midst of Babylon," said Jeremiah, "and go out of the land of the Chaldeans" (*Jeremiah* 50: 8). "Flee from the midst of Babylon, let every man save his life" (*Jeremiah* 51: 6). "Go out of the midst of her people. Let every man save his life from the fierce anger of the Lord" (*Jeremiah* 51: 45). It is a cry which finds its echo in the New Testament. Paul writes to the Corinthians: "Do not be mismated with unbelievers. For what partnership have righteousness and iniquity? Or what fellowship has light with darkness? What accord has Christ with Belial?" (2 *Corinthians* 6: 14, 15). "Do not participate in another man's sins; keep yourself pure" (1 *Timothy* 5: 22).

Swete well points out that this cry and challenge do not involve a coming out at a definite moment. They imply a certain "aloofness of spirit maintained in the very heart of the world's traffic." They describe the essential apartness of the Christian from the world. The commonest word for the Christian in the New Testament is the Greek *hagios*, whose basic meaning is different. The Christian is not conformed to the world but transformed from the world (*Romans* 12: 2). It is not a question of retiring from the world; it is a question of living differently within the world.

## THE DOOM OF PRIDE

*Revelation* 18: 6–8

Repay her in the coin with which she paid others; and repay her double for her deeds. Mix her a double draught in the cup in which she mixed her draughts. In proportion to her boasting and her wantonness give her torture and grief, for she says in her heart: "I sit a queen: I am not a widow; grief is something that I will never see." Because of this her plagues will come upon her in one day—pestilence and grief and famine and she will be burned with fire, because the Lord God who judges her is strong.

THIS passage speaks in terms of punishment. But the instruction to exact vengeance on Rome is not an instruction to men; it is an instruction to the angel, the divine instrument of justice. Vengeance belongs to God, and to God alone. We have here two truths which we must remember.

(i) There is in life a law by which a man sows that which he reaps. Even in the Sermon on the Mount we find an expression of that law: "The measure you give will be the measure you get" (*Matthew* 7: 2). The double punishment and the double reward come from the fact that frequently in Jewish law anyone responsible for loss or damage had to repay it twice over (*Exodus* 22: 4, 7, 9). "O daughter of Babylon, you devastator!" says the Psalmist, "happy shall he be who requites you with what you have done to us" (*Psalm* 137: 8). "Requite her according to her deeds," says Jeremiah of Babylon, "Do to her according to all that she has done; for she has proudly defied the Lord, the Holy One of Israel" (*Jeremiah* 50: 29). There is no getting away from the fact that punishment follows sin, especially if that sin has involved the cruel treatment of fellowmen.

(ii) We meet here the stern truth that all pride will one day be humiliated. Rome's supreme sin has been pride. It is in Old Testament terms that John speaks. He reproduces the ancient judgment on Babylon:

You said, "I shall be mistress for ever," so that you did not lay these things to heart or remember their end. Now therefore hear this, you lover of pleasures, who sit securely, who say in your heart, "I am, and there is no one besides me; I shall not sit as a widow or know the loss of children": These two things shall come to you in a moment, in one day; the loss of children and widowhood shall come upon you in full measure, in spite of your many sorceries and the great power of your enchantments.

Nothing rouses such condemnation as pride, Isaiah speaks grimly: "Because the daughters of Zion are haughty, and walk with outstretched necks, glancing wantonly with their eyes, mincing along as they go, tinkling with their feet the Lord will smite with a scab the heads of the daughters of Zion" (*Isaiah* 3: 16, 17). Tyre is condemned because she has said: "I am perfect in beauty" (*Ezekiel* 27: 3).

There is a sin which the Greek called *hubris*, which is that arrogance, that comes to feel that it has no need of God. The punishment for that sin is ultimate humiliation.

## THE LAMENT OF THE KINGS

*Revelation* 18: 9, 10

> The kings of the earth, who committed fornication with her and who shared in her wantonness, will weep and lament over her, when they will see the smoke of her burning, while they stand afar off because of the fear of her torture, while they say: "Alas! Alas! for the city that seemed so strong, for Babylon the strong city! for in one hour your judgment is come."

IN the rest of this chapter we have the dirges for Rome; the dirge sung by the kings (verses 9 and 10), the dirge sung by the merchants (verses 11–16), the dirge sung by the ship-masters and the sailors (verses 17–19). Again and again we hear of the greatness, the wealth and the wanton luxury of Rome.

We may well ask whether John's indictment is justified or whether he is merely a fanatic shouting doom without any real justification. If we wish to find an account of the luxury and the wantonness of Rome we will find it in such books as *Roman Society from Nero to Marcus Aurelius,* by Samuel Dill, *Roman Life and Manners,* by Ludwig Friedländer, and especially in the *Satires* of Juvenal, the *Lives of the Caesars* by Suetonius, and the works of Tacitus, themselves Romans and themselves appalled by the things about which they

wrote. These books show that nothing John could say of
Rome could be an exaggeration.

There is a saying in the *Talmud* that ten measures of
wealth came down into the world and that Rome received
nine and all the rest of the world only one. One famous
scholar said that in modern times we are babes in the matter
of enjoyment compared with the ancient world; and another
remarked that our most extravagant luxury is poverty
compared with the prodigal magnificence of ancient Rome.

In that ancient world there was a kind of desperate com-
petition in ostentation. It was said of Caligula that "he strove
most of all to realize what men deemed impossible," and it
was said that "the desire of the incredible" was the great
characteristic of Nero. Dill says: "The senator who paid too
low a rent, or rode along the Appian or Flaminian Way with
too scanty a train, became a marked man and immediately
lost caste."

In this first century the world was pouring its riches into the
lap of Rome. As Dill has it: "The long peace, the safety of
the seas, and the freedom of trade, had made Rome the
entrepôt for the peculiar products and delicacies of every
land from the British Channel to the Ganges." Pliny talks
of a meal in which in one dish India was laid under contribution,
in another Egypt, Cyrene, Crete and so forth. Juvenal speaks
of the seas peopled with great keels and of greed luring ships
on expeditions to every land. Aristides has a purple passage on
the way in which things flowed into Rome. "Merchandise is
brought from every land and sea, everything that every season
begets, and every country produces, the products of rivers
and lakes, the arts of the Greeks and the barbarians, so that,
if anyone were to wish to see all these things, he would
either have to visit the whole inhabited world to see them—
or to visit Rome; so many great ships arrive from all over
the world at every hour, at every season, that Rome is like some
common factory of the world, for you may see such great
cargoes from the Indies, or, if you wish, from the blessed
Arabias, that you might well conjecture that the trees there

have been stripped naked; clothing from Babylon, ornaments from the barbarian lands, everything flows to Rome; merchandise, cargoes, the products of the land, the emptying of the mines, the product of every art that is and has been, everything that is begotten and everything that grows. If there is anything you cannot see at Rome, then it is a thing which does not exist and which never existed."

The money possessed and the money spent was colossal. One of Nero's freedman could regard a man with a fortune of £652,000 as a pauper. Apicius squandered a fortune of £1,000,000 in refined debauchery, and committed suicide when he had only £100,000 left because he could not live on such a pittance. In one day Caligula squandered the revenues of three provinces amounting to £100,000 and in a single year scattered broadcast in prodigal profusion £20,000,000. Nero declared that the only use of money was to squander it, and in a very few years he squandered £18,000,000. At one banquet of his the Egyptian roses alone cost £35,000.

Let the Roman historian Suetonius describe his emperors, and remember that this is not a Christian preacher but a pagan historian. Of Caligula he writes: "In reckless extravagance he outdid the prodigals of all times in ingenuity, inventing a new sort of baths and unnatural varieties of food and feasts; for he would bathe in hot or cold perfumed oils, drink pearls of great price dissolved in vinegar, and set before his guests loaves and meats of gold." He even built galleys whose sterns were studded with pearls. Of Nero Suetonius tells us that he compelled people to set before him banquets costing £20,000. "He never wore the same garment twice. He played at dice for £2,000 a point. He fished with a golden net drawn by cords woven of purple and scarlet threads. It is said that he never made a journey with less than a thousand carriages, with his mules shod with silver."

Drinking pearls dissolved in vinegar was a common ostentation. Cleopatra is said to have dissolved and drunk a pearl worth £80,000. Valerius Maximus at a feast set a pearl to drink before every guest, and he himself, Horace tells, swallowed the pearl from Metalla's ear-ring dissolved in wine that he might be able to say that he had swallowed a million sesterces at a gulp.

It was an age of extraordinary gluttony. Dishes of peacocks' brains and nightingales' tongues were set before the guests at banquets. Vitellius, who was emperor for less than a year, succeeded in spending £7,000,000 mainly on food. Suetonius tells of his favourite dish: "In this he mingled the livers of pike, the brains of pheasants and peacocks, the tongues of flamingoes, and the milk of lampreys, brought by his captains and triremes from the whole empire from Parthia to the Spanish strait." Petronius describes the scenes at Trimalchio's banquet: "One course represented the twelve signs of the zodiac. . . . Another dish was a large boar, with baskets of sweetmeats hanging from its tusks. A huge bearded hunter pierced its side with a hunting knife, and forthwith from the wound there issued a flight of thrushes which were dexterously captured in nets as they flew about the room. Towards the end of the meal the guests were startled by strange sounds in the ceiling and a quaking of the whole apartment. As they raised their eyes the ceiling suddenly opened, and a great circular tray descended, with a figure of Priapus, bearing all sorts of fruit and bon-bons."

In the time when John was writing a kind of insanity of wanton extravagance, to which it is very difficult to find any parallel in history, had invaded Rome.

## THE LAMENT OF THE MERCHANTS (1)

*Revelation* 18: 11–16

And the merchants of the earth will weep and lament over her, for no one buys their cargo any more, the cargo of gold and of silver and of precious stones and of pearls, of fine linen and of purple and of silk and of scarlet, all kinds of thyine wood, all kinds of articles of ivory, all kinds of articles of costly wood, and of bronze and of iron and of marble, and cinnamon and perfume and incense, and myrrh, and frankincense and wine and oil, and fine flour, and wheat and cattle and sheep, horses and chariots and slaves, the souls of men.

The ripe fruit your soul desired has gone from you, and all your delicacies and your splendours have perished, never again to be found. The merchants who dealt in these wares, who grew wealthy from their trade with her, shall stand afar off because of the fear of her torture, weeping and grieving. "Alas! Alas!" they shall say, "for the great city, for the city which was clothed in fine linen and purple and scarlet, the city which was decked with gold and with precious stones and with pearls, for in one hour so much wealth is desolated!"

THE lament of the kings and the merchants should be read along with the lament over Tyre in *Ezekiel* 26 and 27 for they have many features in common.

The lament of the merchants is purely selfish. All their sorrow is that the market from which they drew so much wealth is gone. It is significant that both the kings and the merchants stand afar off and watch. They stretch out no hand to help Rome in her last agony; they were never bound to her in love; their only bond was the luxury she desired and the trade it brought to them.

We will learn still more of the luxury of Rome, if we look in detail at some of the items in the cargoes which came to Rome.

At the time during which John was writing there was in Rome a passion for silver dishes. Silver came mainly from Carthagena in Spain, where 40,000 men toiled in the silver mines. Dishes, bowls, jugs, fruitbaskets, statuettes, whole dinner services, were made of solid silver. Lucius Crassus had wrought silver dishes which had cost £50 for each pound of silver in them. Even a fighting general like Pompeius Paullinus carried with him on his campaigns wrought silver dishes which weighed 12,000 pounds, the greater part of which fell into the hands of the Germans, spoils of war. Pliny tells us that women would bathe only in silver baths, soldiers had swords with silver hilts and scabbards with silver chains, even poor women had silver anklets and the very slaves had silver mirrors. At the Saturnalia, the festival which fell at the same time as the Christian Christmas, and at which gifts were given, often the gifts were little silver spoons and the like, and the wealthier the giver the more ostentatious was the gift. Rome was a city of silver.

It was an age which passionately loved precious stones and pearls. It was largely through the conquests of Alexander the Great that precious stones came to the west. Pliny said that the fascination of a gem was that the majestic might of nature presented itself in a limited space.

The order of preference in stones set diamonds first, emeralds—mainly from Scythia—second, beryls and opals, which were used for women's ornaments, third, and the sardonyx, which was used for seal-rings, fourth.

One of the strangest of ancient beliefs was that precious stones had medicinal qualities. The amethyst was said to be a cure for drunkenness; it is wine-red in colour and the word *amethyst* was derived—so it was said— from *a* which means *not* and *methuskein* which means to make drunk. The jasper, or bloodstone, was held to be a cure for haemorrhage. The green jasper was said to bring fertility. The diamond was held to neutralise poison and to cure delirium, and amber worn on the neck was a cure for fever and for other troubles.

Of all stones the Romans loved pearls more than any other. As we have seen, they were drunk dissolved in wine. A certain Struma Nonius had a ring with an opal in it as big as a filbert worth £21,250, but that pales into insignificance compared with the pearl which Julius Caesar gave Servilia and which cost £65,250. Pliny tells of seeing Lollia Paulina, one of Caligula's wives, at a betrothal feast, wearing an ornament of emeralds and pearls, covering head, hair, ears, neck and fingers, which was worth £425,000.

## THE LAMENT OF THE MERCHANTS (2)

*Revelation* 18: 11–16 (*continued*)

FINE linen came mainly from Egypt. It was the clothing of priests and kings. It was very expensive; a priest's robe, for instance, would cost between £40 and £50.

Purple came mainly from Phoenicia. The very word Phoenicia is probably derived from *phoinos,* which means *blood-red*, and the Phoenicians may have been known as "the purple men," because they dealt in purple. Ancient purple was much redder than modern purple. It was the royal colour and the garment of wealth. The purple dye came from a shellfish called *murex*. Only one drop came from each animal; and the shell had to be opened as soon as the shellfish died, for the purple came from a little vein which dried up almost immediately after death. A pound of double-dyed purple wool cost almost £50, and a short purple coat more than £100. Pliny tells us that at this time there was in Rome "a frantic passion for purple."

Silk may now be a commonplace, but in the Rome of the *Revelation* it was almost beyond price, for it had to be imported from far-off China. So costly was it that a pound of silk was sold for a pound weight of gold. Under Tiberius a law was passed against the use of solid gold vessels for the serving of meals and "against men disgracing themselves with silken garments" (Tacitus: *Annals* 2: 23).

Scarlet, like purple, was a much sought after dye. When we are thinking of these fabrics we may note that another of Rome's ostentatious furnishings was Babylonian coverlets for banqueting couches. Such coverlets often cost as much as £7,000, and Nero possessed coverlets for his couches which had cost more than £43,000 each.

The most interesting of the woods mentioned in this passage is thyine. In Latin it was called citrus wood; its botanical name is *thuia articulata*. Coming from North Africa, from the Atlas region, it was sweet-smelling and beautifully grained.

It was used especially for table tops. But, since the citrus tree is seldom very large, trees large enough to provide table tops were very scarce. Tables made of thyine wood could cost anything from £4,000 to £15,000. Seneca, Nero's prime minister, was said to have three hundred of such thyine tables with marble legs.

Ivory was much used for decorative purposes, especially by those who wished to make an ostentatious display. It was used in sculpture, for statues, for swordhilts, for inlaying furniture, for ceremonial chairs, for doors, and even for household furniture. Juvenal talks of the wealthy man: "Nowadays a rich man takes no pleasure in his dinner—his turbot and his venison have no taste, his unguents and his roses seem to smell rotten—unless the broad slabs of his dinner table rest upon a ramping, gaping leopard of solid ivory."

Statuettes of Corinthian brass or bronze were world famous and fabulously expensive. Iron came from the Black Sea and from Spain. For long marble had been used in Babylon for building, but not in Rome. Augustus, however, could boast he had found Rome of brick and left it of marble. In the end there was actually an office called the *ratio marmorum* whose task was to search the world for fine marbles with which to decorate the buildings of Rome.

Cinnamon was a luxury article coming from India and from near Zanzibar, and in Rome it commanded a price of about £65 per pound.

*Spice* is here misleading. The Greek is *amōmon*; Wyclif translated simply *amome*. *Amōmon* was a sweet-smelling balsam, particularly used as a dressing for the hair and as an oil for funeral rites.

In the Old Testament incense had altogether a religious use as an accompaniment of sacrifice in the Temple. According to *Exodus* 30: 34–38 the Temple incense was made of stacte, onycha, galbanum, and frankincense, which are all perfumed gums or balsams. According to the *Talmud* seven further ingredients were added—myrrh, cassia, spikenard, saffron, costus, mace and cinnamon. In Rome incense was used as a perfume with which to greet guests and to scent the room after meals.

In the ancient world wine was universally drunk, but drunkenness was regarded as a grave disgrace. Wine was usually highly diluted, in the proportion of two parts of wine to five parts of water. The grapes were pressed and the juice extracted. Some of it was used just as it was as an unfermented drink. Some of it was boiled to a jelly, and the jelly used to give body and flavour to poor wines. The rest was poured into great jars, which were left to ferment for nine days, then closed, and opened monthly to check the progress of the wine. Even slaves had abundant wine as part of their daily ration, since it was no more than 2½p a gallon.

Myrrh was the gum resin of a shrub which grew mainly in Yemen and in North Africa. It was medically used as an astringent, a stimulant, and an antiseptic. It was also used as a perfume and as an anodyne by women in the time of their purification, and for the embalming of bodies.

Frankincense was a gum resin produced by a tree of the *genus Boswellia*. An incision was made in the tree and a strip of bark removed from below it. The resin then exuded from the tree like milk. In about ten or twelve weeks it coagulated into lumps in which it was sold. It was used for perfume for the body, for the sweetening and flavouring of wine, for oil for lamps and for sacrificial incense.

The chariots here mentioned—the word is *redē*—were not racing or military chariots. They were four-wheeled private chariots, and the aristocrats of Roman wealth often had them silver-plated.

The list closes with the mention of slaves and the souls of men. The word used for *slave* is *sōma,* which literally means a *body*. The slave market was called the *sōmatemporos,* literally *the place where bodies are sold*. The idea is that the slave was sold body and soul into the possession of his master.

It is almost impossible for us to understand how much Roman

civilization was based on slavery. There were some 60,000,000 slaves in the empire. It was no unusual thing for a man to have four hundred slaves. "Use your slaves like the limbs of your body," says a Roman writer, "each for its own end." There were, of course, slaves to do the menial work; and each particular service had its slave. We read of torch-bearers, lantern-bearers, sedan-chair carriers, street attendants, keepers of the outdoor garments. There were slaves who were secretaries, slaves to read aloud, and even slaves to do the necessary research for a man writing a book or a treatise. The slaves even did a man's thinking for him. There were slaves called *nomenclatores* whose duty it was to remind a man of the names of his clients and dependants! "We remember by means of others," says a Roman writer. There were even slaves to remind a man to eat and to go to bed! "Men were too weary even to know that they were hungry." There were slaves to go in front of their master and to return the greetings of friends, which the master was too tired or too disdainful to return himself. A certain ignorant man, unable to learn or remember anything, got himself a set of slaves. One memorized Homer, one Hesiod, others the lyric poets. Their duty was to stand behind him as he dined and to prompt him with suitable quotations. He paid £1,000 for each of them. Some slaves were beautiful youths, "the flower of Asia," who simply stood around the room at banquets to delight the eye. Some were cup-bearers. Some were Alexandrians, who were trained in pert and often obscene repartee. The guests often chose to wipe their soiled hands on the hair of the slaves. Such beautiful boy slaves cost at least £1,000 or £2,000. Some slaves were freaks—dwarfs, giants, cretins, hermaphrodites. There was actually a market in freaks— "men without shanks, with short arms, with three eyes, with pointed heads." Sometimes dwarfs were artificially produced for sale.

It is a grim picture of men being used body and soul for the service and entertainment of others.

This was the world for which the merchants were grieving,

the lost markets and the lost money which they were bewailing. This was the Rome whose end John was threatening. And he was right—for a society built on luxury, on wantonness, on pride, on callousness to human life and personality is necessarily doomed, even from the human point of view.

## THE LAMENT OF THE SHIPMASTERS

*Revelation* 18: 17–19

> And every shipmaster and everyone who sails the sea, and sailors who gain their living from the sea, stood afar off and cried, when they saw the smoke of her burning. "What city was like the great city!" they said, and they flung dust upon their heads, and cried weeping and lamenting: "Alas! Alas! for the great city, in which all who had ships on the sea grew rich from her wealth, because in one hour she has been desolated."

FIRST, the kings uttered their lament over Rome; then, the merchants; and now, the shipmasters. John was taking his picture from Ezekiel's picture of the fall of Tyre, from which so much of this chapter comes. "At the sound of the cry of your pilots the countryside shakes, and down from their ships come all that handle the oar. The mariners and all the pilots of the sea stand on the shore and wail aloud over you, and cry bitterly. They cast dust on their heads and wallow in ashes." (*Ezekiel* 27: 28–30).

Rome, of course, was not upon the sea coast, but its port was Ostia, and, as we have seen, the merchandise of the world flowed into the port of Rome.

It is little wonder that the shipmasters and the sailors will lament, for all the trade which brought so much wealth will be gone.

There is something almost pathetic in these laments. In every case the lament is not for Rome but for themselves. It is one of the laws of life that, if a man places all his happiness in material things, he misses the greatest things of all—love and friendship with his fellowmen.

## JOY AMIDST LAMENTING

*Revelation* 18 : 20

> Rejoice over her, O Heaven, and you dedicated ones of God, and you apostles, and you prophets, because God has given judgment for you against her.

AMIDST all the lamenting comes the voice of joy, the voice of those who are glad to see the vengeance of God upon his enemies and their persecutors.

This is a note which we find more than once in Scripture. "Praise his people, O you nations; for he avenges the blood of his servants, and takes vengeance on his adversaries, and makes expiation for the land of his people" (*Deuteronomy* 32 : 43). Jeremiah says of the doom of ancient Babylon; "Then the heaven and the earth, and all that is in them, shall sing for joy over Babylon; for the destroyers shall come against them out of the north, says the Lord" (*Jeremiah* 51 : 48).

We are here very far from praying for those who despitefully use us. But two things have to be remembered. However we may feel about this voice of vengeance, it is none the less the voice of faith. These men had utter confidence that no man on God's side could ultimately be on the losing side.

Second, there is little personal bitterness here. The people to be destroyed are not so much personal enemies as the enemies of God.

At the same time this is not the more excellent way which Jesus taught. When Abraham Lincoln was told that he was too lenient with his opponents and that his duty was to destroy his enemies, he answered: "Do I not destroy my enemies when I make them my friends?" The real Christian attitude is to seek to destroy enmity, not by force, but by the power of that love which won the victory of the Cross.

## THE FINAL DESOLATION

*Revelation* 18: 21–24

And a strong angel lifted a stone like a great mill-stone, and cast
it into the sea. "Thus," he said, "with a rush Babylon the great
city will be cast down, and will never again be found. The sound
of harpers and minstrels and flute-players and trumpeters will never
again be heard in you. No craftsman of any craft will ever again
be found in you. No more will the sound of the mill be heard in
you. No more will the light of the lamp shine in you. No more
will the voice of the bridegroom and the bride be heard in you; for
your merchants were the great ones of the earth, and because all
nations were lead astray by your sorcery, and because in her
was found the blood of the prophets and of God's dedicated ones
and of all who have been slain upon the earth."

THE picture is of the final desolation of Rome.

It begins with a symbolic action. A strong angel takes a
great millstone and hurls it into the sea which closes over it as
if it had never been. So will Rome be obliterated. John was
taking his picture from the destruction of ancient Babylon.
The word of God came to Jeremiah: "When you finish
reading this book, bind a stone to it, and cast it into the midst
of the Euphrates: and say, Thus shall Babylon sink, to rise no
more, because of the evil that I am bringing upon her"
(*Jeremiah* 51: 63, 64). In later days Strabo, the Greek
geographer, was to say that ancient Babylon was so completely
obliterated that no one would ever have dared to say that the
desert where she stood was once a great city.

Never again will there be any sound of rejoicing. The
doom of Ezekiel against Tyre reads: "And I will stop the music
of your songs, and the sound of your lyres shall be heard no
more" (*Ezekiel* 26: 13). The harpers and the minstrels played
and sang on joyous occasions; the flute was used at festivals
and at funerals; the trumpet sounded at the games and at the
concerts; but now all music was to be silenced.

Never again will there be the sound of a craftsman plying
his trade.

Never again will the sound of domestic activity be heard. Grinding was done by the women at home with two great circular stones one on the top of the other. The corn was put into a hole in the uppermost stone; it was ground between the two stones and emerged through the lower stone. The creak of stone on stone, which could be heard any day at any house door, will never again be heard.

Never again will there be light on the streets or in the houses.

Never again will there be any sound of wedding rejoicing for even love will die. Jeremiah uses the same pictures: "I will banish from them the voice of mirth, and the voice of gladness, the voice of the bridegroom, and the voice of the bride, the grinding of the millstones, and the light of the lamp" (*Jeremiah* 25: 10; cp. 7: 34; 16: 9).

Rome is to become a terrible silent desolation.

And this punishment will come for certain definite reasons.

It will come because she worshipped wealth and luxury and lived wantonly, and found no pleasure except in material things.

It will come because she led men astray with her sorceries. Nahum called Nineveh "graceful and of deadly charms" (*Nahum* 3: 14). Rome flirted with the evil powers to make an evil world.

It will come because she was blood guilty. "Woe to the bloody city!" said Ezekiel of Tyre (*Ezekiel* 24: 6). Within Rome the martyrs perished and persecution went out from her all over the earth.

BEFORE we begin to study the last four chapters of the *Revelation* in detail, it will be well to set out their general programme of events.

They begin with a universal rejoicing at the destruction of Babylon, the power of Rome (19: 1–10). There follows a description of the emergence of a white horse and on it him who is Faithful and True (19: 11–18). Next comes the assembling of hostile powers against the conquering Christ

(19: 19); then the defeat of the opposing forces, the casting of the beast and of the false prophet into the lake of fire, and the slaughter of the rest (19: 20, 21).

Chapter 20 opens with the binding of the devil in the abyss for a period of a thousand years (20: 1–3). There follows the resurrection of the martyrs to reign with Christ for a thousand years, although the rest of the dead are not yet resurrected (20: 4–6). At the end of the thousand years Satan is again loosed for a brief space; there is final conflict with the enemies of Christ who are destroyed with fire from heaven while Satan is cast for ever into the lake of fire and brimstone (20: 7–10). Then comes the general resurrection and the general judgment (20: 11–14); and finally the description of the new heaven and the new earth to take the place of the things which have passed away (21: 1–22; 5).

## THE TE DEUM OF THE ANGELS

*Revelation* 19: 1, 2

> After these things I heard what sounded like a great voice of a vast multitude in heaven. "Hallelujah!" they were saying. "Salvation and glory and power belong to our God, because his judgments are true and just, for he judged the great harlot who corrupted the earth with her fornication, and has avenged upon her the blood of his servants."

IN the description of the total destruction of Babylon, come the words: "Rejoice over her, O heaven, O saints and apostles and prophets, for God has given judgment for you against her!" (18: 20). Here now is the rejoicing which was called for.

It begins with the shout of a vast multitude in heaven. We have already come upon two vast multitudes in heaven, the martyrs in 7: 9 and the angels in 5: 11. Here is most likely the multitude of the angels, first in the *Te Deum* of praise.

This shout of rejoicing begins with *Hallelujah*. *Hallelujah* is a very common word in religious vocabulary but the only time it actually appears in Scripture is on the four occasions in this chapter. Like *Hosanna* it is one of the few Hebrew words which have established themselves in ordinary religious language. It probably came to be so well known to even the simplest member of the Church through its special use as a response of praise in the Easter worship.

*Hallelujah* literally means *Praise God*. It is derived from *halal,* which means *to praise,* and *Jah,* which is the name of God. Although Hallelujah appears only here in the Bible, it occurs in a translated form frequently. It is actually the first phrase in Psalms 106, 111, 112, 113, 117, 135, 146, 147, 148, 149, 150. The series of Psalms from 113–118 were called the *Hallel,* the *Praise God,* and were part of the essential education of every Jewish lad. Where *Hallelujah* occurs in the Old Testament it is translated by *Praise God,* but here in this chapter the original Hebrew form, transliterated into Greek, is retained.

God is praised because *salvation, glory* and *power* belong to him. Each of these three great attributes of God should awaken its own response in the heart of man. The *salvation* of God should awaken the *gratitude* of man; the *glory* of God should awaken the *reverence* of man; the *power* of God is always exercised in the love of God and should, therefore, awaken the *trust* of man. Gratitude, reverence, trust—these are the constituent elements of real praise.

God is praised because he has exercised his just and true judgment on the great harlot. Judgment is the inescapable consequence of sin. T. S. Kepler comments: "The moral law can no more be broken than the law of gravity; it can only be illustrated." It is said that the judgments of God are *true* and *just*. God alone is perfect in judgment for three reasons. First, he alone can see the inmost thoughts and desires of any man. Second, he alone has that purity which can judge without prejudice. Third, he alone has the wisdom to find the right judgment and the power to apply it.

The great harlot is judged because she corrupted the world. The worst of all sins is to teach others to sin.

All forbidden things we've sought,
All the mischief we have wrought,
*All the sin to others taught,*
    Forgive, O Lord, for Jesus' sake.

There is one other reason for the rejoicing. The judgment on Rome is the guarantee that God never in the end abandons his own.

## THE TE DEUM OF NATURE AND THE CHURCH

*Revelation* 19: 3–5

And a second time they said: "Hallelujah! for the smoke from her rises for ever and ever."
    And the twenty-four elders, and the four living creatures fell down and worshipped the God who is seated upon the throne. "Amen," they said, "Hallelujah!" And a voice came forth from the throne. "Praise our God," it said, "all you his servants, you who fear him, small and great."

THE angelic host sings a second Hallelujah. Their praise is that the smoke of Babylon rises for ever and ever. That is to say, never again will she rise from her ruins. The actual picture comes from Isaiah: "The streams of Edom shall be turned into pitch, and her soil into brimstone; her land shall become burning pitch. Night and day it shall not be quenched; its smoke shall go up for ever and ever. From generation to generation it shall lie waste; none shall pass through it for ever and ever" (*Isaiah* 34: 9, 10).

There follows praise from the twenty-four elders and the four living creatures. The twenty-four elders were prominent in the early visions (4: 4, 10; 5: 6, 11, 14; 7: 11; 11: 16; 14: 3) as were the four living creatures (4: 6–9; 5: 6–14; 6: 1–7; 7: 11; 14: 3; 15: 7). We saw that the twenty-four elders represent the twelve patriarchs and the twelve apostles, and, therefore, stand for the totality of the Church. The four living creatures, respectively like a lion, an ox, a man and an eagle, stand for two things, for all that is bravest, strongest, wisest and swiftest in nature—and for the cherubim. Hence a song of praise from the twenty-four elders and the four living creatures is a *Te Deum* from the whole of the Church and the whole of nature.

The voice that comes from the throne is most likely to be understood as the voice of one of the cherubim. "Praise our God," says the voice, "all you his servants, you who fear him." Once again John finds his model in the words of the Old Testament, for that is a quotation from *Psalm* 135: 1, 20.

Two sets of people are called on to praise God. First, there are his *servants*. In the *Revelation* two kinds of people are specially called *the servants of God;* the *prophets* (10: 7; 11: 18; 22: 6), and the *martyrs* (7: 3; 19: 2). First, then, this is the praise of the prophets and the martyrs who have witnessed for God with their voices and with their lives. Second, there are the *small and the great*. H. B. Swete says that this comprehensive phrase embraces "Christians of all intellectual capacities and social grades, and of all stages of progress in the life of Christ." It is a universal summons to praise God for his mighty acts.

## THE TE DEUM OF THE REDEEMED

*Revelation* 19: 6–8

And I heard a voice which sounded like the voice of a vast multitude, and like the sound of many waters, and like the sound of might crashes of thunder.

"Hallelujah!" they said, "because the Lord our God, the Almighty, has entered into his kingdom. Let us rejoice and let us exult, and let us give him the glory, for the marriage of the Lamb has come, and his Bride has prepared herself, and it has been granted to her to clothe herself with fine linen, shining and pure." For the fine linen is the righteous deeds of God's dedicated people.

THE final shout is the praise of the host of the redeemed. John goes out of his way to heap up similes to describe its sound. It was, as H. B. Swete puts it, like "the din of a vast concourse, the roar of a cataract, the roll of thunder."

Once again John finds his inspiration in the words of Scripture. In his mind are two things. First, he is remembering *Psalm* 97: 1: "The Lord reigns; let the earth rejoice." Second, he says: "Let us rejoice and exult." There is only one other place in the New Testament where these two verbs (*chairein* and *agallian*) come together—in Jesus Christ's promise to the persecuted: "*Rejoice* and *be glad*, for your reward is great in heaven" (*Matthew* 5: 12). It is as if the multitude of the redeemed sent up their shout of praise because the promise of Christ to his persecuted ones had come abundantly true.

Next comes the marriage of the Lamb to his bride. That picture stands for the final union between Jesus Christ and his Church. R. H. Charles finely says that the marriage symbolism "denotes the intimate and indissoluble communion of Christ with the community which he has purchased with his own blood" a communion which is "first reached in fulness by the host of the martyrs."

The thought of the relationship between God and his people as a marriage goes far back into the Old Testament. Again and again the prophets thought of Israel as the chosen bride of God. "I will betroth you to me for ever," Hosea hears God say, "I will betroth you to me in righteousness" (*Hosea* 2: 19, 20). "Your Maker is your husband; the Lord of hosts is his name," says Isaiah (*Isaiah* 54: 5). Jeremiah hears God say and appeal: "Return, O faithless children, for I am your master" (*Jeremiah* 3: 14). Ezekiel works out the whole picture most fully in chapter 16.

The marriage symbolism runs all through the Gospels. We read of the marriage feast (*Matthew* 22: 2); of the bridechamber and the wedding garment (*Matthew* 22: 10, 11); of the sons of the bridechamber (*Mark* 2: 19); of the bridegroom (*Mark* 2: 19; *Matthew* 25: 1); of the friends of the bridegroom (*John* 3: 29). And Paul speaks of himself as betrothing the Church like a pure virgin to Christ (2 *Corinthians* 11: 2), and for him the relationship of Christ to his Church is the great model of the relationship of husband and wife (*Ephesians* 5: 21–33).

This may seem to us a strange metaphor. But it conserves certain great truths. In any real marriage there must be four things which must also be in the relationship between the Christian and Christ.

(i) There is *love*. A loveless marriage is a contradiction in terms.

(ii) There is *intimate communion*, so intimate that man and wife become one flesh. The relationship of the Christian and Christ must be the closest in all life.

(iii) There is *joy*. There is nothing like the joy of loving and of being loved. If Christianity does not bring joy, it does not bring anything.

(iv) There is *fidelity*. No marriage can last without fidelity, and the Christian must be as faithful to Jesus Christ as Jesus Christ is to him.

## THE ALMIGHTY AND HIS KINGDOM

*Revelation* 19: 6–8 (*continued*)

THIS passage calls God by a certain name; and says that he has entered into his kingdom.

It calls God the *Almighty*. The word is *pantokratōr*, literally the one who controls all things. The significant thing about this great word is that it occurs ten times in the New Testament. Once it is in an Old Testament quotation in 2 *Corinthians* 6: 18; the other nine times are all in the *Revelation* (1: 8; 4: 8; 11: 17; 15: 3; 16: 7, 14; 19: 6, 15; 21: 22). In other words, this is the characteristic title for God in the *Revelation*.

There was never a time in history in which such forces were

drawn up against the Church as when the *Revelation* was written. There was never a time when the Christian was called upon to undergo such suffering and to accept so continually the prospect of a cruel death. And yet in such times John calls God *pantokratōr*.

Here is faith and confidence; and the whole point of this passage is that that faith and confidence are vindicated.

The Church, the Bride of Christ, is clothed in fine linen, pure and shining. There is a contrast with the scarlet and gold of the great harlot. The white linen represents the good deeds of God's dedicated people; that is to say, it is character which forms the robe which arrays the Bride of Christ.

## THE ONLY WORSHIP

*Revelation* 19: 9, 10a

And he said to me: "Write! Blessed are those who are invited to the feast of the marriage of the Lamb!" And he said to me: "These are the true words of God." And I fell down before his feet to worship him; and he said to me: "See that you do not do this. I am your fellow-servant and the fellow-servant of your brothers who possess the testimony which Jesus gave. Worship God!"

THE Jews had the idea that, when the Messiah came, God's people would, as it were, be entertained by God to a great Messianic Banquet. Isaiah speaks of God preparing for his people "a feast of fat things, a feast of wine on the lees, of fat things full of marrow, of wine on the lees well refined" (*Isaiah* 25: 6). Jesus speaks of many coming from the east and the west and sitting down with the patriarchs in the kingdom of heaven (*Matthew* 8: 11). The word used for *sitting down* is the word for reclining at a meal. The picture is of all men sitting down at the Messianic Banquet of God. Jesus at the Last Supper said that he would not again drink of the cup until he drank it new in his Father's kingdom (*Matthew* 26: 29). That was Jesus looking forward to the great Messianic Banquet.

It may well be from that old Jewish idea that there came the idea of the marriage feast of the Lamb, for that indeed would be the true Messianic Banquet. It is a simple picture, not to be taken with crude literalness, but simply saying very beautifully that in his kingdom all men will enjoy the bounty of God.

But this passage confronts us with something which became of very great importance in the worship of the Church. It was John's instinct to worship the angelic messenger; but the angel forbids him to do that, because the angels are no more than men's fellow-servants. Worship is for God alone. John was forbidding angel worship; and that was a very necessary prohibition, for in the early church there was a well-nigh inevitable tendency to worship angels, a tendency which has never wholly disappeared.

(i) In certain circles of Judaism the angels had a very large place. Raphael tells Tobit that he is the angel who brought his prayer before God (*Tobit* 13: 12–15). In the *Testament of Dan* (6: 2) the angel who intercedes for men is mentioned. In the *Testament of Levi* (5: 5) Michael is said to be the angel who intercedes for Israel. A fourth century A.D. Rabbi, Jehudah, actually gave the odd instruction that men ought not to pray in Aramaic because the angels did not understand Aramaic! The prevalence of all this in Judaism is underlined by the fact that certain Rabbis insisted that prayers must always be offered direct to God, and not to Michael or to Gabriel.

In Judaism there was increasingly stressed the transcendence of God, because of that it was increasingly felt that man needed some intermediary. Hence arose the prominence of angels.

When Jews came over into Christianity, sometimes they brought this special reverence for the angels with them, forgetting that with the coming of Jesus no other intermediary between God and man can be necessary.

(ii) A Greek came into the Church from a world of thought which made angel worship a real danger. First, he came from a world in which there were many gods—Zeus, Hera, Apollo, Aphrodite and the rest. What was easier than to keep the old gods in the form of angels? Second, he came from a world in which it was believed that God did not interest himself directly but made his contact through the *daimons*, by means of whom he controlled the natural forces and acted upon men. What was easier than to turn the *daimons* into angels and to worship them?

John insists that angels are no more than the servants of God; and that God alone must be worshipped. Any other intermediary than Jesus Christ between God and man must be utterly opposed.

## THE SPIRIT OF PROPHECY

*Revelation* 19: 10b

The testimony of Jesus is the spirit of prophecy.

WE take this phrase by itself, because it is both ambiguous and important.

The ambiguity springs from the fact that the testimony of Jesus can bear either of two meanings.

(i) It can mean *the witness which the Christian bears to Jesus Christ*. That is the way in which H. B. Swete takes it. He says: "The possession of the prophetic spirit, which makes a true prophet, shows itself in a life of witness to Jesus, which perpetuates his witness to the Father and to himself." A prophet's message lies in the personal witness of his life, even more than in the spoken witness of his words.

(ii) It can equally mean *the witness which Jesus Christ gives to men*. On that interpretation the phrase will mean that no man can speak to men until he has listened to Jesus Christ. It was said of a great preacher: "First he listened to God, then he spoke to men."

This is the kind of double meaning of which the Greek language is capable. It may well be that John *intended* the double meaning; and that we are meant not to choose between the meanings, but to accept both of them. If so, we can define the true prophet as the man who has received from Christ the message he brings to men, and whose words and works are at one and the same time an act of witness to Christ.

## THE CONQUERING CHRIST

*Revelation* 19: 11

And I saw heaven opened, and, behold, a white horse, and he who is mounted on it is called Faithful and True, and in righteousness he judges and makes war.

HERE is one of the most dramatic moments in the *Revelation*, the emergence of the conquering Christ.

(i) John sees Christ as the conqueror. He is, as H. B. Swete puts it, "a royal commander followed by a dazzling retinue." Here is a picture which is essentially Jewish. Jewish dreams were full of the warrior Messiah, who would lead God's people to victory and smash his enemies. In the *Psalms of Solomon* we have that picture:

Behold, O Lord, and raise up unto them their king the Son of David,
At the time in which thou seest, O God, that he may reign over Israel, Thy servant.
And gird him with strength that he may shatter unrighteous rulers,
And that he may purge Jerusalem from nations that trample her down to destruction.
Wisely, righteously, he shall thrust out sinners from the inheritance,
He shall destroy the pride of the sinner as a potter's vessel,
With a rod of iron he shall break in pieces all their substance,
He shall destroy the godless nations with the word of his mouth;
At his rebuke nations shall flee before him,
And he shall reprove sinners for the thoughts of their hearts
(*Psalms of Solomon* 17: 23–27).

There is a Rabbinic picture of the Messiah: "How beauteous is the king Messiah, who is about to rise from the house of Judah. He hath bound his loins and gone forth to war against those who hate him; kings and princes shall be slain; he will make red the rivers with the blood of the slain . . . his garments will be dipped in blood."

The white horse is the symbol of the conqueror, because it was on a white horse that a Roman general rode when he celebrated a triumph.

It is well to remember that the whole background of this picture lies in Jewish expectations of the future and has little to do with the Christ of the Gospels who was meek and lowly in heart.

(ii) His name is *Faithful* and *True*. Here, on the other hand, is something which is valid for all time. Christ is described by two words.

(*a*) He is *faithful*. The word is *pistos*; it means absolutely to be trusted.

(*b*) He is *true*. The word is *alēthinos* and has two meanings. It means *true* in the sense that Jesus Christ is the one who brings the truth and who never at any time has any falsehood in anything that he says. It also means *genuine*, as opposed to that which is unreal. In Jesus Christ we meet *reality*.

(iii) He judges and makes war in righteousness. Again John finds his picture in the prophetic words of the Old Testament, where it is said of the chosen king of God: "With righteousness he shall judge the poor" (*Isaiah* 11: 4). John's age knew all about the perversion of justice; no one could expect justice from a capricious heathen tyrant. In Asia Minor even the tribunal of the proconsul was subject to bribery and to maladministration. Wars were matters of ambition and tyranny and oppression rather than of justice. But when the conquering Christ comes, his power will be exercised in justice.

## THE UNKNOWABLE NAME

*Revelation* 19: 12

> His eyes are a flame of fire, and on his head are many
> royal crowns, and he has a name written which no one knows
> except himself.

WE begin the description of the conquering Christ.

His eyes are a flame of fire. We have already met this
description in 1: 14 and 2: 18. It stands for the consuming
power of the victorious Christ. On his head he has many
crowns. The word used here for *crown* is *diadēma*, which is
the *royal crown*, as opposed to *stephanos* which is the *crown of
victory*. To be crowned with more than one crown may seem
strange, but in the time of John it was quite natural. It was
not uncommon for a monarch to wear more than one crown
in order to show that he was the king of more than one
country. For instance, when Ptolemy entered Antioch he wore
two crowns or diadems—one to show that he was lord of
Asia and one to show that he was lord of Egypt
(1 *Maccabees* 11: 13). On the head of the victor Christ there
are many crowns to show that he is lord of all the kingdoms
of the earth.

He has a name known to no one but himself. This is a
passage whose meaning is obscure. What is this name?
Many suggestions have been made.

(i) It has been suggested that the name is *kurios*, Lord.
In *Philippians* 2: 9–11 we read of the name above every name
which God has given to Jesus Christ because of his complete
obedience; and there the name is almost certainly *Lord*.

(ii) It is suggested that the name is IHWH. That was the
Jewish name for God. In Hebrew writing there were no
vowels; the I was a Y rather than an I in pronunciation;
the vowels had to be supplied by the reader. No one really
knows what the vowels in IHWH were. The name was in
fact so holy that it was never pronounced. We usually
pronounce it JEHOVAH; but the vowels in Jehovah are

really those of the Hebrew word *Adonai,* which means *Lord,* the name by which the Jews called God in order to avoid pronouncing the sacred name. Many scholars think the name should be IAHWEH. The letters IHWH are called the sacred tetragrammaton, the sacred four letters.

(iii) It may be that the name is one which can be revealed only at the final union of Christ and the Church. In the *Ascension of Isaiah* (9: 5) there is a saying: "Thou canst not bear his name until thou shalt have ascended out of the body." There was a Jewish belief that no man could know the name of God until he had entered into the life of heaven.

(iv) It may be that here is a lingering relic of the old idea that to know the name of a divine being was to have a certain power over him. In two Old Testament stories, the wrestling of Jacob at Peniel (*Genesis* 32: 29), and the appearance of the angelic messenger to Gideon (*Judges* 13: 18) the divine visitor refuses to tell his name.

(v) It may be that we shall never know the symbolism of the unknown name but H. B. Swete has the very fine idea that in the essence of the being of Christ there must always remain something beyond man's understanding. "Notwithstanding the dogmatic helps which the Church offers, the mind fails to grasp the inmost significance of the Person of Christ, which eludes all efforts to bring it within the terms of human knowledge. Only the Son of God can understand the mystery of his own being."

## GOD'S WORD IN ACTION

*Revelation* 19: 13

> He is clothed in a robe dipped in blood, and the name by which he is called is the Word of God.

HERE are two further pictures of the warrior Christ.

(i) He is clothed in a robe dipped in blood, not his own but that of his enemies. As R. H. Charles puts it, it is essential to remember that the Heavenly Leader is this time, not the Slain One, but the Slayer. As usual John takes his picture from the Old Testament and is thinking of the terrible picture in *Isaiah* 63: 1–3, where the prophet pictures God returning from the destruction of Edom; "I trod them in my anger, and trampled them in my wrath; their life blood is sprinkled upon my garments, and I have stained all my raiment." This is the Messiah of Jewish apocalyptic expectation far more than the Messiah whom Jesus claimed to be.

(ii) His name is the Word of God. Although the words are the same as in the first chapter of the Fourth Gospel, the meaning is quite different and much simpler. Here we have the purely Jewish idea of the Word of God. To a Jew a word was not merely a sound; it did things. As Dr. John Paterson puts it in *The Book that is Alive*: "The spoken word in Hebrew was fearfully alive. It was not merely a vocable or sound dropped heedlessly from unthinking lips. It was *a unit of energy charged with power*. It is energised for weal or for woe." We can see that, for instance, in the old story in which Jacob filched Esau's blessing from Isaac (*Genesis* 27). The blessing given could not be taken back.

If that is so of human words, how much truer it is of the divine word. It is by his word that God created the earth and the heavens and everything in them. *And God said* is the recurring phrase in the narrative of creation (*Genesis* 1: 3, 6, 9, 14, 26). The word of God, said Jeremiah, is like a hammer that breaks the rock in pieces (*Jeremiah* 23: 29).

In *Wisdom* there is a description of the plagues in Egypt, and in particular of the slaying of the first-born sons of the Egyptians: "Thine Almighty Word leaped down from heaven out of thy royal throne, as a fierce man of war, into the midst of a land of destruction, and brought thine unfeigned commandment as a sharp sword, and standing up filled all things with death; and it touched the heaven, but it stood upon the earth" (*The Wisdom of Solomon* 18: 15, 16). It is the active word which carried out the commandment of God.

Here is the idea in *Hebrews* 4: 12: "The word of God is living and active, sharper than any two-edged sword."

When John here called the warrior Christ The Word of God, he means that here in action is all the power of God's word; everything that God has said, and threatened, and promised is embodied in Christ.

## THE AVENGING WRATH

*Revelation* 19: 14–16

The armies which are in heaven followed him, on white horses, clothed in fine linen, white and pure.

From his mouth there comes forth a sharp two-edged sword, so that with it he may smite the nations, and he will control them with an iron rod. He will tread the winepress of the anger of the wrath of God the Almighty.

And on his robe, and on his thigh, he has a name written— King of kings and Lord of lords.

THE description of the warrior Christ is further filled in.

He has with him the armies of heaven. With this we may compare Jesus's words at his arrest, when he said he could have had twelve legions of angels to fight for him (*Matthew* 26: 53). The armies of heaven are the hosts of the angels.

From his mouth goes forth a sharp two-edged sword (cp. 1: 16). This description of the warrior Christ comes from two Old Testament passages put side by side. Isaiah says of the heavenly king: "He shall smite the earth with the rod of his mouth, and with the breath of his lips shall he slay the wicked" (*Isaiah* 11: 4). The Psalmist says of the Messianic king: "You shall break them with a rod of iron, and dash them in pieces like a potter's vessel" (*Psalm* 2: 9). Once again we must remember that this picture is demonstrably painted in Jewish terms.

He will tread the winepress of the anger of the wrath of God. The picture is of the warrior Christ trampling the grapes so as to produce the wine of the wrath of God, which his enemies must drink to their doom.

Our most difficult task here is to discover the picture behind the statement that the warrior Christ has the name King of kings and Lord of lords written *on his robe and on his thigh.* Various suggestions have been made. It has been suggested that the name is either embroidered on his girdle or engraved on his sword hilt. It is suggested that it is on the skirt of his general's cloak, for that is where it would be easiest to read on a horseman. It is suggested that it is actually written on his thigh, because it was sometimes the custom to engrave the titles of statues on the thigh. It seems clear that the name is visible to all, and, therefore, probably the likeliest solution is that it was written on the skirt of the warrior Christ's robe, lying over his thigh, as he rode upon the white horse. In any event, the name singles him out as the greatest of all rulers, the only true divine One and the universal King.

## THE DOOM OF THE ENEMIES OF CHRIST

*Revelation* 19: 17–21

And I saw one angel standing in the sun, and he cried with a great voice to all the birds who fly in midheaven. "Come," he said, "assemble for the great feast which God will give you, that you may eat the flesh of kings, and the flesh of captains, and the flesh of mighty men, and the flesh of horses and of those who ride them, and the flesh of all men, both free men and slaves, both small and great."

And I saw the beast and the kings of the earth and their armies assembled to make war with him who rides the horse, and with his army. And the beast was seized, and with him the false prophet, who performed in his presence signs by which he deceived those who had received the mark of the beast, and who worship his image. The two of them were cast alive into the lake of fire which burns with brimstone; and the rest were slain with the sword of him who rides the horse, with the sword which comes out of his mouth; and all the birds were glutted with their flesh.

HERE is a grim picture of birds of prey being invited to come from all over the sky to glut themselves on the corpses of the slain. Again this is a picture taken directly from the Old Testament, from Ezekiel's picture of the slaughter of the forces of Gog and Magog. "Speak to the birds of every sort and to all beasts of the field. . . . You shall eat the flesh of the mighty, and drink the blood of the princes of the earth— of rams, of lambs, and of goats, of bulls. . . . And you shall eat fat till you are filled, and drink blood till you are drunk at the sacrificial feast which I am preparing for you" (*Ezekiel* 39: 17–19). This bloodthirsty picture is again far more in line with Old Testament apocalyptic expectations than with the gospel of Jesus Christ.

Here we have a repetition of the imagery of chapter 13. The beast is Nero redivivus; the false prophet is the provincial organization which administered Caesar worship; those who have the mark of the beast are they who have worshipped at the shrine of Caesar; the kings of the earth and their armies are the Parthian hosts, which Nero was to lead again against Rome and against the world.

So all the forces hostile to God assemble themselves; but the warrior Christ is to conquer. Antichrist and his henchmen are cast into the lake of fire; and all their supporters are slain, to await in Sheol the final judgment.

The cosmic drama is drawing to a close. Nothing has yet been said of the fate of Satan, but now we go on to see that fate.

# THE THOUSAND YEAR REIGN OF CHRIST AND THE SAINTS

*Revelation* 20

SINCE the great importance of this chapter is that it is what might be called the foundation document of Millennarianism or Chiliasm, it will be better to read it as a whole before we deal with it in detail.

1   And I saw an angel coming down out of heaven with the
    key of the abyss, and with a great chain in his hand.
2   And he laid hold of the dragon, the ancient serpent,
    who is the Devil and Satan, and bound him for a
3   thousand years, and cast him into the abyss, and
    locked him in, and set a seal over him, that he might no
    longer deceive the nations, until the thousand years were
    completed. After that he must be set free for a little time.
4   And I saw thrones, and those who had received the privilege
    of judgment sat upon them. And I saw the souls of those
    who had been beheaded because of their witness to Jesus, and
    for the sake of the word of God, and such as had not
    worshipped the beast nor his image, and who had not received
    the mark upon their forehead, and upon their hand. And
    they came to life again, and reigned with Christ for a thousand
    years.
5   The rest of the dead did not come to life again
    until the thousand years were completed. This is the
6   first resurrection. Blessed and holy is he who has a share
    in the first resurrection. Over these the second death has no
    power, but they will be priests of God and of Christ, and
    they will reign with him for a thousand years.
7   And whenever the thousand years shall have been
    completed, Satan will be loosed from his prison, and
8   he will come forth to deceive the nations in the four
    corners of the earth, that is, Gog and Magog, to assemble
    them for war; and their number will be as the sand of the
    sea.
9   And they came up over the broad plain of the
    earth, and they encircled the camp of God's dedicated
    ones, and the beloved city; and fire came down from
10  heaven and devoured them; and the devil who deceived
    them was cast into the lake of fire and brimstone, where
    both the beast and the false prophet were, and they will
    be tortured day and night for ever and ever.
11  And I saw a great white throne and him who sat
    upon it. Earth and the sky fled from his presence,
12  and no place was found for them. And I saw the dead,
    the great and the small, standing before the throne; and
    books were opened. And another book was opened, the

Book of Life; and the dead were judged by that which was
written in these books, according to their deeds.

13  And the sea rendered up the dead in it, and Death
14  and Hades were cast into the lake of fire. This is the
15  second death, the lake of fire; and everyone who was
not found written in the Book of Life was cast into the
lake of fire.

*Millennium* means *a period of one thousand years*; and *chiliasm*
is derived from the Greek *chilios, a thousand*. To put it briefly,
the commonest form of Millennarianism teaches that for a
thousand years before the end Christ will reign upon this
earth in a kingdom of his saints; and after that will come
the final struggle, the general resurrection, the last judgment
and the final consummation.

We note two general facts. First, this was a very common
belief in the early church and it still has its adherents.
Second, this is the only pasage in the New Testament in
which it is clearly taught.

The picture is that first of all the Devil will be bound in
the abyss for a thousand years. Then those who have been
martyred for Christ, although the rest of mankind, even
the Christians among them who did not suffer martyrdom,
will not be resurrected. There will then be a period of
a thousand years in which Christ and his saints will reign.
After that for a brief time the Devil will be released. There
will follow a final struggle and the general resurrection of all
men. The devil will be finally defeated and cast into the
lake of fire; his supporters will be burned up with fire from
heaven; those whose names are in the Book of Life will
enter into blessedness, but those whose names are not in
the Book of Life will also be cast into the lake of fire.

This doctrine does not occur anywhere else in the New
Testament but it was prevalent throughout the early church
especially among those who had received their Christianity
from Jewish sources. Here is our key. The origin of this
doctrine is not specifically Christian but is to be found in

certain Jewish beliefs about the Messianic age which were common in the time after 100 B.C.

Jewish Messianic beliefs were never an unvarying system. They varied from time to time and from thinker to thinker. The basis was that the Messiah would come and establish upon earth the new age, in which the Jewish nation would be supreme.

In the earlier times the general belief was that the kingdom so established would last for ever. God would set up a kingdom which would never be destroyed; it would break in pieces the other kingdoms, but it would stand for ever (*Daniel* 2: 44). It was to be an everlasting dominion (*Daniel* 7: 14, 27).

From 100 B.C. onwards there came a change. It was felt that this world was so incurably evil that within it the Kingdom of God could never finally come; and so there emerged the conception that the Messiah would have a limited reign and that after his reign the final consummation would come. The *Apocalypse of Baruch* foresees the defeat of the forces of evil; then the principate of the Messiah will stand for ever, *until this world of corruption is at an end* (2 *Baruch* 40: 3). One section of *Enoch* sees history as a series of weeks. There are seven weeks of past history. The eighth is the week of the righteous, when a sword is given to the righteous and sinners are delivered into their hands, and the house of God is built. In the ninth week the evil are written down for destruction, and righteousness will flourish. In the tenth week comes judgment; and only then comes the eternal time of goodness and of God (*Enoch* 93: 3–10).

There was much rabbinic discussion of how long the Messianic age would last before the final consummation arrived. Some said 40, some 100, some 600, some 1,000, some 2,000, some 7,000 years.

We look particularly at two answers. 2 *Esdras* is very definite. God is represented as saying: "My Son the Messiah shall be revealed, together with those who are with him, and shall rejoice the survivors *for four hundred years*. And it shall be, after these years, that my Son the Messiah shall die, and all in whom there is human breath. Then shall the world be turned into the primaeval silence seven days, like as at the first beginnings, so that no man is left." And then after that the new age comes (2 *Esdras* 7: 28, 29). This passage is unique in foretelling, not only a limited reign of the Messiah, but the Messiah's death. The period of four hundred years was arrived at by setting side by side two passages from the Old Testament. In *Genesis* 15: 13 God tells Abraham that the period of the affliction of Israel will last for four hundred years. In *Psalm* 90: 15 the prayer is : "Make us glad as many days as thou hast afflicted us, and as many years as we have seen evil." It was, therefore, held that the period of bliss, like the period of affliction, would last for 400 years.

More commonly it was held that the age of the world would correspond to the time taken for its creation and that the time of creation was 6,000 years. "A thousand years in thy sight are but as yesterday" (*Psalm* 90: 4). "One day with the Lord is as a thousand years, and a thousand years as one day" (2 *Peter* 3: 8). Each day of creation was said to be 1,000 years. It was, therefore, held that the Messiah would come in the sixth thousand of the years; and the seventh thousand, the equivalent of the Sabbath rest in the creation story, would be the reign of the Messiah.

Although the reign of the Messiah was to be the reign of righteousness, it was often conceived of in terms of material blessings. "The earth also shall yield its fruit ten thousand-fold, and on each vine there shall be a thousand branches, and each branch shall produce a thousand clusters, and each cluster shall produce a thousand grapes, and each grape a cor (120 gallons) of wine" (2 *Baruch* 29: 5, 6). There will be no more disease, no more untimely death; the beasts will be friendly with men; and women will have no pain in child-birth (2 *Baruch* 73).

Here, then, we have the background of the idea of the Millennium. Already the Jews had come to think of a limited reign of the Messiah, which would be a time of the triumph of righteousness, and of the greatest spiritual and material blessings.

On the basis of this passage of the *Revelation* Millennarianism or Chiliasm was very widespread within the early Church, although it was never universal.

For Justin Martyr it was an essential part of orthodox belief, although he agreed that there were good Christians who did not accept it. "I and others, who are right-minded Christians at all points, are assured that there will be a resurrection of the dead, and a thousand years in Jerusalem, which will then be built adorned and enlarged as the prophets Ezekiel and Isaiah and others declare" (*Dialogue with Trypho* 80). Irenaeus also (*Against Heresies* 5: 32) firmly held to the belief in a Millennium upon earth. One of his reasons was the conviction that, since the saints and the martyrs had suffered upon earth, it was only just that upon earth they should reap the rewards of their fidelity. Tertullian also insisted upon the coming of the Millennium. Papias, the second century collector of so much material upon the Gospels, insisted that Jesus taught the doctrine of the Millennium, and he hands down as the words of Jesus a passage which foretells the wondrous fertility of the earth which is to come: "The days will come in which vines shall grow each having ten thousand shoots, and on each shoot ten thousand branches, and on each branch again ten thousand twigs, and on each twig ten thousand clusters, and on each cluster ten thousand grapes, and each grape when pressed shall yield five and twenty measures of wine. And when any of the saints shall have taken hold of one of their clusters, another shall cry, I am a better cluster; take me, bless the Lord through me. Likewise also a grain of wheat shall produce ten thousand heads, and every head shall have ten thousand grains, and every grain ten thousand pounds of fine flour, bright and clean, and the other fruits, seeds and the grass, shall produce in similar proportions, and all the animals, using these fruits which are products of the soil, shall become in their turn peaceable and harmonious, obedient to man in all subjection." Papias gives this passage as an actual saying of Jesus, but it can be seen that it is very close to the passage of 2 *Baruch* which we have already quoted.

We have already said that, although many in the early church accepted the belief in the Millennium as a part of orthodoxy, many did not. Eusebius almost contemptuously dismisses Papias's report. "I suppose he got those ideas," he says,"through a misunderstanding of the apostolic records, not perceiving that the things said by them were said mystically in figures. For he seems to have been of very limited understanding" (Eusebius: *The Ecclesiastical History* 3: 38).

One of the things which brought discredit upon Millennarianism was the fact that it undoubtedly lent itself to a materialistic interpretation in which it offered physical as much as spiritual pleasures. Eusebius tells how the great scholar Dionysius had in Egypt to deal with a certain much-respected bishop called Nepos who taught "a millennium of bodily luxury upon this earth" (*The Ecclesiastical History* 7: 24). Cerinthus, a heretic, deliberately taught a millennium of "delights of the belly and sexual passion, eating and drinking and marrying" (Eusebius: *The Ecclesiastical History* 3: 28). Jerome spoke contemptuously of "these half-Jews who look for a Jerusalem of gold and precious stones from heaven, and a future kingdom of a thousand years, in which all nations shall serve Israel" (*Commentary on Isaiah* 60: 1).

Origen rebuked those who looked for bodily pleasure in the Millennium. The saints will eat, but it will be the bread of life; they will drink, but it will be the cup of wisdom (*De Principiis* 2.11.2, 3). It was Augustine, however, who, we may almost say, dealt Millennarianism its death blow. At one time he himself had been a Millennarian, although it was always spiritual blessings for which he longed. H. B. Swete summarizes Augustine's position: "He had learned to see in the captivity of Satan nothing else than the binding of the strong man by the stronger than he which the Lord had foretold (*Mark* 3: 27; *Luke* 11: 22); in the thousand years, the whole interval between the first Advent and the last conflict; in the reign of the saints, the entire course of the kingdom of heaven; in the judgment given to them, the binding and loosing of sinners; in the first resurrection, the spiritual share in the Resurrection of Christ which belongs to the baptised" (Augustine: *The City of God* 20: 7). Augustine spiritualized the whole idea of the Millennium.

Millennarianism is by no means extinct within the Church; but it has never been the universally accepted belief of the Church, this is the only passage in the New Testament which unequivocally teaches it, its whole background is Jewish and not Christian, and the literal interpretation of it has always tended to run into danger and excess. It is a doctrine which has long since been left behind by the main stream of Christian thought and which now belongs to the eccentricities of Christian belief.

## THE CHAINING OF SATAN

*Revelation* 20: 1–3

THE abyss was a vast subterranean cavern beneath the earth, sometimes the place where all the dead went, sometimes the place where special sinners were kept awaiting punishment. It was reached by a chasm reaching down into the earth and this the angel locks in order to keep the Devil in the abyss.

It was the abyss which the devils feared most of all. In the story of the Gerasene demoniac the request of the devils was that Jesus would not command them to leave the man and to go out into the deep, that is, the abyss (*Luke* 8: 31).

The seal is set on the chasm to ensure the safe-keeping of the prisoner, just as the seal was set on the tomb of Jesus to make sure that he would not escape (*Matthew* 27: 66).

The Devil is to be kept in the abyss for a period of a thousand years. Even the way in which the word *thousand* is used in Scripture warns us against taking this literally. *Psalm* 50: 10 says that the cattle on a thousand hills belong to God;

and *Job* 9: 3 says that a man cannot answer God once in a thousand times. Thousand is simply used to describe a very large number.

At the end of the period the Devil is to be let loose for a little time. H. B. Swete suggests that the reason for the final loosing of the Devil is this. In a period of peace and righteousness, in a time when the opposition, so to speak, did not exist, it might easily happen that people came to take their faith unthinkingly. The loosing of the Devil meant a testing-time for Christians, and there are times when a testing-time is essential, if the reality of the faith is to be preserved.


## THE PRIVILEGE OF JUDGMENT

*Revelation* 20: 4, 5

IN the first resurrection only those who have died and suffered for the faith are to be raised from the dead. The general resurrection is not to take place until after the thousand year reign of Christ upon earth. There is special privilege for those who have shown special loyalty to Christ.

Those who are to enjoy this privilege belong to two classes. First, there are those who have been martyred for their loyalty to Christ. The word used for the way in which they were killed means *to behead with an axe*, and denotes the most cruel death. Second, there are those who have not worshipped the beast and have not received his mark on their hand or on their forehead. H. B. Swete identifies these, as those who, although they were not actually martyred, willingly bore suffering, reproach, imprisonment, loss of goods, disruption of their homes and personal relationships for the sake of Christ.

In the ancient Church in the days of persecution two terms were used. *Martyrs* were those who actually died for their faith; *confessors* were those who suffered everything short of death for their loyalty to Christ. Both he who dies for Christ and he who lives for Christ will receive his reward.

Those who have been loyal to Christ are to receive the privilege of judgment. This is an idea which occurs more than once in the New Testament. Jesus is represented as saying that, when he returns to sit on the throne of his glory, his twelve apostles will sit on twelve thrones judging the twelve tribes of Israel (*Matthew* 19: 28). Paul reminds the litigious Corinthians that the destiny of the saints is to judge the world (1 *Corinthians* 6: 2). Again we do not need to take this literally. The idea symbolized is that the world to come will redress the balance of this one. In this world the Christian may be a man under the judgment of men; in the world to come the parts will be reversed and those who thought they were the judges will be the judged.

## THE PRIVILEGES OF THE WITNESSES OF CHRIST

*Revelation* 20: 6

VERSE 6 describes the privileges of the Christians who have been true to Christ, even when loyalty was a costly thing.

(i) For them death has been utterly vanquished. The second death has no power over them. Physical death for them is not a thing to be feared, for it is the gateway to life everlasting.

(ii) They are to be the priests of God and of Christ. The Latin for priest is *pontifex*, which means a *bridge-builder*. The priest is the builder of a bridge between God and man; and he, as the Jews saw it, is the one man with the right of direct access into the presence of God. Those who have been loyal to Jesus Christ have the right of free entry into the presence of God; and they have the privilege of introducing others to Jesus Christ.

(iii) They are to reign with Christ. In Christ even the most ordinary man becomes a king.

## THE FINAL STRUGGLE

*Revelation* 20: 7–10

AT the end of the thousand years the Devil is to be loosed, but he has learned no lesson; he begins where he has left off. He will assemble the nations for the final attack on God.

A final attack on Jerusalem by the hostile nations is one of the standard pictures of the last times in Jewish thought. We find it especially in *Daniel* 11 and in *Zechariah* 14: 1–11. *The Sibylline Orders* (3: 663–672) tell how the kings of the nations shall throw themselves against the land in troops, only to be ultimately destroyed by God.

But here we come on a picture which etched itself deeply, if mysteriously, on Jewish thought, the picture of Gog and Magog. We find it first in *Ezekiel* 38 and 39. There Gog of the land of Magog, the chief prince of Meshech and of Tubal, is to launch the great attack upon Israel and is to be in the end utterly destroyed. It may be that originally Gog was connected with the Scythians whose invasions all men feared.

As time went on, in Jewish thought Gog and Magog came to stand for everything that is against God. The rabbis taught that Gog and Magog would assemble themselves and their forces against Jerusalem, and would fall by the hand of the Messiah.

The hostile armies under the Devil's leadership come up against the camp of God's people and against the beloved city, that is, Jerusalem; the hosts are consumed with fire from heaven, the Devil is cast into the lake of fire and brimstone to share the fate of the beast and of the false prophet, and the triumph of God is complete.


## THE FINAL JUDGMENT (1)

*Revelation* 20: 11–15

Now comes the final judgment. God, the Judge, is on his great white throne which symbolizes his unapproachable purity.

It may be that some will find a problem here. The regular picture of the New Testament is that Jesus Christ is judge. *John* 5: 22 represents Jesus as saying: "The Father judges no one, but has given all judgment to the Son." In the Parable of the Sheep and Goats it is the glorified Christ who is the judge (*Matthew* 25: 31–46). In Paul's speech at Athens it is said that God has appointed a day in which he will judge the world by Jesus (*Acts* 17: 31). In 2 *Timothy* 4: 1 Jesus is the one who is about to judge the living and the dead.

There are two answers to this apparent difficulty.

First, the unity of the Father and the Son is such that there is no difficulty in ascribing the action of the one to the other. That is in fact what Paul does. In *Romans* 14: 10 he writes: "We shall all stand before the judgment seat of God." But in 2 *Corinthians* 5: 10 he writes: "We must all appear before the judgment seat of Christ."

Second, it may be that the real reason why God is the judge in John's *Revelation* is that the whole background of the book is Jewish; to a Jew, even when he became a Christian, God stood unique; and it would seem natural to him that God should be judge.

As John tells the story, the judgment begins with the passing away of this present world; earth and sky flee from his presence. John is thinking in pictures which are very familiar in the Old Testament. God laid the foundations of the earth, and the heavens are the work of his hands. None the less it is still true that "they will perish . . . they will all wear out like a garment; thou changest them like raiment, and they pass away" (*Psalm* 102: 25–27). "The heavens will vanish like smoke, the earth will wear out like a garment" (*Isaiah* 51: 6). "Heaven and earth will pass away" (*Mark* 13: 31). "The heavens will pass away with a loud noise, and the elements will be dissolved with fire, and the earth and the works that are upon it will be burned up" (2 *Peter* 3: 10). The new man in Christ must have a new world in Christ.

## THE FINAL JUDGMENT (2)

*Revelation* 20: 11–15 (*continued*)

Now follows the judgment of mankind.

It is the judgment of great and small. There is none so great as to escape the judgment of God, and none so unimportant as to fail to win his vindication.

Two kinds of book are mentioned. The first contains the records of the deeds of men. This is a common idea in Scripture. "The court sat in judgment," says *Daniel*, "and the books were opened" (*Daniel* 7: 10). In *Enoch* the sealed books are opened before the Lord of the sheep (*Enoch* 90: 20). The *Apocalypse of Baruch* foretells the day when "the books shall be opened in which are written the sins of all those who have sinned, and again also the treasuries in which the righteousness of all those who have been righteous in creation is gathered" (2 *Baruch* 24: 1). When the present age passes away, the books will be opened before the face of the firmament, and all shall see together (4 *Ezra* 6: 20).

The idea is simply that a record of all men's deeds is kept by God. The symbolism is that all through life we are writing our own destiny; it is not so much that God judges a man as that a man writes his own judgment.

The second book is the *Book of Life*. This, too, occurs often in Scripture. Moses is willing to be blotted out of the Book of Life if it will save the people (*Exodus* 32: 32). It is the prayer of the Psalmist that the wicked will be blotted out of the Book of the Living and not written with the righteous (*Psalm* 69: 28). Isaiah speaks of those who are written among the living (*Isaiah* 4: 3). Paul speaks of his fellow-labourers whose names are in the Book of Life (*Philippians* 4: 3). It is the promise of the Risen Christ to the Church at Sardis that the name of him who overcomes will not be blotted out of the Book of Life (*Revelation* 3: 5). Those whose names are not written in the Book of Life are given over to destruction (*Revelation* 13: 8). The idea behind this is that every ruler had a roll-book of living citizens under his control; and, of course, when a man died, his name was removed from the roll. Those whose names are in the Book of Life are those who are living, active citizens of the kingdom of God.

At the time of judgment it is said that the sea will give up its dead. The point is twofold. First, in the ancient world burial was all important; if a man did not obtain burial, his spirit would wander, homeless, neither in earth nor in heaven. And, of course, those who died at sea could never be buried. John means that even such as these will appear before the judgment seat of God. Second, H. B. Swete puts the matter in a more general form. "The accidents of death," he says, "will not prevent any from appearing before the judge." No matter how a man dies, he will not escape his punishment nor lose his reward.

Finally, Death and Hades are thrown into the lake of fire. As H. B. Swete puts it, these voracious monsters who have themselves devoured so many are in the end themselves destroyed. In the judgment those who are not in the Book of Life are condemned to the lake of fire with the Devil, their master, but for those whose names are in the Book of Life, death is for ever vanquished.

## THE NEW CREATION

*Revelation* 21: 1

> And I saw a new heaven and a new earth, for the first heaven and the first earth had gone; and the sea was no more.

JOHN has seen the doom of the wicked, and now he sees the bliss of the blessed.

The dream of a new heaven and a new earth was deep in Jewish thought. "Behold," said God to Isaiah, "I create new heavens and a new earth; and the former things shall not be remembered, or come into mind" (*Isaiah* 65: 17). Isaiah speaks of the new heaven and the new earth which God will make, in which life will be one continual act of worship (*Isaiah* 66: 22). This idea is equally strong between the Testaments. It is God's promise: "I will transform the heaven and make it an eternal blessing and light; and I will transform the earth and make it a blessing" (*Enoch* 45: 4). There will be a new creation accomplished which will endure to eternity (*Enoch* 72: 1). The first heaven will pass away, and the new heaven shall appear; the light of heaven will be seven times brighter; and the new creation will last for ever (*Enoch* 91: 16). The Mighty One will shake creation only to renew it (2 *Baruch* 32: 6). God will renew his creation (2 *Esdras* 7: 75).

The picture is always there and its elements are always the same. Sorrow is to be forgotten; sin is to be vanquished; darkness is to be at an end; the temporariness of time is to turn into the everlastingness of eternity. This continuing belief is a witness to three things—to the unquenchable immortal longings in man's soul, to man's inherent sense of sin and to man's faith in God.

In this vision of the future bliss we come on one of the most famous phrases in the *Revelation*—"And the sea was no more." This phrase has a double background.

(i) It has a background in the great mythological beliefs of John's time. We have already seen that the Babylonian story of the creation of the world is of a long struggle between Marduk, the god of creation, and Tiamat, the dragon of chaos. In that story the sea, the waters beneath the firmament, became the dwelling-place of Tiamat. The sea was always an enemy. The Egyptians saw it as the power which swallowed up the waters of the Nile and left the fields barren.

(ii) It has a much more human background. The ancient peoples hated the sea, even though, by the time of John, they were voyaging long and far. They did not possess the compass; and, therefore, as far as possible, they coasted along the shores. It is not till modern times that we come on people who rejoice in being sea-faring.

Matthew Arnold spoke of "the salt, estranging sea." Dr. Johnson once remarked bitterly that no man who had the wit to get himself into gaol would ever choose to go to sea. There is an old story of a man who was weary of battling with the sea. He put an oar on his shoulder and set out with the intention of journeying inland until he reached people who knew so little of the sea that they asked him what strange thing he carried on his shoulder.

*The Sibylline Oracles* (5 : 447) say that in the last time the sea will be dried up. *The Ascension of Moses* (10 : 6) says that the sea will return into the abyss. In Jewish dreams the end of the sea is the end of a force hostile to God and to man.

## THE NEW JERUSALEM (1)

*Revelation* 21 : 2

And I saw the holy city, new Jerusalem, coming down out of heaven from God, like a bride adorned for her husband.

HERE, again, is a dream of the Jews which never died—the dream of the restoration of Jerusalem, the holy city. Once again it has a double background.

(i) It has a background which is essentially Greek. One of the great contributions to the world's philosophical thought was Plato's doctrine of *ideas* or *forms*. He taught that in the invisible world there existed the perfect form or idea of everything upon earth, and that all things on earth were imperfect copies of the heavenly realities. If that be so, there is a heavenly Jerusalem of which the earthly Jerusalem is an imperfect copy. That is what Paul is thinking of when he speaks of the Jerusalem that is above (*Galatians* 4 : 26), and also what is in the mind of the writer to the Hebrews when he speaks of the heavenly Jerusalem (*Hebrews* 12 : 22).

That way of thought left its mark on Jewish visions between the Testaments. We read that in the Messianic Age the Jerusalem which is invisible will appear (2 *Esdras* 7 : 26). The writer of 2 *Esdras* was, he says, given a vision of it in so far as it was possible for human eyes to bear the sight of the heavenly glory (2 *Esdras* 10 : 44–59). In 2 *Baruch* it is said that God made the heavenly Jerusalem before he made Paradise, that Adam saw it before he sinned, that it was shown in a vision to Abraham, that Moses saw it on Mount Sinai, and that it is now present with God (2 *Baruch* 4: 2–6).

This conception of pre-existing forms may seem strange. But at the back of it is the great truth that the ideal actually exists. It further means that God is the source of all ideals. The ideal is a challenge, which, even if it is not worked out in this world, can still be worked out in the world to come.

## THE NEW JERUSALEM (2)

*Revelation* 21 : 2 (*continued*)

(ii) The second background of the conception of the new Jerusalem is entirely Jewish. In his synagogue form of prayer the Jew still prays:

> And to Jerusalem thy city return with compassion, and dwell therein as thou hast promised; and rebuild her speedily in our days, a structure everlasting; and the throne of David speedily establish there. Blessed art thou, O Lord, the builder of Jerusalem.

John's vision of the new Jerusalem uses and amplifies many of the dreams of the prophets. We shall set down some of these dreams and it will be clear at once how the Old Testament again and again finds its echo in the *Revelation*.

> Isaiah had his dream.
> "O afflicted one, storm-tossed, and not comforted, behold, I will set your stones in antimony, and lay your foundations with sapphires. I will make your pinnacles of agate, your gates of carbuncles, and all your wall of precious stones" (*Isaiah* 54: 11, 12).
> Foreigners shall build up your walls, and their kings shall minister to you. . . . Your gates shall be open continually; day and night they shall not be shut. . . . You shall suck the milk of nations, you shall suck the breast of kings. . . . Instead of bronze I will bring gold, and instead of iron I will bring silver; instead of wood, bronze, instead of stones, iron. . . . Violence shall no more be heard in your land, devastation or destruction within your borders; you shall call your walls Salvation, and your

gates Praise. The sun shall be no more your light by day, nor for
brightness shall the moon give light to you by night; but the Lord
will be your everlasting light, and your God will be your glory.
Your sun shall no more go down, nor your moon withdraw
itself; for the Lord will be your everlasting light, and your days
of mourning shall be ended (*Isaiah* 60: 10–20).

Haggai had his dream.

The latter splendour of this house shall be greater than the former,
says the Lord of hosts; and in this place I will give prosperity, says
the Lord of hosts (*Haggai* 2: 9).

Ezekiel had his dream of the rebuilt Jerusalem (chapters
40 and 48) in which we find even the picture of the twelve
gates of the city (*Ezekiel* 48: 31–35).

The writers between the Testaments had their dreams.

The city which God loved he made more radiant than the stars
and the sun and the moon; and he set it as the jewel of the
world and made a Temple exceeding fair in its sanctuary, and
fashioned it in size of many furlongs, with a giant tower,
touching the very clouds, and seen of all, so that all the faithful
and the righteous may see the glory of the invisible God, the
vision of delight (*The Sibylline Oracles* 5: 420–427).

And the gates of Jerusalem shall be builded with sapphire and
    emerald,
    And all thy walls with precious stones,
The towers of Jerusalem shall be builded with gold,
    And their battlements with pure gold,
The streets of Jerusalem shall be paved
    With carbuncle and stones of Ophir,
And the gates of Jerusalem shall utter hymns of gladness,
    And all her houses shall say, Hallelujah!

(*Tobit* 13: 16–18).

It is easy to see that the new Jerusalem was a constant
dream; and that John lovingly collected the differing visions—
the precious stones, the streets and buildings of gold, the ever-
open gates, the light of God making unnecessary the light of
the sun and the moon, the coming of the nations and the
bringing of their gifts—into his own.

Here is faith. Even when Jerusalem was obliterated, the Jews never lost confidence that God would restore it. True, they expressed their hopes in terms of material things; but these are merely the symbols of the certainty that there is eternal bliss for the faithful people of God.

## FELLOWSHIP WITH GOD (1)

*Revelation* 21: 3, 4

And I heard a great voice from heaven. "Behold," it said, "the dwelling-place of God is with men, and he will dwell with them, and they will be his peoples, and God himself shall be with them; and he will wipe away every tear from their eyes, and death will be no more, nor will there be any grief or crying, nor will there be any more pain, for the first things have gone."

HERE is the promise of fellowship with God and all its precious consequences. The voice is that of one of the Angels of the Presence.

God is to make his *dwelling-place* with men. The word used for dwelling-place is *skēnē,* literally a *tent*; but in religious use it had long since lost any idea of an impermanent residence. There are two main ideas here.

(i) *Skēnē* is the word used for the *Tabernacle.* Originally in the wilderness the Tabernacle was a tent, the *skēnē par excellence.* This, then, means that God is to make his tabernacle with men for ever, to give his presence to men for ever. Here in this world and amidst the things of time our realisation of the presence of God is spasmodic; but in heaven we will be permanently aware of that presence.

(ii) There are two words totally different in meaning but similar in sound which in early Christian thought became closely connected. *Skēnē* is one; and the Hebrew *shechinah, the glory of God,* is the other. SKĒNĒ—SHECHINAH— the connection in sound brought it about that men could not hear the one without thinking of the other. As a result, to say that the *skēnē* of God is to be with men immediately brought the thought that the *shechinah* of God is to be with men. In the ancient times the *shechinah* took the form of a luminous cloud which came and went. We read, for instance, of the cloud which filled the house at the dedication of Solomon's Temple (1 *Kings* 8: 10, 11). In the new age the glory of God is not to be a transitory thing, but something which abides permanently with the people of God.

## FELLOWSHIP WITH GOD (2)

*Revelation* 21: 3, 4 (*continued*)

GOD'S promise to make Israel his people and to be their God echoes throughout the Old Testament. "I will make my abode among you . . . and I will walk among you, and will be your God, and you shall be my people" (*Leviticus* 26: 11, 12). In Jeremiah's account of the new covenant the promise of God is: "I will be their God, and they shall be my people" (*Jeremiah* 31: 33). The promise to Ezekiel is: "My dwelling-place shall be with them; and I will be their God, and they shall be my people" (*Ezekiel* 37: 27). The highest promise of all is intimate fellowship with God, in which we can say: "I am my beloved's, and my beloved is mine" (*Song of Solomon* 6: 3).

This fellowship with God in the golden age brings certain things. Tears and grief and crying and pain are gone. That, too, had been the dream of the prophets of the ancient days. "They shall obtain joy and gladness," said Isaiah of the pilgrims of the heavenly way, "and sorrow and sighing shall flee away" (*Isaiah* 35: 10). "I will rejoice in Jerusalem, and be glad in my people; no more shall be heard in it the sound of weeping and the cry of distress" (*Isaiah* 65: 19). Death, too, shall be gone. That, too, had been the dream of the ancient prophets. "He will swallow up death in victory; and the Lord God will wipe away tears from all faces" (*Isaiah* 25: 8).

This is a promise for the future. But even in this present world those who mourn are blessed, for they will be comforted, and death is swallowed up in victory for those who know Christ and the fellowship of his sufferings and the power of his Resurrection (*Matthew* 5 : 4; *Philippians* 3 : 10).

## ALL THINGS NEW

*Revelation* 21 : 5, 6

> And he who is seated upon the throne said: "Behold, I make all things new." And he said: "Write, for these are words that are trustworthy and true." And he said to me: "It is done. I am Alpha and Omega, the beginning and the end. Without price I will give to the thirsty of the fountain of the water of life."

FOR the first time God himself speaks; he is the God who is able to make all things new. Again we are back among the dreams of the ancient prophets. Isaiah heard God say: "Remember not the former things, nor consider the things of old. Behold, I am doing a new thing" (*Isaiah* 43 : 18, 19). This is the witness of Paul: "If any one is in Christ, he is a new creation" (2 *Corinthians* 5 : 17). God can take a man and re-create him, and will some day create a new universe for the saints whose lives he has renewed.

It is not God but the Angel of the Presence who gives the command to write. These words must be taken down and remembered; they are true and absolutely to be relied upon.

"I am Alpha and Omega," says God to John, "the beginning and the end." We have already come upon this claim by the risen Christ in 1 : 8. Again John is hearing the voice that the great prophets had heard, "I am the first, and I am the last; besides me there is no God" (*Isaiah* 44 : 6). *Alpha* is the first letter of the Greek alphabet and *omega* the last. John goes on to amplify this statement. God is the *beginning* and the *end*. The word for *beginning* is *archē*, and does not simply mean first in point of time but first in the sense of the *source* of all things. The word for *end* is *telos*, and does not simply mean end in point of time but the *goal*. John is saying that all life begins in God and ends in God. Paul expressed the same thing when he said perhaps a little more philosophically: "For from him, and through him, and to him are all things" (*Romans* 11: 36), and when he spoke of "one God and Father of us all, who is above all, and through all, and in all" (*Ephesians* 4: 6).

It would be impossible to say anything more magnificent about God. At first sight it might seem to remove God to such a distance that we are no more to him than the flies on the windowpane. But what comes next? "To the thirsty I will give water without price from the fountain of the water of life." All God's greatness is at the disposal of man. "God so loved that he gave . . ." (*John* 3: 16). The splendour of God is used to satisfy the thirst of the longing heart.

## THE GLORY AND THE SHAME

*Revelation* 21: 7, 8

"He who overcomes will enter into possession of these things, and I will be his God and he will be my son. But as for the cowards, the unbelieving, the polluted, the murderers, the fornicators, the sorcerers, the idolaters, and all the liars—their part is in the lake burning with fire and brimstone, which is the second death."

THE bliss is not to everyone but only to him who remains faithful when everything seeks to seduce him from his loyalty.

To such a man God makes the greatest promise of all— "I will be his God and he shall be my son." This promise, or something very near to it, was made in the Old Testament to three different people. First, it was made to Abraham. "I will establish my covenant between me and you and your descendants after you," God said to Abraham,

". . . to be God to you and your descendants" (*Genesis* 17: 7). Second, it was made to the son who was to inherit David's kingdom. "I will be his father," said God, "and he shall be my son" (2 *Samuel* 7: 14). Third, it was made in a Psalm which the Jewish scholars always interpreted of the Messiah. "I will make him the first-born, the highest of the kings of the earth" (*Psalm* 89: 27). Here is a tremendous thing. The promise of God to those who overcome is the same that was made to Abraham the founder of the nation, to David on behalf of Solomon his son, and to the Messiah himself. There is no greater honour in all the universe than that which God gives to the man who is true to him.

But there are those who are condemned. The *cowards* are those who loved ease and comfort more than they loved Christ, and who in the day of trial were ashamed to show whose they were and whom they served. The Authorized Version gives a wrong impression when it translates *deilos* by *fearful*. It is not fear that is condemned. The highest courage is to be desperately afraid and in spite of that to do the right thing and to hold fast to loyalty. What is condemned is the cowardice which denies Christ for safety's sake. The *unbelieving* are those who refused to accept the Gospel or those who with their lips accepted it, but by their lives showed that they did not believe it. The *polluted* are those who allowed themselves to be saturated by the abominations of the world. The *murderers* may well be those who in persecutions slaughtered the Christians. The *fornicators* are those who lived lives of immorality. Ephesus was full of *sorcerers*; *Acts* 19: 19 tells how at the preaching of the name of Christ in the early days the magicians burned their books. The *idolaters* are those who worshipped the false gods of whom the world was full. The *liars* are those who were guilty of untruth and of the silence which is also a lie.

## THE CITY OF GOD

*Revelation* 21 : 9–27

It will be better to read the description of the city of God as a whole before we deal with it in detail.

9   There came to me one of the seven angels who have the seven bowls full of the seven last plagues, and he spoke with me. "Come," he said, "and I will show you the Bride, the wife of the Lamb." And he carried me away in the Spirit to a
10   great and lofty mountain, and showed me the holy city, Jerusalem, coming down out of heaven from God, and it had the glory of God.
11   Its light was like a most precious stone, like a jasper stone, glittering like crystal.
12   It had a wall great and high with twelve gates, and at the gates twelve angels. There were names written on the
13   gates which are the names of the twelve tribes of the sons of Israel. On the east were three gates, and on the north were three gates, and on the south were three gates, and on the west were three gates.
14   The wall of the city had twelve foundations, and on them the twelve names of the twelve apostles of the Lamb.
15   He who was speaking with me had a golden measuring rod, that he might measure the city and its gates and its walls.
16   The city lies four-square, and its length is the same as its breadth. He measured the city with his measuring rod, and the measurement was twelve thousand stades. Its length and breadth and height are equal. And he measured its wall,
17   and the measurement was one hundred and forty-four cubits, by the measurement of a man, that is, of an angel.
18   The building material of the wall was jasper, and the city was of pure gold like pure glass.
19   The foundations of the wall of the city were adorned with every kind of precious stone. The first foundation was a jasper; the second, a sapphire; the third, a chalcedony; the fourth,
20   an emerald; the fifth, a sardonyx; the sixth, a carnelian; the seventh, a chrysolith; the eighth, a beryl; the ninth, a topaz; the tenth, a chrysoprase; the eleventh, a jacinth; the twelfth, an amethyst.

21   The twelve gates were twelve pearls; each one of the gates
     consisted of a single pearl. The street of the city was of pure
     gold, like transparent glass.
22   I saw no temple in it, for the Lord God, the Almighty, is
     its temple, and the Lamb.
23   The city has no need of the sun or the moon to shine for it,
     for the glory of God illumines it, and its lamp is the Lamb.
24   The nations will walk in its light, and the kings of the earth
25   will bring their glory to it. Its gates will never be shut by day,
26   for, as for night, there will be no night there. They shall bring
27   to it the glory and the honour of the nations; but nothing
     unclean shall enter into it, nor shall he who practises
     abominable things or uses falsehood, but only those who are
     written in the Lamb's Book of Life.


## THE BRINGER OF THE VISION

*Revelation* 21: 9, 10

THE personality of the bringer of the vision of the heavenly
Jerusalem must come as a surprise. He is one of the angels
who had the seven bowls filled with the last seven plagues;
and the last time we met such an angel he was the bringer
of the vision of the destruction of Babylon, the great harlot.
It is extraordinary that in 17: 1 the invitation of the angel
is: "Come, I will show you the judgment of the great
harlot," and that in 21: 9 the invitation, perhaps even of the
same angel, is: "Come, I will show you the Bride, the wife
of the Lamb."

No one can say for certain what much of the symbolism
of this chapter stands for. John must have meant something by
making the same angel the bearer of such different messages.
It may be that John wishes us to see that the servant of God
does not choose his task but must do whatever God sends
him to do, and must speak whatever word God gives him
to speak.

The angel, says John, carried him away in the Spirit
to a high mountain. It is in this way that Ezekiel also

describes his experience. "He brought me in the visions of God into the land of Israel, and set me down upon a very high mountain" (*Ezekiel* 40: 2). H. B. Swete points out that it is wrong to take this literally; the lifting up stands for the elevation of spirit in which a man sees the visions and hears the words which are sent to him by God.

## THE CITY'S LIGHT

*Revelation* 21: 11

THERE is a certain difficulty of translation here. The word used for *light* is *phōstēr*. The normal Greek word for *light* is *phōs*, and *phōstēr* is normally the word used for the lights of heaven, the sun, the moon and the stars, for instance, in the Creation story (*Genesis* 1: 14). Does this, then, mean that the body which illumined the city was like a precious stone? Or does it mean that the radiance which played over all the city was like the glitter of a jasper?

We think the word must describe the radiance over the city; it is later quite distinctly said that the city needs no heavenly body like the sun or the moon to give it light, because God is its light.

What, then, is the symbolism? H. B. Swete would find a hint in *Philippians* 2: 15. There Paul says of the Christians at Philippi: "You shine as lights in the world." The holy city is inhabited by thousands and thousands of the saints of God, and it may well be that it is the light of these saintly lives which gives it this glittering glow.

## THE WALL AND THE GATES OF THE CITY

*Revelation* 21: 12

ROUND the city is a great high wall. Again John is thinking in terms of the prophetic pictures of the re-created Jerusalem. The song of the land of Judah will be: "We have a strong city;

God sets up salvation as walls and bulwarks" (*Isaiah* 26: 1). Zechariah hears God say: "I will be to her a wall of fire round about" (*Zechariah* 2: 5). The simplest interpretation of the wall is that it is "the insurmountable bulwark of faith." Faith is the wall behind which the saints of God are secure against the assaults of the world, the flesh and the devil.

In the wall are twelve gates, and on the gates the names of the twelve tribes of the sons of Israel. The word for gate is interesting. It is not the normal word which is *pulē*; it is *pulōn*. The *pulōn* could be either of two things. A large house was built round an open courtyard. It opened on to the street by a great gate in the outer wall, leading into a spacious vestibule. That could be the picture here. *Pulōn* can also mean the gate-tower in a great city, like the gate leading into a battlemented castle.

There are two things to note.

(i) There are twelve gates. Surely this stands for the *catholicity* of the Church. A man can come by many roads into the kingdom, for "there are as many ways to the stars as there are men to climb them."

(ii) On the gates are the names of the twelves tribes. Surely this stands for the *continuity* of the Church. The God who revealed himself to the patriarchs is the God who also, and far more fully, revealed himself in Jesus Christ; the God of the Old Testament is the God of the New Testament.


## THE GATES OF THE CITY

*Revelation* 21: 13

THERE are three gates on each of the four sides of the city of God. Part at least of that picture John got from Ezekiel (*Ezekiel* 48: 30–35). What John meant to symbolize by this arrangement other than the catholicity of the Church we do not know. There is one symbolic interpretation which was unlikely to be in his mind, but which is none the less very beautiful and very comforting.

There are three gates on the *east*. The east is the place of the rising sun and the beginning of the day. These gates could represent the way into the holy city of those who find Christ in the glad morning of their days.

There are three gates on the *north*. The north is the cold land with a certain chill in it. These gates could stand for the way into the holy city of those who come to Christianity by the intellectual exercise of thought, and have found the faith through their minds rather than through their hearts.

There are three gates on the *south*. The south is the warm land, where the wind is gentle and the climate soft. These gates could stand for the way into the holy city of those who have come to Christ through their emotions, whose love ran over at the sight of the cross.

There are three gates on the *west*. The west is the land of the dying day and the setting sun. These gates could stand for the way into the holy city of those who come to Christ in the evening of their days.

## THE MEASURING OF THE CITY

*Revelation* 21: 15–17

JOHN takes his picture of the man with the measuring rod from *Ezekiel* 40: 3.

(i) We must note the city's *shape*. It was four-square. It was common enough for cities to be built in the form of a square; both Babylon and Nineveh were like that. But the holy city was not only square; it was in the form of a perfect cube. The length, breadth and height were the same. This is significant. The cube was the symbol of perfection. Both Plato and Aristotle refer to the fact that in Greece the good man was called "four-square" (Plato, *Protagoras* 339 B; Aristotle, *Nicomachean Ethics* 1.10.11; *Rhetoric* 3.11).

It was the same with the Jews. The altar of the burnt offering, the altar of the incense, and the High Priest's breast-plate were all in the form of a cube (*Exodus* 27: 1; 30: 2;

28: 16). Again and again this shape occurs in Ezekiel's visions of the new Jerusalem and the new temple (*Ezekiel* 41: 21; 43: 16; 45: 2; 48: 20). But most important of all, in Solomon's temple the Holy of Holies was a perfect cube (1 *Kings* 6: 20).

There is no doubt of the symbolism which John intends. He intends us to see that the whole of the holy city is the Holy of Holies, the dwelling-place of God.

(ii) We must note the city's *dimensions*. Each side of the city was twelve thousand *stades*. A stade is very nearly a *furlong*; therefore, each side was 1,500 miles long, and the total area of the city was 2,250,000 square miles. The rabbinic dreams of the re-created Jerusalem were vast enough. It was said that it would reach to Damascus and would cover the whole of Palestine. But a city with that area would stretch nearly from London to New York. Surely we are meant to see that in the holy city *there is room for everyone*. Men are so apt to limit their Churches, to shut out those who do not believe as they do or who do not administer as they do.

Strangely enough it is different when we come to the wall. The wall is 144 cubits high, that is, 266 feet, not very high. The wall of Babylon was 300 feet high, and the walls of the porch of Solomon's temple were 180 feet high. There is no comparison between the height of the wall and the size of the city. Again there is symbolism here. The wall cannot be for defence, for all hostile beings, spiritual and human, have been obliterated or cast into the lake of fire. The only thing the wall can do is delimit the area of the city; and the fact that it is so low shows that delimitation is comparatively unimportant. God is much more eager to bring men in than to shut them out—and his Church must be the same.


## THE PRECIOUS STONES OF THE CITY

*Revelation* 21: 18–21

THE city itself was of pure gold, so pure that it seemed like transparent glass. It is possible that John is here accentuating a feature of the earthly Jerusalem. Josephus describes Herod's temple: "Now the outward face of the temple in its front lacked nothing that was likely to surprise either men's minds or their eyes; for it was covered all over with plates of gold of great weight, and, at the first rising of the sun, reflected back a very fiery splendour, and made those who forced themselves to look upon it to turn away their eyes, just as they would at the sun's own rays. But this temple appeared to strangers, when they were at a distance, like a mountain covered with snow, for as to those parts that were not golden, they were exceeding white" (Josephus: *Wars of the Jews* 5.5.6).

John goes on to speak of the twelve foundations of the city. Between the twelve gates there were twelve spaces, and the idea is that between these spaces there was one vast foundation stone. Again John may have been thinking of the vast stones in the foundations of the Jerusalem Temple. In the passage which we have just quoted Josephus speaks of stones in the Temple foundation walls of almost 70 feet in length, 8 feet in height, and 9 feet in breadth. In verse 14 John has said that the stones are inscribed with the names of the twelve apostles. They were both Jesus's first followers and his ambassadors, and they were literally the foundations of the Church.

In the city of God these foundation stones were all precious stones. The *jasper* was not the modern opaque jasper but a translucent rock crystal, green in colour. The *sapphire* appears in the Old Testament story as the stone of the paving on which God stood (*Exodus* 24: 10). Again, it was not the modern sapphire. Pliny describes it as sky-blue, flecked with gold. It was most likely the stone now known as lapis lazuli. The *chalcedony* was a green silicate of copper, found in mines near Chalcedon. It is described as being like the sheen of green on a dove's neck or in a peacock's tail. The *emerald* was the modern emerald, which Pliny describes as the greenest of all green stones. The *sardonyx* was an onyx in which the white was broken by layers of red and brown; it was specially used for cameos. The *sard* or *carnelian* took its name from Sardis. It was blood-red, and was the commonest of all stones used for engraving gems. The identification of the *chrysolite* is uncertain. Its Hebrew name means *the stone of Tarshish*. Pliny describes it as shining with a golden radiance. It could be a yellow beryl or a gold-coloured jasper. The *beryl* was like an emerald; the best stones were sea-blue or sea-green. The *topaz* was a transparent, greenish-gold stone, very highly valued by the Hebrews. *Job* speaks of the topaz of Ethiopia (*Job* 28: 19). The *jacinth* is described by ancient writers as being a violet, bluish-purple stone. It is likely that it was the equivalent of the modern sapphire. The *amethyst* is described as being very similar to the jacinth, but more brilliant.

Have these stones any symbolism?

(i) It may be noted that eight of them are the same as the stones in the breast-plate of the High Priest (*Exodus* 28: 17). John may simply have used the breast-plate as his model.

(ii) It may well be that the only intention of John is to stress the splendour of the city of God in which even the foundations were stones beyond price.

(iii) There is another interesting possibility. In the east there was the idea of the city of the gods in the skies. There the gods dwelt; the sun and the moon and the stars were its lights; the Milky Way was its great street; there were twelve gates through which the stars went in and out upon their business. Connected with the city of the gods there are the signs of the Zodiac, the signs of the parts of the heavens through which the sun passes. The curious thing is that the signs of the Zodiac have as their corresponding precious stones exactly these twelve.

The table is as follows:

> The Ram — amethyst.
> The Bull — jacinth.
> The Twins — chrysoprase.

The Crab — topaz.
The Lion — beryl.
The Virgin — chrysolite.
The Balance — carnelian.
The Scorpion — sardonyx.
The Archer — emerald.
The Goat — chalcedony.
The Water-carrier — sapphire.
The Fishes — jasper.

There is at least the possibility that John was thinking of the city of God as the consummation of the old idea of the city of the Gods, but far outshining it.

But there is one curious point. If that be so, John gives the signs of the Zodiac in precisely the reverse order! What the symbolism of that would be it is impossible to tell, unless it is John's way of saying that the city of the gods is made new in the city of God.

The most staggering use of precious stones in this picture is that the gates of the city of God each consist of one vast pearl. In the ancient world pearls were of all stones most valued. All his life the merchantman would seek the pearl of great price and then count it worth selling all his possessions to buy it (*Matthew* 13: 46). Gates of pearl are a symbol of unimaginable beauty and unassessable riches.

## THE PRESENCE OF GOD

*Revelation* 21: 22, 23

IN verse 22 John lays down a unique feature of the city of God; in it there is no temple. When we remember how precious the Temple was to the Jews, this is amazing. But we have already noted that the city is built in the shape of a perfect cube, indicating that it itself is the Holy of Holies. The city needs no temple because the presence of God is continually there.

Here is symbolism which is plain for all to see. Buildings

do not make a Church nor liturgy, nor form of government, nor method of ordination to the ministry. The one thing which makes a Church is the presence of Jesus Christ. Without that there can be no such thing as a Church; with that any gathering of people is a real Church.

The city of God needed no created light, because God the uncreated light was in the midst of her. "The Lord," said Isaiah, "will be your everlasting light" (*Isaiah* 60: 19, 20). "In thy light," said the Psalmist, "do we see light" (*Psalm* 36: 9). Only when we see things in the light of God, do we see things as they are. Some things which seem vastly important are seen to be unimportant when seen in the light of God. Some things which seem permissible enough are seen to be dangerous when seen in the light of God. Some things which seem unbearable are seen to be a path to glory when seen in the light of God.

## THE WHOLE EARTH FOR GOD

*Revelation* 21: 24–27

A PASSAGE like this enables us—and even compels us—to redress a wrong which is often done to Jewish thought. Here is a picture of all nations coming to God and of all kings bringing him their gifts. In other words, here is a picture of universal salvation. It is often said that the Jews looked for nothing but the destruction of the Gentiles. It is true that we find sayings like: "God created the Gentiles to be fuel for the fires of hell." It is true that there is a strain of Jewish thought which expected the annihilation, or at least the enslavement, of the Gentiles; but there is much on the other side, and voice after voice speaks of the time when all men shall know and love God.

Isaiah has a picture of the day when all nations will go up to Mount Sion to be taught the law and to learn to walk in the ways of God (*Isaiah* 2: 2–4). God will set up an ensign to which all the nations will come (*Isaiah* 11: 12). It is God's word of privilege to Israel: "I will give you for a light to the nations, that my salvation may reach to the ends of the earth" (*Isaiah* 49: 6). The isles will wait upon God and in his arm will they trust (*Isaiah* 51: 5). Nations who never knew God will run to him (*Isaiah* 55: 5). The sons of the stranger will learn to love God and to serve him. God will gather others to him (*Isaiah* 56: 6–8). It is Israel's task to declare God's glory among the Gentiles (*Isaiah* 66: 19). The ends of the earth are invited to look to God and to be saved (*Isaiah* 45: 22). All nations shall be gathered to Jerusalem, and shall recognize it as the throne of the Lord, and will no more stubbornly follow their evil heart (*Jeremiah* 3: 17). The Gentiles will come to God from the ends of the earth, confessing and repenting of the previous errors of their ways (*Jeremiah* 16: 19–21). All peoples, nations and languages will serve the one who is like a son of man (*Daniel* 7: 14). All men shall worship God, everyone from his place, even all the isles of the heathen (*Zephaniah* 2: 11). God will give all men a pure language in which they may with one consent call upon him (*Zephaniah* 3: 9). All flesh will be silent before God (*Zechariah* 2: 13). Many people and the inhabitants of many cities will come to Jerusalem. People of all races and tongues shall "take hold of the robe of a Jew, saying, Let us go with you, for we have heard that God is with you" (*Zechariah* 8: 20–23). The day will come when the Lord will be king over all the earth; in that day there will be one Lord (*Zechariah* 14: 9).

What is true of the Old Testament is true of the literature between the Testaments. The vision in *Tobit* is:

A bright light shall shine unto all the ends of the earth;
Many nations shall come from afar,
And the inhabitants of the utmost ends of the earth unto thy holy name;
With their gifts in their hands unto the king of heaven
(*Tobit* 13: 11).

All the nations which are in the whole earth, all shall turn and fear God truly, all shall leave their idols (*Tobit* 14: 6). *Enoch* writes nobly of God's chosen one:

He shall be a staff to the righteous whereon to stay themselves
and not fall,
And he shall be a light of the Gentiles,
And the hope of those who are troubled of heart.
All who dwell on earth shall fall down and worship before him,
And will praise and bless and celebrate with song the Lord of
Spirits (*Enoch* 48: 4, 5).

The writer of *Enoch* hears the voice of God say: "All the
children of men shall become righteous, and all nations shall
offer adoration, and shall praise me, and shall worship me"
(*Enoch* 10: 21).

*The Testaments of the Twelve Patriarchs* is full of this
universal hope. When the Messiah comes "in his priesthood
the Gentiles shall be multiplied in knowledge upon the earth,
and enlightened in the grace of the Lord" (*Testament of Levi*
18: 9). It is the word of God: "If ye work that which is
good, my children, both men and angels will bless you; and
God shall be glorified among the Gentiles through you." It is
Israel's task "to gather the righteous from among the Gentiles"
(*Testament of Naphtali* 8: 3, 4). God will save all Israel and
all the Gentiles (*Testament of Asher* 7: 3). *The Sibylline
Oracles* has a noble passage which tells of the reaction of the
Gentiles when they see the goodness of God to Israel:

Then all the isles and the cities shall say, How doth the Eternal
love those men! For all things work in sympathy with them and
help them, the heaven, and God's chariot the sun, and the moon.
A sweet strain shall they utter from their mouths in hymns. Come,
let us all fall upon the earth and supplicate the Eternal King, the
mighty, everlasting God. Let us make procession to his Temple,
for he is the sole Potentate. And let us all ponder the law of the
Most High God, who is the most righteous of all upon the earth.
But we had gone astray from the path of the Eternal, and with
foolish heart worshipped the work of men's hands, idols and images
of men that are dead (*Sibylline Oracles* 3: 710–723).

Nations shall come from the ends of the earth to see the
glory of God (*Psalms of Solomon* 17: 34).

When John pictured the nations walking in the light of the
city of God and the kings bringing their gifts to it, he was

foretelling the consummation of a hope which was always in the hearts of the greatest of his countrymen.

## RECEPTION AND REJECTION

*Revelation* 21 : 24–27 (*continued*)

WE gather up three further points before we leave this chapter.

(i) More than once John insists that there will be no night in the city of God. The ancient peoples, like children, were afraid of the dark. In the new world the frightening dark will be no more, for the presence of God will bring eternal light. Even in this world of space and time, where God is, the night is as bright as the day (*Psalm* 139: 12).

H. B. Swete sees further symbolism here. In the city of God there will be no darkness. Again and again it has happened that an age of brilliance has been followed by an age of darkness. But in the new age the darkness will be gone and there will be nothing but light.

(ii) John, like the ancient prophets, repeatedly speaks of the Gentiles and their kings bringing their gifts to God. It is true that the nations did bring their gifts to the Church. The Greeks brought the power of their intellect. To them, as Plato said, "the unexamined life was the life not worth living," and so the unexamined faith was the faith not worth having. To the Greeks we owe theology. The Romans were the greatest experts in government the world has ever seen. To the Church they brought their ability to organize and to administer and to formulate law. When a man enters the Church, he must bring his gift with him; the writer his power in words, the artist his power in colour, the sculptor his mastery of line and form and mass, the musician his music, the craftsman his craft. There is no gift which Christ cannot use.

(iii) The chapter ends with a threat. Those who will not lay aside the evil of their ways are barred from the city of God. There is a sinner who sins against his will; there is a sinner who deliberately sins. It is not the repentant sinner, but the defiant sinner, who is barred from the city of God.

## THE RIVER OF LIFE

*Revelation* 22: 1, 2

> And he showed me the river of the water of life, shining like crystal, coming out from the throne of God and of the Lamb, in the midst of the city street. And on either side of the river was the tree of life, which produced twelve kinds of fruit, rendering its fruit according to each month; and the leaves of the tree were for the healing of the nations.

So far the description has been of the exterior of the holy city; now the scene moves inside.

First, there is the river of the water of life. This picture has many sources in the Old Testament. At its back is the river which watered the Garden of Eden and made it fruitful (*Genesis* 2: 8–16). Still closer is Ezekiel's picture of the river which issued from the Temple (*Ezekiel* 47: 1–7). The Psalmist sings of the river whose streams make glad the city of God (*Psalm* 46: 4). "A fountain," says Joel, "shall come forth from the house of the Lord" (*Joel* 3: 18). "Living waters," says Zechariah, "shall flow out from Jerusalem" (*Zechariah* 14: 8). In *Second Enoch* there is the picture of a river in Paradise, which issues in the third heaven, which flows from beneath the tree of life, and which divides into four streams of honey, milk, wine, and oil (2 *Enoch* 8: 5).

Closely allied with this is the picture so common in Scripture of the *fountain of life*; we have it in 7: 17; 21: 6 in the *Revelation*. It is Jeremiah's complaint that the people have forsaken God who is the fountain of living waters to hew themselves out broken cisterns which can hold no water (*Jeremiah* 2: 13). The warning in *Enoch* is:

> Woe to you who drink water from every fountain,
> For suddenly shall ye be consumed and wither away,
> Because ye have forsaken the fountain of life (*Enoch* 96: 6).

The mouth of a righteous man is a well of life (*Proverbs* 10: 11). The teaching of the wise is a fountain of life (*Proverbs* 13: 14). The fear of the Lord is a fountain of life (*Proverbs* 14: 27).

Wisdom is a fountain of life to him who has it (*Proverbs* 16: 22). With God, says the Psalmist, is the fountain of life (*Psalm* 36: 9). "God," said the rabbis in their dreams of the golden age, "will produce a river from the Holy of Holies, beside which every kind of delicate fruits will grow."

H. B. Swete identifies the river of life with the Spirit. In the Fourth Gospel Jesus says: "He who believes in me, out of his heart shall flow rivers of living water." John goes on to explain: "This he said about the Spirit which those who believed in him were to receive (*John* 7: 38, 39).

But it may well be that there is something simpler here. Those who live in a civilization in which the turn of a tap will bring cold, clear water in any quantity can scarcely understand how precious water was in the East. In the hot lands water was, and is, literally life. And the river of life may well stand for the abundant life God provides for his people which is there for the taking.

## THE TREE OF LIFE

*Revelation* 22: 1, 2 (*continued*)

In this passage there is an ambiguity of punctuation. *In the midst of the city street* may be taken, not as the end of the first sentence, but as the beginning of the second. It will then be not the river which is in the midst of the street but the tree of life. Taking the phrase with the first sentence seems to give the better picture.

John takes his picture of the tree of life from two sources— from the tree in the Garden of Eden (*Genesis* 3: 6); and even more from Ezekiel. "And on the banks, on both sides of the river, there will grow all kinds of trees for food. Their leaves will not wither nor their fruit fail, but they will bear fresh fruit every month. Their fruit will be for food, and their leaves for healing" (*Ezekiel* 47: 12). Here again the rabbinic dreams of the future are very close. One runs: "In the age to come God will create trees which will produce fruit in any month; and the man who eats from them will be healed."

The tree gives many and varied fruits. Surely in that we may see the symbolism of the fruit of the Spirit (*Galatians* 5: 22, 23). In the different fruit for each month of the year may we not see symbolized that in the life which God gives there is a special grace for each age from the cradle to the grave? The tree of life is no longer forbidden; it is there in the midst of the city for all to take. Nor are its fruits confined to the Jews; its leaves are for the healing of the nations. Only in the Spirit of God can the wounds and the breaches of the nations be healed.

## THE BEAUTY OF HOLINESS

*Revelation* 22: 3–5

No longer shall there be any accursed thing. And the throne of God and of the Lamb shall be in it, and his servants shall worship him, and shall see his face, and his name shall be on their foreheads. And night will be no more, for they have no need of the light of a lamp, or the light of a sun, for the Lord God will be a light to them, and they will reign for ever and ever.

HERE is the final culmination of the description of the city of God.

There will be no accursed thing there. That is to say, there will be no more of the pollutions which harm the Christian life.

God's servants shall see his face. The promise will come true that the pure in heart will see God (*Matthew* 5: 8). We may best understand the greatness of that promise by remembering that the Christian is promised a privilege which was denied even to Moses to whom God's word was: "You cannot see my face; for man shall not see me and live" (*Exodus* 33: 20, 23). It is in Christ alone that men can see God.

The sight of God produces two things. It produces the perfect worship; where God is always seen, all life becomes an act of worship. It produces the perfect consecration; the inhabitants of the city will have the mark of God upon their foreheads, showing that they belong absolutely to him.

John returns to his vision that in the city of God there can never be any darkness nor need of any other light, for the presence of God is there.

The vision ends with the promise that the people of God will reign for ever and ever. In perfect submission to him they will find perfect freedom and the only true royalty.

## FINAL WORDS

*Revelation* 22: 6–9

And he said to me: "These words are trustworthy and true, for the Lord, the God of the spirits of the prophets, has sent his angel to show to his servants the things which must speedily happen."

"And, behold, I am coming soon. Blessed is he who keeps the words of the prophecy of this book."

It is I John who am the hearer and the seer of these things. And, when I heard and saw them, I fell down to worship before the feet of the angel who was showing them to me. And he said to me: "See that you do not do this. I am your fellow-servant, and the fellow-servant of your brothers the prophets, and of those who keep the words of this book. Worship God."

WHAT remains of the last chapter of the *Revelation* is curiously disjointed. Things are set down without any apparent order; there are repetitions of what has gone before; and it is often very difficult to be·sure who is the actual speaker. There are two possibilities. It may be that John is deliberately sounding again many of the themes which run through his book, and bringing on the stage many of the characters for a final message. It is perhaps more likely that he did not finally set in order this last chapter and that we have it in unfinished form. We have three speakers.

The first is one of the angels who have been the interpreters of the divine things to John. Once again he stresses the truth of all that John has seen and heard. "The God of the spirits of the prophets" means the God who inspired the minds of the prophets. Therefore the messages John received came from the same God as inspired the great prophets of the Old Testament, and must be treated with equal seriousness.

The second speaker is Jesus Christ himself. He reiterates that his return is not to be long delayed. Then he pronounces his blessing on the man who reads and obeys the words of John's book. Swete aptly calls this "the felicitation of the devout student." The devout student is the best of all students. There are too many who are devout, but not students; they will not accept the discipline of learning and even look with suspicion upon the further knowledge which study brings. There are also too many who are students, but not devout; they are interested too much in intellectual knowledge and too little in prayer and in service of their fellow-men.

The last speaker is John. He identifies himself as the author of the book. Then, strangely enough, he delivers exactly the same warning against angel worship as in 19: 10. Either John would have removed this passage as a needless repetition, if he had had opportunity fully to revise his book; or he was so aware of the danger of angel worship that he believed it necessary to give the same warning twice. He certainly leaves us in no doubt that worship of angels is wrong and that worship must be given to God alone.

## THE TIME IS NEAR AND THE TIME IS PAST

*Revelation* 22: 10, 11

And he said to me: "Do not seal the words of the prophecy of this book; for the time is near. Let the wrong-doer continue in his wrong-doing; let him who is filthy continue in his filthiness; let the righteous man continue in his righteousness; let him who is dedicated to God continue in his dedication."

THIS passage insists that the coming of Christ is close at hand; it must be the Risen Christ who is speaking.

In the older Apocalypses, written between the Testaments, the instruction is always to seal them and lay them up for a distant future. In *Daniel,* for instance, we read: "Seal up the vision, for it pertains to many days hence" (*Daniel* 8: 26). But now it is not the time to seal but it is the time to open and read; for the coming of Christ will take place at any moment.

What, then, is the meaning of this curious passage which seems to say that men must remain as they are? There are two possibilities.

(i) There comes a time when it is too late to change. In *Daniel* we read: "The wicked shall do wickedly" (*Daniel* 12: 10). As Ezekiel had it: "He that will hear, let him hear; and he that will refuse to hear, let him refuse" (*Ezekiel* 3: 27). A man can so long refuse the way of Christ that in the end he cannot take it. That is the sin against the Holy Spirit.

(ii) The ancient commentator, Andreas, says that the Risen Christ is saying: "Let each man do what pleases him; I will not force his choice." This, then, would be another warning that every man is writing his own destiny.

## THE CLAIMS OF CHRIST

*Revelation* 22: 12, 13

> Behold, I am coming soon, and I have my reward with me, to render to each man, as his work is. I am Alpha and Omega, the first and the last, the beginning and the end.

THE Risen Christ once again announces his speedy coming; and he makes two great claims.

(i) He has his reward with him and will render to every man according to his work. H. B. Swete says: "Christ speaks as the Great Steward, who in the eventide of the world will call the labourers to receive their day's wages."

(ii) He is Alpha and Omega, the first and the last, the beginning and the end. This is a repetition of titles used in 1: 17; 2: 8; 21: 6. There is more than one idea here.

(*a*) There is the idea of *completeness*. The Greeks used

*from alpha to omega* and the Hebrews *from aleph to tau* to indicate completeness. For instance, Abraham kept the whole Law from aleph to tau. Here is the symbol that Jesus Christ has everything within himself and needs nothing from any other source.

(*b*) There is the idea of *eternity*. He includes in himself all time, for he is the first and the last.

(*c*) There is the idea of *authority*. The Greeks said that Zeus was the beginning, the middle, and the end. The Jewish rabbis took over this idea and applied it to God, with their own interpretation. They said that, since God was the beginning, he received his power from no one; since he was the middle, he shared his power with no one; and since he was the end, he never handed over his power to anyone.

## THE ACCEPTED AND THE REJECTED

*Revelation* 22: 14, 15

Blessed are those who wash their robes, that they may have the right to the tree of life, and that they may enter into the city by the gates. Outside are the dogs and the sorcerers and the fornicators and the murderers and the idolaters and everyone who loves and acts falsehood.

(i) Those who wash their robes have the right of entry into the city of God; the Authorized Version has: Blessed are they that do his commandments. In Greek the two phrases would be very like each other. *Those who have washed their robes* is *hoi plunontes tas stolas,* and *those that do his commandments* is *hoi poiountes tas entolas.* In the early Greek manuscripts all the words are written in capital letters and there is no space left between them. If we set down these two phrases in English capital letters, we see how closely they resemble each other.

HOIPLUNONTESTASSTOLAS
HOIPOIOUNTESTASENTOLAS

"Those who have washed their robes" is the reading of the best manuscripts, but it is easy to see how a scribe could make a mistake in copying and substitute the more usual phrase.

This phrase shows man's part in salvation. It is Jesus Christ who in his Cross has provided that grace by which alone man can be forgiven; but man has to appropriate that sacrifice. To take a simple analogy, we can supply soap and water, but we cannot compel a person to use them. Those who enter into the city of God are those who have accepted the sacrifice of Jesus Christ.

(ii) There follows the list of those who are debarred from the city of God. We have already considered a very similar list in 21: 8 of those who were cast into the lake of fire. The new phrase here is the dogs. This can have two meanings.

(i) The dog was the symbol for everything that was savage and unclean. H. B. Swete says: "No one who has watched the dogs that prowl in the quarters of an eastern city will wonder at the contempt and disgust which the word suggests to the oriental mind." That was why the Jews called the Gentiles dogs. There is a rabbinic saying: "Whoever eats with an idolator is the same as he who would eat with a dog. Who is a dog? He who is not circumcised." Andreas suggests that the dogs are not only the shameless and the unbelieving, but also Christians who after their baptism "return to their vomit." The dog may, then, be a symbol of all that is disgusting.

(ii) But there is another possibility. There is a strange phrase in *Deuteronomy* 23: 18. The full verse runs: "You shall not bring the hire of a harlot or the wages of a dog into the house of the Lord your God in payment for any vow." The first part is clear enough. It is forbidden to offer to God money that has been made by prostitution. But *the wages of a dog* is more difficult. The point is this. In the ancient temples there were not only female sacred prostitutes, there were also male sacred prostitutes; and these male prostitutes were commonly called *dogs*. *Dog* can denote a thoroughly immoral person, and that may be its meaning here.

Every one who loves and acts falsehood is shut out. Here is an echo of the Psalmist: "No man who practises deceit shall dwell in my house; no man who utters lies shall continue in my presence" (*Psalm* 101: 7).

## THE GUARANTEE OF TRUTH

*Revelation* 22: 16

> I, Jesus, sent my angel to you to testify to these things for the sake of the Churches. I am the root and the offspring of David, and the bright morning star.

JESUS guarantees the truth of all that John has seen and heard. The point of this guarantee is this. The book begins by promising a revelation to be given by Jesus (1: 1); this is the attestation of Jesus that, however the vision came, it came from him.

He then goes on to give, as it were, his credentials. "I am the root and the offspring of David," he says. That is a reference to *Isaiah* 11: 1: "There shall come forth a shoot from the stump of Jesse, and a branch shall grow out of his roots." Jesus is saying that in him is the fulfilment of this prophecy, that he is at one and the same time the eternal source of being from which David came and his promised descendant.

"I am the bright morning star," he says. To call a man a morning star was to class him very high among the heroes. The rabbis, for instance, called Mordecai by that name. More than that, this would recall the great Messianic prophecy: "A star shall come forth out of Jacob" (*Numbers* 24: 17).

This would awaken other realms of thought. The morning star is the herald of the day which chases away the darkness of the night; before Jesus the night of sin and death flees away.

Surely this would awaken still another memory. In the days of his flesh Jesus had said: "I am the light of the world; he who follows me will not walk in darkness, but will have the

light of life" (*John* 8: 12). When the Risen Christ said that
he was the morning star, he claimed again to be the light
of the world and the vanquisher of all the world's darkness.

## THE GREAT INVITATION

*Revelation* 22: 17

> The Spirit and the Bride say: Come! And let him that hears say:
> Come! Let him who is thirsty come and let him who wishes take
> the water of life without price.

THERE are two different interpretations of this passage.

H. B. Swete takes the first two parts as an appeal to Christ
to fulfil his promise and come quickly back to this world;
and he takes the third part as an invitation to the thirsty soul
to come to Christ. But it seems very improbable that there
should be such a difference between the first two parts and
the third. It is much more likely that the whole passage is a
great invitation to all men to come to Christ. It falls into
three sections.

(i) There is the invitation of the Spirit and the Bride. The
Bride, we know, is the Church. But what are we to understand by the Spirit? It may be the Spirit who is operative
in all the prophets and who is always calling men back to
God. Much more likely, John uses the Spirit for the voice
of Jesus himself. The regular ending of the letters to the seven
Churches is an invitation to hear what the Spirit is saying
(2: 7, 11, 17, 29; 3: 6, 13, 22). Now, the speaker to the seven
Churches is the Risen Christ; and, therefore, quite clearly there
the Spirit and the Christ are identified. "The Spirit and the
Bride say: Come!" probably means that Christ and his Church
join in the invitation to accept all that he has to offer.

(ii) "Let him that hears say: Come!" symbolizes the great
truth that every Christian is to be a missionary. He who has
been found by Christ must find others for Christ.

(iii) The third section is an invitation to all thirsty souls to come to Jesus Christ that their need may be satisfied. It must remind us of God's great invitation, "Ho, every one who thirsts come to the waters, and he who has no money; come, buy and eat! come, buy wine and milk without money and without price" (*Isaiah* 55: 1); and also of the great word of Jesus himself. "He who comes to me shall not hunger; and he who believes in me shall never thirst" (*John* 6: 35). In Christ alone the longing of the soul can be satisfied.

> O Christ, in thee my soul hath found,
>> And found in thee alone,
> The peace, the joy, I sought so long,
>> The bliss till now unknown.
>>> Now none but Christ can satisfy,
>>> None other Name for me!
>> There's love, and life, and lasting joy,
>> Lord Jesus found in thee.

## THE WARNING

*Revelation* 22: 18, 19

> I give this warning to everyone who hears the words of the prophecy of this book. If anyone adds to them, God will add to him the plagues which are written in this book. And, if anyone takes away from the words of the book of this prophecy, God will take away his share in the tree of life and in the holy city, which are described in this book.

THERE are certain things to note about this solemn warning.

(i) It is not to be interpreted with absolute literalness. It does not refer to every individual word of the *Revelation*. It so happens that the text is, in fact, in bad condition and we do not know for certain what the actual wording is. What it does warn against is distorting the teaching which the book contains. It is very much what Paul meant, when he said: "If any one is preaching to you a gospel contrary to that which you received, let him be accursed" (*Galatians* 1: 8, 9). It is the truth, and not the wording of the truth, which must not be changed.

(ii) This is far from being an unique ending to an ancient book. It is, in fact, the kind of ending that ancient writers commonly added to their books. We find similar warnings in the Bible in other places. "You shall not add to the word which I command you, nor take from it; that you may keep the commandments of the Lord your God, which I command you" (*Deuteronomy* 4:2). "Every word of God proves true. . . . Do not add to his words, lest he rebuke you, and you be found a liar" (*Proverbs* 30: 5, 6). In the *Book of Enoch* the writer demands that no one should "change or minish ought of my words" (*Enoch* 104: 10).

The *Letter of Aristeas* tells how the Septuagint, the Greek version of the Hebrew Bible, was made by seventy Jewish scholars at the request of the King of Egypt. When the task was done "they bade them pronounce a curse in accordance with their custom upon any who should make any alteration either by adding anything or changing in any way whatever any of the words which had been written or making an omission" (*Letter of Aristeas* 310, 311). In the preface to his book *On Origins*, Rufinus adjures in the sight of God, the Father, the Son and the Holy Spirit, anyone who reads or copies his book, not to add, subtract, insert, or alter anything. Eusebius (*The Ecclesiastical History* 5.20.2) quotes the way in which Irenaeus, the great second century Christian scholar, ends one of his books: "I adjure thee who mayest copy this book, by our Lord Jesus Christ, and by his glorious advent, when he comes to judge the quick and the dead, to compare what thou shalt write, and correct it carefully by this manuscript, and also to write this adjuration, and to place it on your copy."

In the ancient days, since all books were hand-copied by scribes and everyone knew how easy it was for a scribe to make mistakes in the copying, it was a regular custom to insert at the end of a book a solemn warning against change.

It is in the light of that regular custom that we must read

John's words. To use this passage as an argument for verbal inspiration is an error.

One final word must be said about this passage. R. H. Charles points out that this warning may not be part of the original book at all. We must be impressed by the number of times John insists that Christ will come at any moment (verses 7, 10, 12, 20). "Behold, I am coming soon" is the very refrain of the chapter. And yet this warning would seem to imply the expectation of a long time of reading and copying the book, a time which John himself clearly did not expect. It is, therefore, by no means impossible that these words are the words not of John but of a later scribe, anxious that none should alter the book in the days to come.

## LAST WORDS

*Revelation* 22: 20, 21

> He who testifies to the truth of these things says: "Yes, I am coming soon." So let it be! Come, Lord Jesus!
> The grace of the Lord Jesus Christ be with you all.

THERE is both pathos and glory in the way in which the *Revelation* ends. Amidst the terrible persecution of his day, the one thing which John longed for was the speedy return of Christ. That hope was never realized in the way in which he expected, but we can never doubt that Christ nevertheless abundantly kept his promise that he would be with his own even to the end of the world (*Matthew* 28: 20).

Then comes the glory. Come what may, John was sure of the grace of the Lord Jesus Christ and equally sure that it was sufficient for all things.

It is surely symbolic, and it is surely fitting, that the last word of the Bible should be GRACE.

# FURTHER READING

G. B. Caird, *The Revelation of Saint John the Divine* (ACB; *E*)
R. H. Charles, *Revelation* (ICC; *G*)
T. S. Kepler, *The Book of Revelation*
H. B. Swete, *The Apocalypse of St John* (MmC; *G*)

## *Abbreviations*

ACB : A. and C. Black New Testament Commentary
ICC : International Critical Commentary
MmC: Macmillan Commentary

*E* : English Text
*G* : Greek Text